# PAINTED

········································

# POMEGRANATES

········································

# AND

········································

# NEEDLEPOINT

········································

# RABBIS

········································

D1560036

WHERE RELIGION LIVES

Kristy Nabhan-Warren, editor

*Where Religion Lives publishes ethnographies of religious life. The series features the methods of religious studies along with anthropological approaches to lived religion. The religious studies perspective encompasses attention to historical contingency, theory, religious doctrine and texts, and religious practitioners' intimate, personal narratives. The series also highlights the critical realities of migration and transnationalism.*

*A complete list of titles published in this series appears at the end of the book.*

# Painted

# Pomegranates

## and

*How Jews Craft Resilience
and Create Community*

# Needlepoint

# Rabbis

Jodi Eichler-Levine

THE UNIVERSITY OF

NORTH CAROLINA PRESS

Chapel Hill

© 2020 The University of North Carolina Press
All rights reserved
Manufactured in the United States of America
Designed by Richard Hendel
Set in Miller and Didot types by Tseng Information Systems, Inc.

The University of North Carolina Press has been a
member of the Green Press Initiative since 2003.

Cover illustrations: (foreground) detail of *Pomegranate in
Surface Embroidery with Beads* (2017) by Arlene Diane Spector;
(background) detail of Torah mantel *Anochi—I Am* by N. Amanda
Ford. The embroidered Hebrew word is "Anochi," a biblical form for
"I am," which is found at the beginning of the Ten Commandments.

Library of Congress Cataloging-in-Publication Data
Names: Eichler-Levine, Jodi, author.
Title: Painted pomegranates and needlepoint rabbis : how Jews
craft resilience and create community / Jodi Eichler-Levine.
Other titles: Where religion lives.
Description: Chapel Hill : The University of North Carolina Press, 2020. |
Series: Where religion lives | Includes bibliographical references and index.
Identifiers: LCCN 2020010717 | ISBN 9781469660622 (cloth : alk. paper) |
ISBN 9781469660639 (paperback : alk. paper) | ISBN 9781469660646 (ebook)
Subjects: LCSH: Jewish crafts—United States. | Jews—United States—
Identity. | Handicraft—Social aspects—United States. | Handicraft—
United States—Religious aspects.
Classification: LCC BM729.H35 E33 2020 | DDC 745.5089/924073—dc23
LC record available at https://lccn.loc.gov/2020010717

Portions of the conclusion appeared earlier in somewhat
different form in Jodi Eichler-Levine, "Mediating Moses and
Matzah," in "The Old and New Media" issue, *AJS Perspectives*
(Spring 2018): 16–18.

*For the knitters, weavers,*

*spinners, potters, stitchers,*

*woodworkers, quilters, and*

*all who craft, in solitude,*

*in community, in love:*

*may the work of your*

*hands prosper.*

# CONTENTS
. . . . . . . . . . . . . .

# ILLUSTRATIONS

· · · · · · · · · · · · · · · · · · · · ·

# PAINTED

........................

# POMEGRANATES

........................

# AND

........................

# NEEDLEPOINT

........................

# RABBIS

........................

# PROLOGUE

. . . . . . . . . . . . . . . . . . . . . .

## *The Needlepoint Rabbi*

An old man draped in blue and white robes rests on my office windowsill. He is there because of Grandma Salle. This needlepoint rabbi in a golden frame is the precise sort of bearded old sage I often wish I could displace from the center of imagined Jewishness. I grew up at a time when women were at long last becoming rabbis in America but female faces in the pulpit were rare. This rabbi reminds me of the centuries before those changes. In that same ancient vein, even the color palette feels Old World—reds and oranges and bits of bright, garish yellow adorn the background and the Torah he holds. Despite my dread and revulsion for that yellow, I admire the stitches that created the man: just one kind of stitch, on the diagonal, they slant so neatly, and the threads are all the same weight. I see none of the more complex, multidirectional stitches or beading that stymied me when I attempted needlepoint at a workshop in Atlanta. Yet, Grandma Salle crafted this man from a *ton* of stitches, hundreds, thousands, so even, with nuances up close that I can't see at a distance.

A few years ago, in November 2017, I was in the midst of moving, and my parents accompanied me as I cleaned out the rental house basement. They had come about some of my childhood toys, but then they saw Grandma Salle's needlepoint propped against a baseboard in the dust-bunny-filled suburban gloom.

My father—Grandma Salle's son—said I should get rid of it. "It's ugly." His statement carried the weight of other things, including my mother's inability to let go of my childhood toys, which now even my own daughter has outgrown. "Throw it out," he suggested, grumpily, urging me to let it go.

My mother was aghast. "But she *made* it!" she insisted.

*But she made it.* Hands and emotions matter. I touched its dusty frame. Something of the essence of my grandmother lingered in that piece decades after her death. It was "vibrant matter," a way to *feel* a tactile, crafted Judaism.[1] "Touch," writes cultural historian Constance Classen, "is the hungriest sense." It is through touch and vibrant matter that the people you will meet in the following pages—Jewish artists and crafters—engage with Jewish life.[2]

Rather than emphasizing texts and rabbis, which have long been at the center of how we think about Judaism, this book calls our attention to crafts and laypersons, mostly women. In that process, I have found both new practices and new styles of objects made by people who are crafting a Judaism of feeling on multiple levels. It is a Judaism of literal "feeling," one attuned to the sense of touch, and a Judaism of "feeling" emotions, a Judaism of affect.[3] This Judaism is one of waves, not static substances, one of subtle frequencies, of sensations that cannot always be expressed in language. Those feelings accrue at the intersections of bodies, objects, and the making of those objects. It is a Judaism in which matter has tremendous power. At the same time, this is a Judaism that is always in motion, always being constructed, never finished.

For Grandma Salle, needlepoint was a daily devotion, then a visual, everyday presence signaling her Jewish identity in her home. As much as I know that making Jewish homes in America is an ambivalent, layered process, that day in the basement I found myself of two minds about what to do with the rabbi.[4] On the one hand, I was the one who had *kept* the needlepoint for so many years, dragging it across the country to multiple jobs, though I had never hung it up. On the other hand, I had too much stuff. As we quibbled in the basement, I thought of the many artists and crafters I had already encountered, how their objects hold tremendous power linked to identity, memory, and Jewishness. How could I throw away my own ancestor's careful stitches?

It was decided. "It's *totally* ugly," I said, "but she *made* it. I'm keeping it. It can go to my office." My campus office is filled with objects: a Star of David quilted mat; a *Fraggle Rock* puppet; the Judah Maccabee "Huggable Hanukkah Hero" doll that inspired my dissertation; a bobblehead of Bernie Brewer knitting from a "Stitch 'n Pitch" night in Milwaukee. Grandma Salle's needlepoint rabbi would fit right in.

I imagined what my colleagues would think when they saw him perched among my collection. "Isn't it *awful*?" I would chirp, beaming. "My grandmother made it."

So now, Grandma Salle's needlepoint rabbi lives on the windowsill of my office, behind a stack of new books I haven't had time to read, a shorter stack of completed books, and numerous tchotchkes, including a miniature Cheesehead and a Wonder Woman bobblehead (fig. P.1).

FIGURE P.1. *Salle Eichler, needlepoint rabbi. Photograph by the author.*

It really is an ugly needlepoint, and yet, I continue to find myself arrested by it.

Who *is* he, this old man clutching a holy scroll, and why did my paternal grandmother purchase a needlepoint canvas emblazoned with this image, then spend untold hours filling in his visage with slants of brightly colored fiber? She was so different from some of the feminist artists I have met in my research, my Grandma Salle.... She died when I was thirteen, and in truth I mainly recall her in snippets from childhood and nostalgia-drenched postmemories.[5] Though a traditionalist and an ardent Hadassah supporter, she rarely attended synagogue. She was similar, in generation and organizational sensibility, to some of the women who founded the Pomegranate Guild of Judaic Needlework—one of the groups with which I have done my research—yet less focused on artistic originality. Before she married, Grandma Salle was a professional singer with high musical standards, but when it came to crafting, she appears to have been happy to follow along with the colors on the canvas, whereas many of my interviewees take pride in their original designs or the special twists they added to an existing pattern.

How strange, this imagined, bearded man in a woman's creation. The midcentury middlebrow performance of piety graced the walls of her crowded, perennially overheated Kew Gardens Hills apartment. Pictures from a small fiftieth-anniversary celebration for Grandma Salle and Grandpa Phil confirm this. There they are, opening up their presents; there I am, about ten years old, looking on skeptically, then reading in a corner; and there is the needlepoint rabbi, smack in the middle of the apartment, behind Grandma Salle in the chair I rarely saw her leave. Why did she choose to create the rabbi? Perhaps because he was popular or simply available: mass produced in roughly the 1950s, the rabbi was purchased in the thousands and worked up by women all over the United States. These days I can find the same needlepoint for sale on eBay and Etsy; people in Pennsylvania, Long Island, and England are all willing to part with their framed copies of this image, for a fee.[6] Nor is he the only popular rabbi needlepoint image.

In 1973, fiber artist Mae Rockland Tupa, author of *The Work of Our Hands: Jewish Needlecraft for Today*, wrote, "Too much of what has recently been called Jewish art has consisted of depictions of mournfulness masquerading as spirituality. Beloved as he may be, the praying, bearded rabbi is not the only subject matter available to Jewish art."[7] Perhaps she had seen many needlepoints like Grandma Salle's and wanted to push Jewish craft and art in a new direction. This has certainly happened in the decades since; the Torah cover pictured in Grandma Salle's mass-produced needlepoint kit is not at all the colorful, modern, innovative sort of Torah mantle I have beheld in my interviews all over the country. Instead, it is a deep burgundy, emblazoned with the tablets of the covenant. I imagine it made of velvet, were it real. I can practically smell the camphor as I gaze on it. The rabbi's gnarled hands, shaded tan and brown, grasp the Torah. By the time I knew Grandma Salle, her own hands shook and stuck, riddled with arthritis. I have no conscious memories of watching her sew. I did not remember that she did needlepoint until I began working on this book and my mother reminded me.

### CROCHET HOOKS AND CHUPPAH BEES

No single activity or life event led to the writing of this book. If I am honest, though, thinking through craft objects in my own homes entails grappling with relationships and moments of great loss. Therein lies the connection with what I call generative resilience, the act of coping through the process of creation that I have seen in my research and has roots and resonance in my own story.

This force is found in everyone's lives.

Relationships form the crux of generative resilience, especially relationships across generations and communities. Although I started this story with Grandma Salle, it was my maternal grandmother, Grandma Ettie, with whom I actually crafted. Grandma Ettie usually had a crochet hook in hand. Her work was not elaborate or elegant, but it was functional: endless hats, scarves, and coverings for hangers to keep the clothes from slipping off, as well as small blankets for my dolls' beds. She tried to teach me to crochet, but it didn't take, perhaps because I was left-handed, or perhaps because I simply lacked the fine motor skills at that age. I do remember sitting with her and doing other kinds of handwork while she crocheted—using a crochet hook and knitting nobby to make endless lengths of tubed, stockinette braid or doing free-form embroidery or a bit of cross-stitch.

Grandma Ettie's daughter—my mother, Miriam—was *always* doing something with her hands: oil painting most frequently (the smell of turpentine always brings back my childhood), but also bargello, some knitting and crochet, and the creation of a fine set of clothes for my second-grade star turn as the Pied Piper. But although I dabbled in many things, I did not become a crafter until 2004, when, midway through graduate school, my best friend taught me how to knit and we both got caught up in that decade's hip knitting revival. In contrast to the amorphous nature of intellectual work, I was hooked on the tactile reward of making row after row of stitches. Scarves and baby blankets, hats and socks all came to life on my knitting needles.

When I married, I decided that our chuppah (marriage canopy) should be hand-knit. With a mere six weeks of notice, friends and family from all over the country contributed knit and crochet squares. For the centerpiece, I repurposed a blanket I had been knitting and furiously knit more squares on gigantic, size 17 wooden needles. A week or two before the nuptials, I convened a chuppah bee at my mother-in-law's apartment. The friends and family who attended transformed the day into a surprise bridal shower. Women from my childhood, graduate school pals, and relatives, some Jewish, some not, all joined together around a giant dining room table to sew the squares into one body. Even my mother-in-law, who normally does not do anything of a crafty variety, went to her local yarn store and learned how to knit a square. I photographed each woman present with her square; others had arrived via mail.[8] My mother brought a piece of Grandma Ettie's crochet to incorporate, making the chuppah an object which, in those stitches, stretched beyond the mortal world. Munching red velvet cake prepared by my best friend, we worked late into the night.

The chuppah bee created a temporary community quite similar to the ones I study; it also generated a ritual object. No one *needs* a hand-knit, crazily colored chuppah for a Jewish wedding; any piece of fabric would do. (For that matter, the chuppah is not part of the legal requirements for a Jewish wedding; rather, like the glass crushed at the end of the ceremony, it's a tradition, one with immense staying power.) In addition to cementing social bonds, our wedding chuppah resembled an act of *hiddur mitzvah*, or the beautification or enhancement of a commandment—in this case, the commandment of marriage. This is not how I framed the chuppah bee in my head at the time, but it is a notion I have encountered many times since in my ethnographic exploits. It is a value-added action.

While the chuppah bee was a celebration of life and community, generative resilience also finds itself deeply enmeshed in the opposite force—great loss. When my Grandma Ettie was in her twenties, her fiancé was killed in a truck accident. She later met and married my grandfather, Ralph Friedman, during World War II. In 1964, when my mother was just seventeen and Grandma Ettie was fifty, my grandfather died of a pulmonary embolism. A few years later, their son Jerry, just twenty years old, was killed in a motorcycle accident on Long Island; he was missing for weeks before his body was finally found when the leaves fell off the bushes above him. Then it was just Grandma and my mother until my father, and, ultimately, I, came along.

Grandma Ettie persevered. She carried on. She worked, she learned finances, she crocheted. My mother did, too, but each coped with her grief in different ways. Grandma Ettie had a motto: "When in doubt, throw it out." She even threw out my grandfather's diploma from Columbia University Teachers College. In contrast, my mother holds onto objects, whether it is the beautiful Hanukkah apron Grandma Ettie sewed or last year's *New York Times*. I grew up in a home abundant in objects—purchased ones, personally created ones—a home in which my own childhood creations, however humble, were always retained, even framed. I thus come to the study of objects, art, and craft with a keen personal sense of the power they wield as repositories of sentiment. For my Grandma Ettie they held, perhaps, too much. For my mother, Miriam, they can never hold enough. Thus, when it came to Grandma Salle's needlepoint rabbi, it was my mother who defended the retention of the piece.

Not long ago, when I interviewed my parents for this book, my mother told me another story about my family and its objects. The story resembles many of those sprinkled throughout *Painted Pomegranates and Needlepoint Rabbis*. It is the story of three generations of handwork, a story of objects saved, retained, and used to celebrate decades' worth of Jewish holidays.

In my mother's story, there is a matzah deckle (a cloth matzah cover)

FIGURE P.2. *Ceil Godfrey, matzah deckle. Photograph by the author.*

that my family has used every Passover since I was a child, and before then
(fig. P.2). My mother has relayed its tale many times. Most recently, this is
how she told it. When she was around twenty-four years old, her aunt Ceil
offered to make a set of a hand-embroidered matzah and challah covers,
with a matching bag for hiding the afikomen (a piece of matzah that is
part of the Passover ritual) for anyone in the family who wanted one. My
mother recounted,

> Anyway, my aunt Ceil told my mother she wanted to make me one,
> and my mother said, "Don't bother, Miriam will never make a seder."
> My aunt Ceil was smarter than that. She came to me or called me
> up or something, or we saw each other, and she said, "Would you
> like . . . ?" She explained to me what she wanted to make me. I said,
> "I'd love it!" She said, "All I need to know is what color you want it
> to be. A lot of people want them in blue because that's traditional."
> I said, "Could you make it in orange, please? That's my favorite
> color." She said, "Absolutely I can make it in orange." . . . Getting
> orange thread wasn't difficult, but she actually got what she needed
> to crochet the edge in orange, and she made it for me in white fabric
> with orange wording and pictures and edging. My mother was

absolutely shocked when I started making seders. I use these things. My mother was surprised.

My mother, Miriam, not only "made" seders in the sense of cooking; she also led them. I never really knew my great-aunt Ceil, who died when I was three or four years old. Yet I grew up with this delicate but robust white-and-orange object like a talisman of family connections hovering over my childhood. My mother still keeps the matzah deckle in the original box in which it was given, a handwritten note from her aunt tucked beneath it. Now that our family seders have shifted from my mother and father's home to my own, it graces my Passover table. The Judaism of our matzah deckle is a *felt* one, laden with sentiment but also one that we can literally grasp: it is the sensation of crisp, white Aida cloth and orange silken bumps. I handle it carefully, but it does not reside in my house. My mother keeps it in hers, holding onto it in a way I find both moving and heartrending. In a family that has sustained great losses, the embroidered matzah cover endures.

The matzah deckle did not inspire this book any more or less than my hand-knit chuppah or Grandma Salle's needlepoint rabbi. It is a part of my story, and ethnographers are enmeshed in our own family histories as much as we try to attend carefully to the stories of others. No one object or moment clearly causes another, yet they are linked like the loops of stitches on a knitting needle. I started the journey toward *Painted Pomegranates and Needlepoint Rabbis* during my graduate school knitting phase when I stumbled across books like *Zen and the Art of Knitting*. Then there were books on quilting and kabbalah and mindful knitting, and I thought: Hmm, religion and crafting—there's something going on there.[9] Although my fieldwork and purposeful research happened later, I know that the needlepoint rabbi, the chuppah, and the deckle shaped me along the way, and so I have shared them with you. Whatever your background, your objects and their stories—or perhaps, your dearth of objects and stories—have shaped you, too.

As I write these words, I am deeply aware of how easy it is to romanticize such processes. It would be dishonest to suggest that my engagement with this subject did not emerge from my own captivation with its possibilities, with my own sense, when I was twenty-five, that in yarn I could find salvation. I appreciate that my family history speaks of generative resilience, a personal process through which I see, in all of my foremothers' creations, an insistent thriving in the face of loss. My hope is to draw out the fine line between idealizing what crafting and objects can do, on one pole, and so dramatically deconstructing such practices that I render them meaningless. In my engagement with the needlepoint rabbi who looks down upon the office where I write, I seek a middle ground. By holding on to this crafted, bearded visage, I both participate in nostalgia and become aware of its presence; I marvel at the mass consumer production of needlepoint kits while appreciating the countless hours Grandma Salle must have spent pushing her needle in and out of the canvas; I engage in sentiment with an ironic twist. In the pages that follow, I hope to bring this blend of appreciation and insight, of analysis tempered by empathy, to the creations and creators of a deeply vibrant and felt Judaism.

# INTRODUCTION

. . . . . . . . . . . . . . . . . . . . . . . . . .

*Suturing the Mortal World*

On a hot Sunday morning in May 2017, excitement hummed through a suburban Atlanta hotel as groups of women rushed to morning workshops at the Pomegranate Guild of Judaic Needlework's biennial convention. I arrived seven minutes early for my very first class, "Drawing with Scissors," with local Atlanta artist Flora Rosefsky. Despite the guild's name, this workshop would not involve sewing or needles of any kind. Instead, we would wield scissors, learning techniques in paper collage that could inspire future designs for needlework. It was a theory workshop, meant to inspire us toward open-ended creations rather than sending us home with a finished product.

Though I was prompt, most of the other participants were already seated at U-shaped conference tables. Before each of us rested two blank pieces of paper, black and white, with a notepad on top. Most important, we each had what Flora called a "pizza box": a white, ten-inch-square bakery box topped with one of Flora's beautiful postcards. Near the front of the room, Flora had propped inspirational art books on an easel; a side table displayed a colorful throw that one guild member had crocheted from Flora's designs; and in another corner, a table glowed with a glorious rainbow of paper in different sizes and textures.

Flora, a petite woman with short brown hair and a wise face, counted. "Nine is good and I'm ten so we have a minyan," she announced, referring to the quorum of ten adult Jews required for certain prayers and rituals. (There is no quorum for crafting; it was a good joke, though.) She began our session by quoting from a piece on the American Guild of Judaic Art website about making art. Flora then emphasized one of her own mantras for us: "It's your vision and your voice." She also asked us, "Is everyone born with a creative soul?" Finally, she talked about Buddhism and about being present in the moment. All of the women listened intently, and I felt a sense of nervous anticipation, but also freedom. Here was a Jewish practice that was generative, not prescriptive. A frisson of energy, a mixture of solemnity and revelry, filled the room.

At last, Flora permitted us to open our boxes. Inside rested a wide assortment of paper squares—some of heavy stock, others light, some velvety and soft, others crisp, a few so thin and tissuey as to be nearly translucent. I was captivated by a pale purple sheet flecked with bits of gold. The box also contained a glue stick and a pair of scissors. Our first task was to start playing with something abstract—maybe a feeling—and make a collage on a small piece of card stock. Our second task would be to use an inspirational quotation or text of our own selection to work on a larger collage.

At first, I aimlessly cut out a mix of curves and then some triangles in orange, green, and blue, scattering them around my page. But it didn't seem to be going well. I heard Flora talking to the other participants as if they were really, well, *artists*, discussing things like color dominance. I glanced at the work being done by my next-door neighbor—an established quilter—and decided that she was doing a much better job. Competitive by nature, I continued to compare my collage to others around the table. It did not measure up well, and Flora didn't really say anything about my work, which I took as a bad sign. When we put up our first round of pictures on the wall, I saw that other folks had found ways to somehow, magically, make all of those little paper scraps into extraordinary designs. One woman's picture already looked like a vivid desert scene. Mine was just a random shape jumble. You could call it abstract, but I felt like a failure.

Next, it was time for the "real" piece, and I felt the pressure of the blank page before me. I reread the inspirational text, which, per our instructions, I had brought with me. I had chosen Marge Piercy's poem "The Art of Blessing the Day." It is very long and contains so many images that I couldn't choose just one, let alone figure out how to capture the glorious poem on a mere nine-and-a-half-by-eleven-inch sheet of paper. I was just one hour into the convention and fading fast.

In the poem, I had always lingered on the lines, "This is the blessing for a ripe peach: / This is luck made round."[1] Should I dare to collage a peach? We were in Georgia, after all. The convention's logo even featured a peach intimately nestled against a pomegranate. Was a peach a bit too much?

I went to the "paper store"—that colorful buffet at the front—for inspiration. I loved seeing all the colors together. I pulled out some of the pieces cut from magazines, with patterns and texture in the prints, and a mix of metallic and cool colors. I went back to my seat and shuffled the papers nervously. Flora seemed to read my mind. "Don't overthink it," she said. "But that's what I do for a living!" I replied, getting a successful laugh from the woman on my right.

In my head, without realizing what I had done, I misremembered the poem and combined the two lines together, muttering to myself, "This is the blessing for luck made round." Ok. Luck made *round*. I could cut only with curves, then. Round. I picked up the most beautiful piece of paper, that translucent, tissuey purple with the gold flecks, and I started to cut, frightened of ruining such a beautiful item, but more scared not to try. *This is the blessing for luck made round.* I sliced it into a loose, spherical form and set it in the center of my page, slightly off center. I cut sinuous curves of blue and gray from the magazine pages, arranging them like spokes around the central axis. Then I dared to cut into the most expensive—*eight dollars a sheet*—piece of paper. It was green and black and felt like velvet.

I started to get into the zone. *This is the blessing for luck made round.* Flora periodically said how *intent* I looked. I watched the individual veins and fibers of the paper as I cut and cut, around and around in whorls. One bit of the green became an orb in the center of the purple. Other bits became spirals. I wanted more space between the curving lines. I chipped away and away at the paper, noticing each grain, each bit of pulp, and thought I might understand why people like woodworking: the whittling away. I decided the piece had too many cool colors. I added some red, some angles. In a semimystical trance, I felt as if I could dive right into the paper itself.

At the end of the class, we all hung our pictures on the wall for a group critique. Mine was still not particularly striking, but it was more purposeful than the first. It was, ineffably, *art*—or at least *artsy*. The experience surprised me. The blessings of Marge Piercy's earthy take on Judaism were now something I could touch and hold. Flora seemed very pleased. "Jodi, I think you really grew," she told me.

## CRAFTING A JUDAISM OF FEELING

In this book, "Judaism" functions as a horizon, not as a container.[2] These artists and crafters demonstrate that Judaism is, to build loosely off mid-twentieth-century thinker, Rabbi Mordecai Kaplan, always evolving.[3] It is in endless action, best understood as process, not product, though many of its products are beautiful to behold. It is as messy and material as the sacrifices and smoke that littered the Jerusalem temple before normative or rabbinic Judaism fully came to be, and yet it is also as spiritual as any Judaism forged in a Protestant-dominated American cauldron might inevitably be.[4] Sometimes, it is as stereotypically, classically Jewish as it gets: sometimes it is a rabbi depicted in needlepoint, a familiar sage, the Ashkenazi male authority American Jews still romanticize even as they supplant him. Sometimes crafting Judaism is revolutionary, and sometimes it follows familiar patterns—just in threads on fabric, rather than in ink on parchment.

*Painted Pomegranates and Needlepoint Rabbis* examines Jewish material culture with a focus on creativity, gender, and religion in North America.[5] It is a book about the power of craft in relation to Jewish identities. By focusing on generative resilience, a process in which acts of creation become a crucial part of their makers' ways of being and coping in the world, we can better understand how craft sustains and embellishes Jewish life. Many other themes—technology, gifts, community, resistance, and generations—also emerge from these explorations. All of these concepts, however, can be understood in tandem with this overarching narrative line, which moves from individual to collective understandings of creating objects. This interdisciplinary study of Jewish creations and creators at the turn of the twenty-first century focuses on the power to persevere that is found in quotidian actions. To generate resilience through the sutures of everyday craft is to perform an existential act of survival.

I was first inspired to study crafts and materiality because I was seeking comfort after writing a book about violence and suffering. What I found, though often beautiful, was not always comfortable. This book attempts to do justice to the ambivalence and ambiguity at the heart of our romance with objects. "Here at the end of all things"—here in late capitalism, amid a shaky age of global empires and a warming planet—these homespun cultures provoke a reckoning with what it means to create in a fragile world: with the attempt to roll entropy backward armed primarily with needle and thread.[6]

In this story, Jewish practices of creative freedom are part of larger trends in the United States. Throughout *Painted Pomegranates and Needlepoint Rabbis*, I use Jewish examples to examine such key ideas as gender, technology, and the gift in the study of North American religions. In other words, though this book focuses on Jews, it is not just about Judaism. Examining this Judaism of feeling and resilience gives us a more robust picture of religion, ethnicity, and religio-racial overlaps in North America.[7] It takes up and expands upon the important work already produced on material religion.[8] Finally, though Jews are a small portion of the U.S. population, studying a minority group disrupts dominant understandings of religion, helping us to see these concepts in a new light. In this way, *Painted Pomegranates and Needlepoint Rabbis* challenges those of us in the field of religious studies to keep grappling with our terms.

But what do I mean by Jewish examples? Words like "Jew," "Judaism," "Jewish," and "religion" have long and complex histories. None are static; as I wrote about Judaism, above, all are in process. Nonetheless, it is helpful briefly to explore what I am talking about when I use these terms.

The term "Jew" is certainly fraught. It is a word that has been defined as much by non-Jews as by Jews themselves, including long, often derogatory histories, particularly in Christian Europe. The modern English word "Jew" can be traced back to the Greek *ioudaios* (based on the Hebrew *yehudi*), which was used in the late first millennium B.C.E. and early first millennium C.E. to mean either Judean or Jew.[9] After the second century of the common era, when the last hopes for Judean self-rule ended with the failure of the Bar Kochba revolt, the word "Jew," translated into various languages, retained both ethnic and religious overtones, although it was not the term Jews most typically used to refer to themselves: terms like "Hebrew" or "children of Israel" were more common.[10] It is also important to remember that since antiquity there have been procedures for converting to Judaism, indicating that being a Jew has always involved complicated layers and inroads. It is *not* a simple matter of descent. In the nineteenth and early twentieth centuries, as race "science" arose, the term "Jew" also took on racialized connotations (and, with that phenomenon, further negative stereotypes and anti-Jewish violence). Today, "Jew," as used in North America, has stronger religious overtones but also retains an ethnic sense. Yet there is no one Jewish ethnicity. Broadly speaking, in the contemporary United States, Jews, who make up approximately 2 percent of the population, may identify as Jewish ethnically, culturally, religiously, or some combination of all of these. In this study, I include anyone who self-identifies as Jewish, which ends up including Jews who have matrilineal and patrilineal descent, as well as converts, and Jews who focus on both religious and ethnic understandings of their identity. To put it even more simply: Jews are a far-flung people who may share ancestry, religious practices, histories, or texts—but *all* of those things vary across time and space. "Jewish"—an adjective form—is a fuzzy and capacious category, one that the Jews described within these pages employ to describe objects, practices, foods, feelings, and themselves. I eschew notions of a fixed Jewish identity or a timeless Jewish tradition.[11] Jewishness—like craft—is a process, an endless making, unmaking, and refashioning.

Judaism is, in its simplest form, the religion of the Jews. It is something Jews *do*. However, Jews have not always framed their practices, sacred texts, or beliefs as a stable religious "-ism." Modern Jewish thinkers initially resisted the notion of religion, which they saw as a Christian concept. Over the last few centuries, however, Jews increasingly enunciated the aspects of Judaism that looked like other religions in order to make themselves legible to Christians. They also molded those very practices into formations that more closely resembled the religions of their neighbors, building seminaries and, for a brief moment in the nineteenth century, writing Jewish "catechisms." (Of course, cultures are always hybrid and fluid, so this is not *just* a modern phenomenon; ancient, pre-Jewish Israelites had many practices that resembled Canaanite ones, even though later biblical authors would decry those rites.)[12]

This became particularly pronounced in the modern United States. Reeling from the horrors of the Holocaust, amid the rise of American mainstream religiosity against the backdrop of the Cold War, Jewish Americans sought to minimize the association of Jewishness with race and to enumerate the ways that Judaism was a religion, something neatly compartmentalized in the home and synagogue, with greater emphasis on conscience and ethics than ritual: part of a Catholic-Protestant-Jewish "trifaith America," cementing a process that began around World War I.[13] Following the 1970s, however, as ideas about multiculturalism and revived ethnic pride became part of U.S. cultures, Jews, too, began to reassert their ethnic identities and to revive many ritual, linguistic, and material practices that had been lost, particularly among Ashkenazim (eastern European Jews), focusing on eastern European folk practices and languages such as Yiddish; one similar example is the return of the prayer shawl in some synagogues where it had, for a time, been discouraged.[14] Intertwined with these revivals, Judaism remains, developing with and as part of the rich religious ferment of the contemporary United States. Judaism displays many characteristics of other world religions—prayers, laws, rituals, theologies, stories—with a particular emphasis on ritual and complex notions about peoplehood.

What, then, is this thing called religion? In the history of the United States, Americans, influenced by Protestant Christianity, have tended to think of religion as synonymous with belief, but that is a small part of the picture. Defining religion is a challenging enterprise.[15] It is a moving, fluid target that can be thought of in terms of practice, community, texts, sounds, and feelings, to name just a few angles. I take a broad approach; as with Judaism, I envision religion as a process, not an eternal phenomenon. Religion is a profoundly social thing. Humans make things religious through their actions and interactions. Whatever the sacred might be, it is a status that people confer upon aspects of the world around them, from such familiar examples as a Torah scroll or worship service to less obvious, but no less real, experiences, such as a pilgrimage to Disney World or the collective effervescence of "the church of baseball."[16] Many of our daily actions are religious. Examining what we become through both creation and consumption—and creating often also entails *consuming* raw materials—is one of our vital contemporary tasks; we are always "being consumed by the social inevitability of consumer decision. *Religion* is a word to intensify what we do when we name authority, practice interactions, and interpret life itself."[17]

Another helpful way to think about religion is as a quality of specialness.[18] Yet that does not mean that it is completely set aside from the rest of life. These are porous boundaries. The line between religious and secular is never neat, and what we call "the secular" is co-constituted by religion.[19] Furthermore, religion is not always an obvious presence, or a loud one. In fact, many of the stories in *Painted Pomegranates and Needlepoint Rabbis* are examples of everyday religion: the quotidian actions, conversations, objects, stories, and other moments that flow throughout the tides and currents of social and material worlds.[20] They show us how Jewish lives and Jewish meaning making are subtle yet powerful practices.

*Painted Pomegranates and Needlepoint Rabbis* helps us to understand everyday religious lives in the increasingly postdenominational age of the American "religious nones."[21] Jewish Americans provide a case study of an internally heterogeneous group where these trends are particularly relevant but remain understudied.[22] Apprehending Jewish American history and sociology means recognizing how denominations, along with other major twentieth-century Jewish institutions (Jewish community centers, schools, summer camps), are only one small piece of the puzzle of American Jewish communities. It is also crucial for those of us who study Jewish American phenomena to inform our work with insights from the broader field of religions in North America and for us to provide insights that speak back to that field. Both of these ways of studying Jews have become an important part of recent scholarship.[23] Although my informants in this study do at times come together in formal organizations like the Pomegranate Guild, or in groups that overlap with official Jewish spaces (synagogue knitting circles), attending to craft and creativity allows me to study the granular nature of everyday Jewish life.[24]

## HOW I WROTE THIS BOOK
This study builds upon three years of fieldwork, including participant observation and long-form interviews, with Jewish Americans in a variety of locations, including Pennsylvania, New York, Maryland, Georgia, and California, as well as extensive research of online crafting communities.

The overwhelming majority of the people featured below hail from the United States. My informants are primarily women, alongside a few men and some individuals who identify as nonbinary or genderqueer. All are people who make things: predominantly in the fiber arts (knitting, sewing, crochet, quilting, cross-stich, needlepoint, embroidery), but also in clay, wood, and ink. Some of the objects that they make are specifically Jewish ritual objects, such as challah covers and prayer shawls; some are objects created for charitable causes for what interviewees identified as Jewish reasons, such as *mitzvot* (commandments); other items are primarily decorative or are more about process than a specific product. Other sources for this study include crafting manuals, memoirs, and ephemera, along with craft blogs and archival materials.

I followed many paths to locate the people, stories, and objects that populate *Painted Pomegranates and Needlepoint Rabbis*. This is an interdisciplinary study that is primarily—but not entirely—ethnographic in its orientation. That means it is about the study of people. In early 2016, I conducted a qualitative online survey that resulted in more than three hundred responses, primarily from the United States but also from Canada and other Anglophone countries; this survey gave me an initial sense of important themes and popular creative activities, which I ended up narrowing to activities that entailed creating objects. Using snowball sampling, I organized more than thirty face-to-face and phone interviews with Jews in a variety of regions from 2016 to 2019. I also conducted participant observation by spending time with synagogue knitting circles and attending the Pomegranate Guild of Judaic Needlework's biennial convention. My work also makes use of online ethnographic techniques through the study of crafting blogs and Pinterest, and through examination of craftivist actions that spread through Internet-based communication, particularly the Pussyhat phenomenon, which was cofounded by a Jewish woman, and Jewish Hearts for Pittsburgh, an art installation begun in the wake of the October 2018 shootings at the Tree of Life synagogue in Pittsburgh, Pennsylvania. Conversations, including the interviews, tended to be open-ended; although I entered them with some questions in mind, I did my best to follow the interviewees' leads as much as possible.

Stylistically, some aspects of this book differ from either a traditional ethnography or a study of professional artists. Initially, I assumed that, as in most works of qualitative sociological research, the people I interviewed would have their identities hidden, with first name pseudonyms replacing their real names. Several of my interviewees did, indeed, prefer to speak anonymously or pseudonymously, a request that I have of course honored, so some parts of this book follow that pattern, with some other minor changes to occlude their identities. What surprised me—but, of course, should not have—was the fact that many of my informants did *not* wish to remain anonymous. They are, rightly, quite proud of their work and wish to remain known by their real names. In some cases, especially if an interviewee has shown their work publicly or had their work (art, activism, or both) appear in news media, I have used the individual's full name (and refer to them by last name in subsequent mentions). In other cases, I have used just the individual's first name. This had to do in part with the *feel* of the text, too. These were intimate conversations in homes and gathered around sewing, so I have trended toward the use of first names, not as a sign of disrespect, but as a way of conveying the warmth of these conversations. (Sometimes, especially when artists shared the same first name, last names were the best choice.)

Ethnography is an interpersonal process; it is a series of encounters as we stumble toward a more nuanced understanding of the world around us. When I entered these spaces, I was not just a professor; I was also a Jewish American woman in my late thirties, then in my early forties. I was a liberal, practicing Ashkenazi Jew who hailed from the Northeast (with a long stint in the Midwest), and a mother. I was also not the only one asking questions. Throughout the years that I worked on this book, interviewees always queried me about my own craft practice and, frequently, about my young daughter. They asked me about my Jewish background and my academic work, which was of course what had brought me to their doors. I disclosed many careful tidbits as openly as I could in this ethnographic give-and-take. In these conversations, I felt a strong sense of an identity layering, of how my value in these homes signified something more than a person who wanted to touch objects and hear stories. My presence as an ethnographer was one way of preserving these stories and these objects—of which I have hundreds of photographs. I am keenly aware, however, that, when it comes to those interviewees who are older than me—a large number of subjects—I am also of interest to them precisely *because* I am a younger Jewish woman who knits, embroiders, and crochets, as someone who can be a bearer of memory not just in words but also in thread.

Age matters. Four decades ago, anthropologist Barbara Myerhoff conducted years of groundbreaking fieldwork with the elderly Jewish residents of Venice, California. Not all of the crafters portrayed throughout *Painted Pomegranates and Needlepoint Rabbis* are senior citizens, but a preponderance are. I have frequently found myself turning to Myerhoff during this project. Like me, she was a middle-aged Ashkenazi Jewish woman interacting with Ashkenazi Jews of an older generation who found her Jewish identity of interest. In one of her opening anecdotes, a woman named Basha asks her: "Are you Jewish? . . . Are you married? . . . You got children? . . . Are you teaching them to be Jews?" "I'm trying," Myerhoff replies.[25]

Myerhoff was speaking primarily with Holocaust survivors and their contemporaries. In my work, I have talked with a large number of women of her generation, the baby boomers. Had she lived, and not died of cancer in 1985, she, too, would now be a senior citizen. As Riv-Ellen Prell evocatively writes, Myerhoff drew a direct connection between her embodied self and the people she studied: "Anthropologist Barbara Myerhoff looked at the camera in her documentary film *Number Our Days* and explained, 'Someday I will be a little old Jewish lady.'"[26] Alas, this did not come to pass. Like Myerhoff, I am keenly aware of my subject position in studying a group so close to my own experience, and I have wondered, like her, how much of my work is a personal quest. Writing decades after groundbreaking works of feminist anthropology that changed the researcher's place in the text from a disembodied voice to a character within the story, I have been directly influenced by the reflexive ethnographic turn. I am still puzzling over what to make of the significant overlaps of the personal and the academic in this project.[27] It is not a memoir, but it does contain some of my stories within its pages.

Although *Painted Pomegranates and Needlepoint Rabbis* is thorough and far reaching, it does not and could not attend to the thousands of objects and attendant stories being produced daily in Jewish houses, by Jewish hands or hands that are Jewish adjacent, all over the world. It does attempt, though, to dive richly and deeply into this ferment of creativity, and the book's accompanying online exhibit will extend its reach and longevity in this regard. Every time I travel to a new place, I learn of more crafters. I am humbled by the vast quantity and quality of this world.[28]

Crucially, my informants come from many segments of Jewish life. When they affiliate denominationally, they are Reform, Reconstructionist, Conservative, and Orthodox. Many others, like a large number of Jewish Americans, identify as "just Jewish," culturally Jewish, or as otherwise Jewishly engaged but unaffiliated. In this way, they reflect an increasingly postdenominational moment in Jewish American life.[29] They include millennials, Gen Xers, baby boomers, and some interviewees born before World War II, although on the whole they skew heavily toward the older side of that spectrum.

Snowball sampling—the sociological practice of starting with a few informants and then building upon their suggestions to find further ones, like a snowball that grows as you roll it down the hill—does have limitations. Notably, my informants are relatively homogenous in terms of class, ethnicity, gender identity, sexual orientation, and, to some extent, age. The majority of my informants are Ashkenazi middle- to upper-class women, between roughly the ages of fifty and ninety. I did not ask my informants about sexuality, but many voluntarily reported being in heterosexual relationships. I cannot say that my interlocutors fully reflect the internal diversity of the Jewish American community, which is made up of at least 12 to 15 percent Jews of color, and a sizable LGBTQ community.[30] Although my online survey is more diverse and I was ultimately able to speak with some informants who do not pass as white, there is still more similarity than difference among my long-form interviewees, which is a methodological limitation for which I hold myself fully accountable. My chief goal has been to intervene along axes of age (intentionally seeking older informants) and sex (seeking women's voices), but this sampling method has limitations. On the other hand, focusing on particular networks, especially the Pomegranate Guild of Judaic Needlework, has given me a deeper and richer account than a random sample might have done.

A BRIEF WORD ABOUT ART AND CRAFT

Defining "art" is notoriously slippery. One evocative phrase, "Art asks a question," is helpful. "Art is the containment of sense" and "The work of art signifies an increase in being" also apply to many of my encounters.[31] "Craft," which derives from the Old English *cræft*, is similarly difficult to pin down. Archaeologist and historian Alexander Langlands writes that "it has something to do with making, and making with a perceived authenticity: by hand, with love … to a desired standard"; he argues that we should "embrace it as a form of knowledge, not just a knowledge of making but a knowledge of being."[32] I treat the terms "art" and "craft" as two poles at the ends of a continuum, rather than as a binary, although this book does skew much more toward the study of craft.

The notion of a divide between art and craft is itself a politicized construction with a difficult history. "Art" has tended to be defined, per *Webster's*, as "the conscious use of skill and creative imagination, especially in the production of aesthetic objects."[33] Contemporary art has tended to focus on process and action as much as on product.[34] In contrast, the term "craft" has often been used in a derogatory manner, denoting work that is more common or folk in its nature, lacking aesthetic refinement. Craft objects were also distinguished from art ones if they had a specific use, rather than existing for their aesthetic qualities alone. This distinction was also a deeply gendered one. Thus, oil paintings created by men became fine art while quilts sewn by women became craft. Since the 1960s and the rise of second-wave feminism, both artists and critics have sought to trouble this distinction. Most famously, perhaps, Judy Chicago's installation *The Dinner Party* employed multiple forms of craft, including embroidery, to draw attention to the ways that women's art and intellectual contributions have been overlooked. More recently, Margo Jefferson and other critics have drawn our attention to the rising importance of work previously understood as craft, with reference to the enormous success in 2002–3, at the Whitney Museum of American Art and then on a national tour, of *The Quilts of Gee's Bend*, which hailed from generations of work in a small black community in Alabama. As Jefferson argues, "Happily, institutions and individuals are deciding to throw out the old debates about the relative values of art designated fine, folk, high or utilitarian. The point is to understand each tradition. The point is to open one's eyes to any artist who, as Joseph Conrad said, can make us hear, feel and above all see."[35]

This study is not a history of the distinctions between art and craft, though they are both terms my subjects used to describe their work, to varying degrees. In my fieldwork, I intentionally did not distinguish between the study of art and craft. Some of my interviewees identify primarily as crafters. Others are artists whose work has appeared in exhibits or juried shows. A few of my informants reflected overtly on the art/craft notion itself, referring to some of their pieces as "art" and others as "craft." I use the term "craft" in its broadest sense, encompassing many sorts of creative acts. As a student of lived religions, I do have a slight bias toward "craft" because of its connotations of the everyday, its more accessible nature. Everyone, regardless of skill level, can do both craft *and* art, but as I learned in my workshop with Flora, tiptoeing into art—opening oneself up to critique, a hallmark of artistic processes—can be humbling.

FROM GENDER TO GENERATIONS

The pages that follow allow you to engage with a tactile account of what it means to be Jewish, a creator, a religious person, a member of an ethnic group—in short, to be human—in an age and region where material creation has become associated with leisure more than with economic necessity. The continuing power of such practices and objects owes a debt to their emotionally charged nature. Objects, from delicately embroidered prayer shawls to prepainted needlepoints of rabbis, constitute containers for emotion and also a kind of betweenness, a site where narratives and memories are transmitted.[36]

These stories follow a sequence. They move from tales of individuals to narratives of communities. The book opens by delving into crafters' reflections on the meaning of creation, as well as interviewees' discussions of parenthood, fertility, and infertility. Here, the concept of generative resilience helps us to wend a path that negotiates between two common pitfalls in the characterization of crafts and gender. On the one hand, portrayals of women's art and craft, as well as women's religious experiences, sometimes trend toward romantic ideas about so-called feminine crafts.[37] The earliest anecdotes in *Painted Pomegranates and Needlepoint Rabbis* wrestle with concepts like creation and with the relationship between being in a gendered body and creating objects that are themselves gendered. Rethinking Jewish objects entails finding new ways to disentangle notions of gender, creation, and craft by noticing the subtle ways in which contemporary Jews attach meaning to their objects and their craft processes, rather than seeing such activities through an idealized lens.

Next, I open up the story by looking at the technologies that enable creation and by attending to craft processes on blogs and other forms of social media, a form through which individuals interface with various kinds of publics.[38] Here, the virtual and the material, the digital and the tactile, are symbiotic in the diverse world of Jewish crafts. Technology and Jewish fiber arts are not at odds; indeed, they "mingle promiscuously" in many of the cases I am studying, though not without moments of tension.[39] In the middle of the book, I turn from the literal technologies of blogs and spindles to the ritual technologies associated with gift giving. Gifts are often strongly associated with life-cycle rituals such as weddings, enunciating their power as bearers of affect. They are also at the heart of how we theorize religion. Focusing on the notion of the gift requires us to think about how Jews and other Americans generate resilience through forms of exchange.[40]

The ensuing sections of *Painted Pomegranates and Needlepoint Rabbis* consider community in its many incarnations. My time spent with the Pomegranate Guild of Judaic Needlework and with Pennsylvania knitting circles is central to this story, as are modern imaginings of the figure of Bezalel, the mythical chief artisan of the tabernacle in the Hebrew Bible. Here, we see how resilience is generated in the conversations that accompany creation, in the ways that stitchers share their work with one another, and in the relationships they develop over time. Sometimes, resilience is transformed into resistance, into acts that some of my informants call "craft activism" or "craftivism." Through them, I explore how collective movements ranging from the pink Pussyhats that accompanied the 2017 Women's March to the more recent installation of Jewish

Hearts for Pittsburgh are understood, by many participants, through the Jewish notion of *tikkun olam*, or repairing the world.[41] Although many of my informants express liberal political leanings, politically conservative crafters also engage in an understanding of their work as having redemptive social value. Jewish American political life is heterogeneous, but the notion of generative activities as reparative ones links these disparate efforts. Finally, I close *Painted Pomegranates and Needlepoint Rabbis* by thinking about resilience through the dimension of time. One longtime Pomegranate Guild member told me that she creates Jewish textiles to replace all of the ones "lost in the fires" of the Holocaust. She is not the only one. To create objects is to engage in a quest for continuity.

To begin, we must enter into the world where objects and people intersect. We must listen to their stories in search of unlikely artifacts and images of motherhood hanging on by a thread. Stitching the generations is an action that is sutured, conceptually, to how we think about bodies, especially the bodies of women. For all women, that discourse is a fraught one—and for Jewish women, it comes with extra baggage. We turn now to stories of full and empty spaces, of excess and scarcity, and begin with a birth.

# 1 : IN THE BEGINNING

. . . . . . . . . . . . . . . . . . . . . . . . . . . . .

*Generative Resilience and
the Creation of Gender*

In the beginning, there was a handkerchief. It is October 2016. I am in a sunny, white-walled studio talking with Heather Arak-Kanofsky, a professionally trained artist who now has a thriving business creating customized gifts for corporate and private events. Heather—who, like me, is a late Gen Xer—is reflecting on how art and creativity connect with her sense of meaning in the world. "I've always thought, 'Why be an artist? Is it really important to be an artist? Does it really make a difference?' But if you look all the way back, people needed those things. They wanted to create beauty, they needed to have that in their lives. And I feel like for me, the idea of something being transformed from profane to sacred ...." Excited, she interrupts herself to get an object from one of the low bookshelves that line the sides of the room. It is a white handkerchief covered with colorful embroidery, laid out on a red book cover (fig. 1.1). Then she tells me the story of the piece:

> I had this fight with my grandma when I was six years old. I think it was when my sister was being born ... and I didn't wanna get out of my nightgown. I like being in my PJs all day. It's comfortable. And so she was like, "Get up, you need to get up." And I said something, and then I said, "You're fat." We were having an argument. "You're fat." And she said, "Wow, that was very hurtful." So I felt really bad ... you know, I loved her so much.... So I said, "I need a handkerchief," and she said, "Okay." So she gave me the handkerchief and I drew this for her, and then she embroidered it.[1]

I am awed by the care with which this item has been preserved, and by the way in which she framed its story. For Heather, the handkerchief was the site of transforming the profane into the sacred. The aesthetic style here is homey and collaborative. On the left-hand side is a person—a person who looks a bit like a snowman—wearing a hat and scarf. On

FIGURE 1.1. *Heather Arak-Kanofsky and Muriel Kamins Lefkowitz, embroidered handkerchief. Photograph by the author.*

the right-hand side, her grandmother, pictured in profile, is an amalgamation of abstract curves and lines, filled in with browns and blacks and greens, with hints of orange and a delicate, tiny sun. Arak-Kanofsky's grandmother used pink embroidery floss to stitch over the carefully lettered phrase "Fat is Good" on the left and "Love Heather" on the right; a similar mauve shade was used in a blanket stitch all around the border. The air around us feels still, its quietness almost palpable, as we contemplate this heirloom.

Arak-Kanofsky describes how her grandmother kept the piece for years, using it as a book cover, then gave it back to her when she became engaged. In turn, on her wedding day—which was also her grandmother's wedding anniversary—she had the piece mounted and gave it back to her, once more, as a gift. Eventually, after her grandmother's death, she inherited it. Now it is one of the many carefully curated objects that reside in her airy workspace, a memento. She sums up some of what she learned from the experience. In part, it showed her that family was a place where you could push limits, where a moment of discomfort was transformed into something different through the meaning making process of family life. Here, "fat" was turned from a pejorative term into a valued descriptor. Ultimately, she says, it taught her this: "You can take a terrible moment and make it into something that is really amazing."[2]

You could say that the practice of religion is frequently about taking a terrible moment and make it into something that is really amazing—or, at the very least, into something that is abundant in meaning. Many

Jewish holidays, such as Purim and Passover, commemorate moments of persecution and transform them into days of feasting and revelry. The handkerchief does this, too, in a way that is less obviously Jewish than a Passover seder and yet no less vital for how Jewish Americans make profound religious meaning in their lives. It is an everyday Judaism of feeling. It tinkers with meaning in a way that is similar to the move made in midrash, Jewish traditions of interpretation. A six-year-old remade the world in crayons, and her grandmother added the next stratum in thread, like the layered deliberations of rabbinic thought. The word "fat"—a pejorative, painful term for modern American women—became re-rendered as a sign of capacious love and intergenerational bonding via an iterative creative process.[3] In this handkerchief form, the portraiture created by a child—an ephemeral practice that, in many homes, is relegated to recycling bins across the continent, ad infinitum, each day—is inscribed as a permanent keepsake instead. The grandmother's bulky body is refigured by the hand of the child who descended from the child who descended through those hips. It is seen anew as a beautiful one. The bond built by the handkerchief was so important to Heather that the handkerchief itself became a part of her life-cycle rituals. The item is also materially lasting, lingering here in the studio long after the grandmother's death. What is this act, if not a religious one?

In this object and its attendant story, we see the myriad processes we will encounter throughout this book: the transmission of affect, technological mediation, the promotion of gift culture, the bonds of community, a moment of repair, and the hold of memory. It speaks of a kind of activism, too, a body positivity that is hard won but enduring. The "Fat is Good" handkerchief encapsulates generative resilience, the process of struggle, adaptation, and intimate production that I have found so frequently in the diverse stories contained herein. To generate resilience is to perform an existential act of survival. To create any item at all is a profound act of strength, perhaps even chutzpah, in a world that has always been falling a little bit apart at the seams.

In psychological literature, resilience denotes both processes and capacities of positive adaptation in the face of stressors and adversities.[4] In the field of religious studies, resilience often indicates survival and the ability to endure.[5] In the stories that make up this book, acts of creation constitute resilient actions that are, in their way, religious, particularly when we focus on religion as a social process. That is to say, they help their creators to "make homes" and "confront suffering," and for some of my interlocutors, they also buttress "a network of relationships between heaven and earth involving humans of all ages and many different sacred figures together."[6] Even when these actions don't engage directly with formal rituals or institutions, they intersect with the broad category we call religion on multiple subtle frequencies. This does not happen in a systematic way. In fact, the value of approaching these objects and moments as examples of religion—and Judaism—comes because they form a loose network, not a neat arrangement. Religion, like the yarn at the bottom of my knitting bag, is a messy tangle of feelings, relationships, and attunements, shot through with taut fibers of tradition.

The "Fat is Good" handkerchief also asks that we think about gender. This is not just because it is about women's bodies—all human beings live in bodies of varying sexes, and they all "do gender," performing a wide range of culturally bounded signals that other humans interpret as signs of identity (including not just masculinity and femininity but also a host of other possibilities, including nonbinary ones).[7] These are "intimate engagements": snapshots of gender and Jewish crafts with a measure of interiority and reflection, but also with a subtle awareness of broader publics and social contexts.[8] How crafters discuss acts of creation, parenting, and generations are all deeply enmeshed with the making of gender among Jewish Americans. On the one hand, interpretations of art and craft, as well as women's religious experiences, sometimes trend toward romanticized ideas about so-called feminine crafts.[9] On the other hand, deconstructing that interpretation does an injustice to its power in many lives. In other words, even though it is important to notice such rhetorical patterns, I do not want to notice them out of existence; the traditional gender norms that I want us to understand historically are still meaningful ideas that animate the religious lives of many Jewish Americans. Similarly, the power of creation—so laden with theological overdetermination—is often thought through as emblematic of women's procreative capabilities. This metaphor has pitfalls for those who literally or figuratively struggle with creation and procreation, production and reproduction. Can we find a way to disentangle and revise our notions of gender, creation, and craft—and, alongside these, our notions of Jewishness and religion?

GENDERING GENERATIVITY

Generativity is gendered. This happens in many ways. There are times when it is gendered as masculine—think of the word "seminal," from "semen"—times when it is pictured in terms that are feminine—"a pregnant pause"—and other times when the imagery is more complicated. Consider this verse from the Hebrew Bible, Psalm 139:13: "You knit me together in my mother's womb."[10] This verse addresses a male creator deity who is anthropomorphic, described as performing a skilled craft that takes place within the body of a woman.[11] That psalm in full, which emphasizes the intimacy between the deity and the speaker, details the wonders of God's creation and contains myriad Hebrew synonyms for fashioning, making, and forming, along with a great deal of nature imagery and an emphasis on God's knowledge of humans' innermost thoughts. To create is thus associated with divine power, but even in this version, the divine being does not create in a vacuum: the God of this psalm does his work in the depths of female bodies and deep caves, working in concert with embodied and earthly materials, however hidden. In Jewish descriptions of creation, from ancient Canaanite phallic pillars to kabbalistic ideas of the divine phallus emanating into the feminized *sefirot* ("luminosities," the ten emanations of divinity), images of male bodies as the givers of life abound.[12]

Not all notions of reproduction or life-giving creation have a masculine agent. In a variety of cultural contexts, we find examples where the bodies of women were celebrated for their fecundity in ways that might have been religious. Think, for example, of the Venus of Willendorf, a statue found in Austria, dating to the Upper Paleolithic period, which was celebrated by many second-wave feminists—those most active in the 1960s through the 1980s—as an emblem of the maternal divine. (Today, you can also find a lovely pattern online to crochet your very own Venus of Willendorf, and it made the social media rounds as recently as July 2018, so she must still hold some cultural cachet.)[13] When modern feminist spirituality movements emerged in the 1960s and 1970s, both women's bodies and feminized creative processes became foci in metaphorical *and* literal ways. Jewish feminists reclaimed Lilith, Adam's legendary first wife who, in various rabbinic tellings, had been exiled before the creation of Eve and characterized as a demoness.[14] Some Jewish feminists echoed other second-wave feminists in their attention to fertility images, reviving attention to the ancient Near Eastern fertility goddesses that the male authors of the Hebrew Bible and, later, the rabbinic tradition, had castigated. They celebrated feminist seders and created new theologies, prayer language, and rituals that spoke to a craving for ways of being Jewish women in the context of second-wave feminism, paralleling related developments in other religious communities throughout the United States.[15] Many of my informants came of age during this time and carry that language forward with them.

By the 1990s, however, some feminists questioned what it meant to make women's reproductive capacities so central to their religious identity, or to elide the nuanced history of weaving, knitting, and other trades, which were not always conducted by women, nor were these activities always pleasurable for the women who performed them. As we entered the twenty-first century, unpacking gender as a binary notion also entered more powerfully into this conversation. Many people moved toward thinking about gender as both a social process and a continuum; they noted how sex-gender systems varied across time and space, including the recognition that many cultures have more than two gender identities.[16] We have also begun to fathom that biological sex is not a simple either/or but rather an assignment built upon myriad factors.[17] My ethnographic data doesn't always reflect these nuances. In my discussions with crafters, I could not escape a valorization of various arts, especially the needle arts, as women's work, even as I *also* sometimes encountered the work of male and gender nonbinary crafters, as well as forms of ritual innovation that trouble gender norms.

In my online survey, conducted in 2016, a few questions prompted respondents to reflect upon whether there were connections between gender and craft in their lives. Some responses reinforce an association between women and creativity:

> I feel that I am part of a special heritage of women, and a continuing link in a chain of women creating art. I feel that there is a long tradition of women beautifying practical, everyday items.... On a practical level, I am pretty sure that every craft I know how to do has been taught to me by a woman. I feel that it is a powerful way for women to connect with one another, as teachers, students, and fellow artists. I'm not exactly sure how to explain it, but I often feel that my art expresses my femininity.[18]

This statement frames crafting as women's work while also celebrating the importance of the everyday, as Arak-Kanofsky did at the beginning of this chapter. Another respondent wrote: "Sewing and knitting make me feel feminine, in a way, and powerful. It's a way of combining femininity and empowerment for me. I can CREATE beautiful, meaningful, useful things. It makes me feel like a meaningful, useful woman—more than a wife, more than a mother. It's a part of my identity as a person."[19] This statement simultaneously celebrates crafting as feminine while also indicating that it is something *beyond* traditional roles of being a wife or mother.[20] For her, craft imbues power, and it is not the power of a heavy-bellied ancient fertility goddess—it is the power of a modern woman who can create "beautiful, meaningful, useful things": a producer, rather than a consumer.

For Jews, creation and generativity are also special categories in terms of ritual practice and narrative meaning. Productions and reproductions, creations and creativity, are theoretically, theologically, and ritually intertwined. The very notion of resting on the Sabbath is done in imitation of God, the ultimate creator. Understanding Jewish art and craft requires attending deeply to *how* things are made. Artist and professor Ben Schachter compares these Jewish definitions of "work" with art criticism that attends to "process." He draws our attention to the *melakhot*, the thirty-nine categories of work forbidden on the Sabbath that are enumerated in the Talmud. These are then linked with both notions of divine creation and the actions of Bezalel, the chief artisan of the Tabernacle, whose actions are described in the book of Exodus and who looms large in many Jewish artists' self-understanding. Many of the verbs included among the melakhot correspond to the activities in which my informants take part, including "spinning, weaving, making two loops, sewing two stitches," and more.[21] Most crucially, as Schachter argues, "The exclusion of the *melakhot* from the Sabbath is the human parallel of divine creation and highlights the idea that creation—creating—at any level is important. Ultimately, then, Judaism sees work in a radically different way than mainstream society does; work is synonymous with creativity."[22] Though Judaism is not a monolithic actor—religious traditions as such lack agency, or, to put it another way, Jews do things, whereas Judaism is a concept—Schachter's observation demonstrates an ethos that I have seen firsthand many times. Many Jews see creation as a holy gift.

Simultaneously, reproducing Jewish bodies in the form of literal bioproductions—children—is a theme present from ancient Israelite literature to post-Holocaust, pronatalist imperatives to repopulate the Jewish people.[23] What happens when we examine the confluence of artistic generation and the creation of further humans via fertility and infertility, parenting and unparenting, connection and rupture? Deeply gendered experiences around bodies, infertility, parenting, and circumcision emerge here, showing how Jewish genders are crafted and reinforced.

## HORROR VACUI AND THE EXCESSES OF JEWISH WOMEN

In her 1979 classic *The Art of Judaic Needlework*, Ita Aber places the narrative origins of Jewish fabric arts in assorted biblical texts, including the story of Bezalel and the creation of the Tabernacle as described in Exodus 35–39. She writes, "From this we know that the plastic and graphic artist held a singular position in the Jewish community. What is most extraordinary is that while the people of Israel were still in the desert, they prepared all of the materials for the making of the Tabernacle. They were even asked to stop, because *too much had been prepared*."[24]

In this telling, even amid the privations of the desert, Israelites were ever the overachievers, preparing more raiment and adornments than necessary. What does material abundance mean in relation to Jewish creativity?[25] I thought of Aber's interpretation of the Israelites when I spoke with artist and professor Laurel Robinson about the notion of *horror vacui*. Robinson is a Georgia-based painter and wood-carver. Referring to her own work in contrast with another creative Jew who had a "very Zen" aesthetic, Robinson told me:

> Jews don't need that. We're all full of horror vacui. I have horror vacui supremely. I do not like empty places, I like it all cluttered with as much junk in it as possible. And I think Jews are ... Part of the slam of Jewish art is that it's bad because it's horror vacui. It's like folk art. It's like horror vacui. No, horror vacui is great. I think it is why we have Talmud pages designed in a particular, complex way with commentary on the border and then drawings on the outside of the margins because we're perfectly capable, as a group of people, of isolating an interesting tidbit in the midst of the chaos.[26]

This statement is situated in a particular time, place, and class, but when I returned to my office, I found myself thinking about Robinson's words in relation to so many of the homes I have visited while writing this book, homes filled with stuff: literal piles upon piles of quilted challah covers, woven prayer shawls, crocheted *kippot* (prayer caps), holiday decorations, and the raw materials needed to craft them. To have too much stuff, of course, is an act of class privilege. To create, for some, is to fight against empty spaces by filling them up. *Horror vacui* is Latin for, literally, the fear of a vacuum: the fear of white, empty spaces on a canvas or a computer screen, accompanied by the attendant desire to fill that void with color, light, and chaos. In the history of art criticism, the term arose in response to — and critique of — the Victorian age of hyperadornment.

Thinking with horror vacui helps us to shed new light on the ethnizing and gendering of Jewish art, craft, and bodies. Jews, particularly Jewish women, have often been understood and stereotyped in relation to excess and abundance.[27] This brings us back to where we began this chapter: with fat. In both European and American history, Jewish women's bodies were often derided as simply too much: too large, too loud, too uncouth. Jewish noses, of course, were also too much.[28] Jewish mothers served too much food. Robinson aptly connected this with denigrations of Jewish art as *also* too much, too folk, too filled with images (ironically, given the fact that Jewish tradition is also at times misunderstood as aniconic), lacking in white space: as being what even my own mother — an avid collector of objects—would call *ongepotchket*, a Yiddish word for that which is excessively elaborate, overly decorated. I think about Robinson and horror vacui in concert with the story of Bezalel and friends wandering in the desert, somehow making too much art for the Tabernacle even in the midst of vast, sun-bleached emptiness. What would it mean to lean into this excess of creation and of holding onto creations, this drive to fill the void of empty spaces with luminous, bedazzled materiality? What would it mean to embrace excess rather than to try to shrink oneself into a smaller space?[29]

The makers I have met while writing this book are all generating resilience through their push into this horror, even when their artistic aesthetic is more minimalist. They fill up the voids of existence with "the comfort of things."[30] Things ground, though they can also overwhelm. Louise Silk, a Pittsburgh-based quilt artist and author of *The Quilting Path: A Guide to Spiritual Discovery through Fabric, Thread, and Kabbalah*, told me, "There's always a purpose for a quilt. There's always a reason to have a quilt. And there's always another present, another wall, another table. . . . It's endless, it's absolutely endless." She paused, then deadpanned: "You can have too many needlepoint pillows, for sure."[31] One year later, I visited Arlene Spector, of the Philadelphia chapter of the Pomegranate Guild, and sat among dozens of intricately designed needlepoint pillows, some of which had won awards. Evidently, there *was* no such thing as too many needlepoint pillows, either, I thought, marveling at the time it had taken Arlene and her fellow designers to chart those patterns, the tiny, vivid hieroglyphics-inspired figures on some of those cases.

For those Jewish women who can afford to do so, acquiring things— and making even more things with their hands—is also a way of claiming space they are not supposed to take up, of embracing the capaciousness for which they are typically mocked. Heather Arak-Kanofsky's "Fat is Good" handkerchief revalues larger Jewish women's bodies on a literal level, but the piles of quilted challah covers and stacks of embroidered prayer shawls do this kind of work, too. Ritual objects do not *need* to be enhanced with quilted trompe l'oeil matzah fabric, and a Torah cover does not require decoration, but these productions incorporate the Jewish concept of hiddur mitzvah, the beautification, enhancement, or adornment of a commandment. Though that is an old Jewish idea, it takes on new meaning if we think about this rapid multiplication of handmade Jewish objects in contemporary America in order to reclaim excess, to marvel at a capacious spirit of creation. By taking up space, by bringing too much to the table, the makers of these objects are perennially crafting a new Judaism, one that makes room for multiple colorful emanations of selfhood.

At the same time, creating these objects is an activity with strong dimensions of class, race, and consumerism at play. Creating and collecting in abundance is simultaneously a radical, subversive act *and* a neoliberally conforming one. This is fraught with layers of class privilege, especially in terms of acquisition. As I was writing *Painted Pomegranates and Needlepoint Rabbis*, Marie Kondo's *The Life-Changing Magic of Tidying Up* climbed the *New York Times* best-seller list, and her Netflix series, *Tidying Up with Marie Kondo*, launched a thousand think pieces, as middle- and upper-class Americans sought to purge their homes of items that did not "spark joy," a privilege not given to those who cannot afford to meet all of their needs or who save everything they can for reuse and repurposing. (The Marie Kondo fad was also not without some problematic racialized overtones about "Asian sages," either.)[32]

Most contemporary crafted objects are not created ex nihilo. They require yards of fabric, skeins of yarn, and equipment ranging from a humble eight-dollar set of knitting needles to fancy sewing machines that can cost thousands of dollars. Most crucially, they require time. Time is, of course, a financial luxury. Thus, though these acts of creation are subversive in ways that are both conscious and unintended, they also reproduce power structures and an American approach to both identity and religiosity that is enmeshed with consumer habits. Acts of creation are never simple. They are not isolated from the act of consuming, and consuming, in a hypercapitalist culture, has itself taken on a religious valence. Those who can afford to do so revel in their possessions but are also possessed by them, leading to a sense of claustrophobia that sparked the latest minimalism purge.[33]

## CREATING CHILDREN, LOSING CREATIONS

What happens when, rather than excess, one is confronted with emptiness? Heather Arak-Kanofsky made explicit connections between her experience with several years of infertility and her identity as an artist. She told me, "I spent five years trying to get pregnant, and I couldn't, I had trouble. And there was nothing really wrong with me, whatever that means, but I just couldn't get pregnant, and the way that that kind of relates to my creativity is, I was like, 'I can make anything, but I can't make a baby. How is that possible?' We were the most fertile, fabulous couple, but it doesn't make any sense, you know? Like why? Why can't I do this?"[34]

Today, Arak-Kanofsky is the parent of two sons. Her memory of infertility, though colored by her identity as an artist, is a common one among

Jewish women in twenty-first-century North America: demographically speaking, Jewish American women marry somewhat later and often experience infertility, which accords with broader national trends regarding age of first marriage and later onset of childbearing among all Americans, not just Jews.[35]

In a similar kind of doubling, the many-seeded pomegranate, an ancient emblem of fertility, is in the very name of one of the main organizations with which I did fieldwork: the Pomegranate Guild of Judaic Needlework. The pomegranate is a widely used motif in both historical and contemporary Jewish art. A Pinterest search for the terms "Pomegranate," "Jewish," and "art" yields hundreds of hits, including paintings, cloisonné enamel pendants, ceramic vases, and elaborate embroidered samplers. Some Jewish women have reckoned directly with infertility in their art, including Philadelphia playwright Lisa Grunberger. Photographer Abigail Glass created a striking, piercing photograph of a hundred of the needles used in her fertility treatments, geometrically arranged against a vivid red background.[36]

Infertility is deeply relevant for this chapter because of the ways it unsettles our notions of generativity and because it is, in part, about empty spaces. Emotionally, infertility is a massive, embodied experience of horror vacui. For some women, it entails a keen awareness of an empty womb and of empty rooms planned for children who are not there. This inspires some very beautiful, and very painful, art and craft. It is also an explicit counterpoint to both the pomegranate symbol and a host of other Jewish natalist ritual images and foods—eggs on Passover, for example—that are meant to evoke so-called natural images of fertility. The ancient Israelite agricultural origins of what later became Jewish traditions bleed through into modern Jewish lives in a host of ways. Making space in Jewish art, thought, liturgy, and ritual for the profoundly painful empty spaces of infertility is a communal work in progress.[37] Fertility images saturate the classical lexicon of Jewish visual culture; the time has come for new grammars in Jewish American collective culture.

On the flip side of Glass's needle image and Arak-Kanofsky's remembered experience, which entailed feeling a mismatch between her own artistic generativity and her sense that her body was failing to create a human life, are the experiences of artists who become parents and then find difficulties balancing the work of parenting with their desire to make new art. As one of my online survey respondents puts it: "I tried to embroider a Hebrew wall hanging for my son when he was born. That was before I realized that having children would end, for a while at least, my embroidery career." Similarly, Stacey, one of the Generation X members of the Pomegranate Guild, recalls beginning a needlepoint creation for her twins' room when she was pregnant . . . and finishing it when they were two.

The ability to make time for crafting is often at odds with the practice of raising young children, especially doing so while working outside the home. This tension is explored vividly in a series of quilts by New York–based fiber artist Heather Stoltz. Stoltz, who has an undergraduate degree in engineering, developed her combined interest in both quilting and Jewish studies while pursuing a master's degree at the Jewish Theological Seminary; her work has appeared in a number of professional shows. Today, she creates commissioned pieces and runs educational fabric workshops.

When I interviewed Stoltz early in 2018, one theme we discussed was how her experience of making art had changed once she became a parent, a theme that she explored at length in a group of projects she calls her *Parenthood* series. Many of these pieces, as well as Stoltz's statements about them, reveal a mix of struggle and synthesis in her roles as Jewish mother and Jewish artist. As she put it, most of her prior work "had been either related directly to Jewish texts or social justice issues or both." Then, she said, "I really made this conscious decision to get back to the artwork and make new work, because with the kids and the outside job, trying to juggle it all, the artwork just kind of fell away. I needed to reclaim that space and to start creating again."[38]

*Parenthood* consists of thirteen pieces, with themes ranging from the bifurcation of parenting and art to that most stereotypical of Jewish themes: guilt. She describes her process this way: "It started with the first piece that I designed. It's called *Torn*. It's that division of my life between my artistic life and my mother side. So half of it is a reflection of me as an artist and the other side of me as a mom. There's a division between the two sides. From that came all of the other pieces, including the piece about feeling bottled up, the artistic side being bottled inside and not having a way to get out. And then pieces about mom guilt."[39]

Stoltz's motherhood series candidly illustrates the deep ambivalences and challenges surrounding American parenting in the twenty-first century. *Torn*'s vivid colors and juxtaposition of dark, chaotic curves with bright, geometrically refined segments suggest a contrast between introspective solitude and abundant-but-jarring extroversion, a dividing line within a parent's personality as she learns to code-switch between multiple worlds and notions of self.

*Torn*, which is one of the earliest pieces in this series, started with Stoltz thinking about a bifurcation between her artist self, which is represented in cool batiks, and her parent self, represented by more vivid, whimsical colors. The process of making a piece—which Stoltz details on her blog—is key here, as her grappling with parenthood changed during the project. Early on, when a mentor suggested that she link both sides of the piece, her response was that she "felt that the two pieces of myself were so disparate that there was no connection between them." As her work continued, her feelings evolved: "By now, I had been working on art about parenthood for a few months and creating these pieces was bringing together the two sides of my life. I no longer felt quite so torn apart by these two worlds. While the tension remains, there is at least some connection between my artist self and my parent self, so I edited the design to connect the two halves by a united backing fabric."[40]

Here, we see an emotional alchemy akin to what happened with Arak-Kanofsky and her grandmother's handkerchief. For Stoltz, the passing of time but also the activity of quilting alters her feelings about parenthood, which are then made material in the final abstract piece. There is a back-and-forth process of creation and feeling afoot here. Stoltz built resilience—and emotional integration—through the method of quilting and the time elapsed in creating an art quilt.

If *Torn* ultimately integrates two aspects of Stoltz's life, some of her other work reveals areas of pain and neglect. Her 2018 piece *Hanging by a Thread* depicts the way that parenthood has attenuated her connection to prayer and other aspects of Jewish practice (fig. 1.2). As she describes the work:

> Judaism and prayer had been a central part of my life and a real source of spirituality before I had kids. I am now finding that my connection to prayer and the community is slipping away. This piece represents the slow erosion of my Jewish identity and how I feel like there's very little left to keep me connected. The piece takes the shape of a tallit with part of the prayer before putting on the tallit painted on the *atarah* [decorated area around the neck]. The embroidered lines start out like stripes on a traditional tallit but are broken and fraying as they get further from the top. The tallit itself is also coming undone with large tears and the knots on the tzitzit untying. And finally, a figure at the bottom clutches onto the tzitzit, trying to hold on to what's left of her Judaism.[41]

Stoltz wrote an essay about the piece on Kveller, a popular Jewish parenting site. Here, she elaborated her thoughts on both the artwork and how parenting had altered her synagogue experience. She described the difficulties in getting children to sit quietly in synagogue and the differences

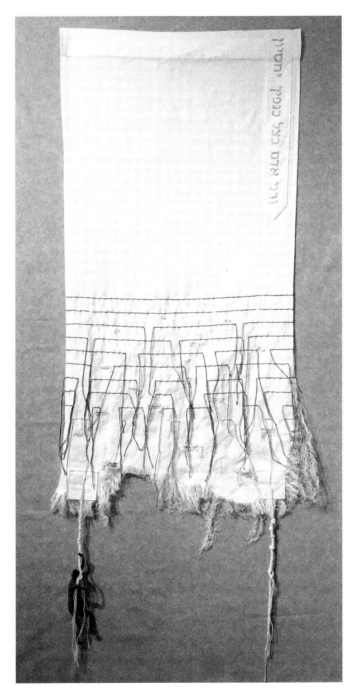

FIGURE 1.2.
*Heather Stoltz,*
Hanging by a
Thread. *Courtesy*
*of the artist.*

between being able to pray with her full attention and with a divided self, and all of the small customs that she had found falling away from her Sabbath practice, including feeling cloistered from the main community and distracted when attending the service geared for young children: "What had happened to those spiritual moments I used to have? I missed the songs, the communal prayer, the ability to close my eyes for the *Shema* without wondering if both kids would still be in the room when I opened them."[42] By expressing this rupture in art, Stoltz contributes to a Judaism that makes new room for *feeling*. There is no prayer for the conflicted emotion a new parent feels when she cannot concentrate on prayer because her children require attention. As Jewish studies scholar Mara Benjamin writes, "To live with and be responsible for a newborn, a baby, a toddler, is to suddenly wake up to one's un-freedom.... Maternity lifts, sometimes rips, the veil from our eyes, opening us to recognizing our conditionality." Stoltz's crafted Judaism reveals a portrait of an "obligated self, a self radically bound up with someone else."[43]

In Jewish tradition, the rending of clothing signifies mourning, a practice that Stoltz plays on in the torn prayer shawl of this piece, where the tallit itself is coming undone, and the tzitzit, the knotted ritual fringes that are commanded in the Torah and which make it a special garment, are coming untied, sacred threads unspooled, unwound, reversed. In the Kveller article, she concludes: "I am still holding on. I see what had been meaningful about Judaism slipping away. I'm mourning that loss, but I'm hoping that we can discover new ways to make Judaism meaningful for all of us, together, as a family."[44] Her work acknowledges how parenting is not always celebratory, even under the best of circumstances. It also entails grief over what is lost in this major life change, the aspects of self that are sometimes repressed when caring for others.

To return to Robinson and the horror vacui: children take up space—sometimes a great deal of it—but the gaps in Stoltz's torn prayer shawl are a kind of empty space, a void once filled with *kavanah*, or intention in prayer, now emptied through the stresses of shepherding two children through the Saturday rituals. *Hanging by a Thread* reveals the paradoxical pain contained within modern Jewish pronatalist communal imperatives.[45] For decades, Jewish American leaders have urged Jews to marry other Jews and have urged them to have Jewish children, a seemingly perennial theme that has become amplified by contemporary anxieties about intermarriage, "continuity" (one of the biggest Jewish buzzwords of the 1990s), and a perceived lack of "Jewish engagement" (I would argue that the problem is not an engagement gap but, rather, that today's Jews are simply engaging in new and different ways that contrast with their parents' communal patterns). Stoltz's work gets at the embodied results of natalist imperatives. When women's bodies are enlisted in the reproduction of new Jews, the women themselves may find their ability to meaningfully practice Judaism curtailed. An avid debate in the comments section of her Kveller piece, along with endless tomes of collective handwringing over Jewish continuity and the status of Jewish families, makes it evident that although the leaders of major Jewish institutions (and their attending rhetoric) value offspring, the full equality and engagement of involved parents of young children remains a challenge on a pragmatic level in many spaces. Stoltz's resilience comes on multiple levels: a refusal to sacrifice art *or* prayer, however challenging that might be. Though she has lost quiet moments of prayer in her day-to-day life, she also created a new cultural expression, an artwork that may not be a substitute for the act of prayer but remains a powerful, different kind of Jewish expression, one that provoked recognition from many of her readers. Through her art and her blogging, we witness a refusal to have these ambivalent pains go unheard.

STITCHES THAT BIND: ON WIMPELS

Heather Stoltz's recent work gives us a highly conceptual vision of modern Jewish parenting. We turn now to a much older craft that has reemerged in our contemporary moment, one where women affixed their stitches to a liminal moment between being a parent and not, to an object that links home and synagogue in a different way—namely, to the *wimpel*, or Torah binder.

The wimpel is an object that emerges out of early modern European Jewish traditions; though they are extant from many countries, including Spain, Italy, and France, wimpels are most heavily associated with eighteenth-century Germany.[46] The swaddling cloth that was used on the day of a baby boy's circumcision (*b'rit milah*) was cut into strips and then sewn together to form a lengthy band of material. New mothers and their friends and relatives then covered these strips with decorations, including elaborate embroidery. Ultimately, they donated the cloth to their local synagogue as a beltlike binder, used to wrap around the Torah scroll, holding it closed underneath a large cloth cover when it was not opened for reading. Though women typically did the handiwork, the husband offered the cloth in synagogue, with the mother present in the women's section. The timing of this donation varied. In some cases, it took place on the first Sabbath that the parturient (new mother) returned to synagogue, about a month after the child's birth.[47] In other cases, the wimpel was brought at the time of weaning or at the time of the child's first haircut.

Like so many other objects described in this book, the wimpel is a *minhag* (tradition), not something required by halacha, Jewish law. There is great variation among wimpels, but they usually include the baby's name, date of birth (and, at times, a visualization of its horoscope), and a formula from the b'rit milah ceremony welcoming the baby into the *b'rit* (covenant), and into a life of Torah, the marriage canopy (chuppah), and good deeds (*ma'asim tovim*). Illustrations of this trifecta—particularly images of the chuppah—abound. If you have been to a modern museum of Jewish art and culture, you have probably seen a wimpel.

In recent years, the wimpel has been making a comeback, profiled in a feature in the *Forward*, among other places. As Rachel Geizhals writes, wimpels in the United States have spread beyond their original context of being primarily used among German-descended Jews (called *yekkes* in slang): "Artists in Pennsylvania, Oregon, and California have painted, quilted, and embroidered wimpels of silk, needlepoint, and velvet for pluralistic clients around the country."[48] Wimpels are now used not just at the time of a child's birth and not just for boys; they are also created for bar and bat mitzvah ceremonies and a host of other occasions, though typically for life-cycle rituals of some kind.

Two of my informants were well ahead of this revival trend, making wimpels for their family members in the 1970s and 1980s. I interviewed Robin, a baby boomer, and Zelda, her aunt, separately at their respective homes in Southern California. Both were avid stitchers before they began making wimpels; Zelda was one of the earliest members of the California chapter of the Pomegranate Guild. Along with Robin's mother, each had made wimpels for baby boys born into their family.

Early in our interview, Robin showed me the elaborate Elijah's pillow used to back the chair on which *all* of the babies in the family—boy or girl—had rested when each was named on the eighth day. This was an innovative practice in the 1970s, at a time when the need for ceremonies to welcome baby girls into the covenant was becoming more evident among American Jews, yet practices like the *simchat bat* (joy in a daughter) ceremony were not yet widespread. Next, she displayed a different Elijah's pillow, used only for the b'rit milah, with the names of dozens of baby boys in the family, and the date of each of their ceremonies, carefully embroidered on the back of the pillow. Finally, she showed me one of the wimpels that were made for her sons, bright red embroidery on stark, shining white silk, and told me their stories (fig. 1.3). Although early modern German Jews worked on the elaborate embroidery *after* the b'rit milah for anywhere from thirty days to three years, in her family, the

FIGURE 1.3. *Robin Kessler Einstein, wimpel. Photograph by the author.*

goal was to complete the decorations on the wimpel *before* the circumcision: in other words, within eight days of the child's birth.

Flabbergasted at this short time frame, I asked her how this had worked. Many Ashkenazi Jews are superstitious about preparing items for a baby that has not been born, with practices ranging from not bringing *anything* for the baby into the house before its birth, to, in some contrasting recent examples, having a baby shower and the entire nursery ready. Robin never knew if each of her four children would be a boy or a girl—they were born before the widespread use of ultrasounds and, thus, the assignment of a sex identity before birth. In terms of superstition, she forged a middle path of sorts. Gesturing toward the generic parts of the wimpel text—the traditional formulations for Torah, marriage, and good deeds—she explained that those parts, her mother had prepared. Then Robin had stenciled—but did not stitch—the lettering for the expected Hebrew month and year of the birth. The name, however, was left blank.

Showing it to me, she said, "Then, once the baby is born you've got eight days to make *this*!" She gestured to the Hebrew name, composed of dozens of tiny red stitches. (Red was considered a lucky color and, in Jewish folklore, is one that can ward off the evil eye). She would not dare, she said, commit a bit of the dates or name to fabric until the baby emerged, whole and healthy. She had actually expected to have another girl. But then, "Lo and behold, my first son was born! My husband quickly made a stencil for the little one's name, my mom lined the whole thing onto the fabric, penciled it onto the fabric, and she and my husband brought fabric, thread, and scissors to me in the hospital within a few hours of our little one's birth. And I began happily stitching away!"[49]

Then she told me the rest of the story. "Fortunately, my boys were born in the days when you were in the hospital for five days, so I could do all the stitching." Robin lobbied to remain in the hospital, where nurses helped new parents to care for the baby, for extra days after the birth. She joked, pantomiming, "So, I'm stitching. I always had a Jewish gynecologist and obstetrician, so I said, 'I need one more day!'" She imitated the doctor, "'Okay, put down she needs one more day.' And I'm stitching there. This was a long time ago. Now, you can't get away with that."[50]

I was captivated by this story, reflecting on how, no, you certainly can't get away with that anymore. When my own child was born in 2011, not only were hospital stays shorter, but rooming in as standard practice meant you spent your immediate postpartum days feeding, diapering, and rocking your baby—hardly conducive to fine stitching. Consequently, I didn't finish my daughter's baby blanket until she was six months old. Robin's story evoked a time when the hospital was a place where the new mother rested while nurses took on the bulk of childcare. Hospitals and child-rearing practices, of course, have their own complex histories, beyond the focus of this study, but one method was clearly superior if one wanted to produce the perfect wimpel after the birth but *before* the circumcision.[51] Her story also spoke of Jewish class norms and career stereotypes, providing a slightly altered twist on Jewish doctor jokes. To finish the story, Robin showed me a picture of one of her sons in the early 1990s, now grown to thirteen, beside his father on the day he became a bar mitzvah. His wimpel was there, wrapped proudly around the Torah scroll as father and son both beamed.

The next day, elsewhere in the greater Los Angeles area, Robin's aunt Zelda showed me the wimpel she made, not for her son, but for her grandson. Zelda had read a book about wimpels in the Magnes Collection of Jewish Art and Life at the University of California at Berkeley and was inspired to create one. Although by 1988, ultrasound had come into slightly wider use, her son and daughter-in-law chose not to learn the baby's sex assignment, which complicated her plans for elaborate appliqué. Nevertheless, the piece she unrolled for me in her cozy living room was a marvel, a colorful array of images. We spread the wimpel out along the back of her couch so that I could photograph it in full, but my favorite image from our interview is of her holding it up as she first revealed it to me (fig. 1.4). Her smile beamed with the joy of this accomplishment. Every image stitched onto the fabric is laden with meaning. A rainbow links the word *b'rit*, for covenant, with the rest of the formula, evoking the sign of the

FIGURE 1.4. *Zelda, portrait with wimpel. Photograph by the author.*

rainbow as a covenantal symbol (the rainbow appears at the end of the
Noah narrative in the book of Genesis). Peacocks are affixed to each end
of the text, "facing out," she told me, "because when they come together,
they face each other, and there are peacocks at the gates of heaven."[52]
Elsewhere on the wimpel are pomegranates—a whole one near the beginning, and a tree filled with pomegranates near the words for "good deeds,"
because the seeds of a pomegranate are rumored to number 613, the total
number of commandments enumerated in Jewish tradition. The wimpel also features a tiny Torah scroll, a chuppah, and doves, among other
images. Even the grandchild's name is flanked by a variety of finely embroidered embellishments. The overall effect is of immense care, attention to detail, study, and pride in Jewish heritage.

What are we to make of these wimpels, old and new? How do practices of gender flow around the wimpel? Thinking with the wimpel requires us to engage with ideas of both increase and loss, presences and absences.

When a child is safely delivered in modern America—and certainly much more so when one was born in early modern Europe—it is still in a fragile state, in great danger of illness and death, as is the mother, which is what gave rise to so many folk practices protecting mother and child. There is much fear and anxiety in these "blessed events."[53] Even if the child survives, there is potential for a different kind of horror vacui: the womb, the space made empty again after birth. The wimpel is a new object created by the mother (or a relative) who, even if all went well, has a new human creation before her but is also, on a different level, bereft. The child that was intimately within her is now elsewhere. Then, in the ceremony of b'rit milah, it is taken into the synagogue, a historically male-dominated space, to be named. In Jewish tradition, women have been excluded from the action of marking the covenant through circumcision, both because cisgendered female bodies lack a penis and because the command to circumcise is directed at the father.[54] Jewish women are considered part of a covenant with God but are not included in this ritual. Yet on some level, the wimpel intervenes in this process and its gendering. Out of a swaddling cloth associated with the rending of flesh comes a mending in fabric, a new kind of binding.

The wimpel also provokes us to think about gender, the binding of Isaac, and women in Jewish American cultures. The story of Genesis 22, in which Abraham is told by God to sacrifice his son Isaac on a mountain—only to have an angel stay his hand at the last moment—is of pivotal importance in both Jewish and Christian traditions. For Jews, who reread the story ritually each Rosh Hashanah (Jewish New Year), it is known as the *akedah*, literally the binding of Isaac, for the way that the boy was trussed up on the altar, quivering beneath his father's enormous knife (*maachelet*).

Reading Torah binders alongside the binding of Isaac evokes many ironies, and makes spaces for resistant, transformative interpretations of earlier traditions. Sarah, Isaac's mother, is left out of the binding of Isaac story, a fact that is noted by rabbinic interpreters, who speculated that Sarah's death in the next section of the Torah was caused by her grief at what Abraham had nearly done. Feminist scholars, poets, and liturgists have all done much to bemoan and at times reimagine Sarah's occlusion from the akedah narrative.[55] In early modern Germany, women could not be called up to the Torah—yet their handiwork, specifically their handiwork tied to the birth of a new community member—quite literally bound the sacred scroll they could not approach.

Twentieth-century and contemporary wimpels, of course, are a slightly different thing. A small moment in my conversation with Robin hangs with me. As she showed me the wimpel, she indicated that there had not been enough room to include both of the baby's parents' names upon it, so she just included her husband's. "We decided we didn't have enough room for my name, so we would just leave it the father; it's the *bris*, leave it the father, it's alright."[56]

"It's the *bris*, leave it the father." On the one hand, the issue did not seem to have been a fraught one; on the other, it was still recalled over thirty years later. Robin ceded the space of the b'rit milah over to her husband. Circumcisions are about the male body; let the male name predominate. Yet here, too, was *her* presence, materially, marked so boldly in those bright stitches, on the day of the circumcision and in the photo of the Torah scroll, bound by that same strip of fabric, from thirteen years later. In the picture of the father and son beaming as the son becomes a bar mitzvah, the brilliant red stitching on the wimpel is the *punctum*, that spot in the picture which pins you and draws you in.[57]

The wimpel would seem to be an object that reinforces traditional gender roles, but I wonder if it might in fact be more fluid than its history would suggest. On the one hand, of course, it is an artifact of binary complementarity, an object originally created by women to honor men and boys. Reclaimed, reinterpreted, it can be understood as a reparative act, an insertion of the mother into a space—proximity to the Torah scroll—that she was normally, at that time in history, denied. Sarah was not present at the binding of Isaac, but her metaphorical descendants stitch their way into a different kind of all-male setting.

As discussed earlier, however, not all bodies create new life. Further, not all bodies are defined as either male or female. To further untangle our way out of these gendered bindings, we need to return to the concept with which we began: resilience.

EVERYDAY RESILIENCE

An overwhelming number of my interviewees and survey respondents describe creation as a requirement of their existence. Crafting new objects is something they simply *have* to do, akin to breathing, a means of survival. Peachy Levy, a renowned Los Angeles–based fiber artist, told me, "An artist has to work all the time. So if I don't have commissions from synagogues for ceremonial pieces, I create decorative art with Jewish themes."[58] More dramatically, one survey respondent wrote, "Creativity is crucial to our survival as humans, and we especially need it as Jewish women."

On levels that are sometimes mundane and sometimes mystical—or both—many of my respondents took part in crafting "a utopia of ordinary habit," one in which craft and other daily rituals help us to "insist that daily life in all its ordinariness can be a basis for the utopian project of building new worlds in response to both spiritual despair and political depression."[59] These crafters did indeed voice sentiments of despair. They grieved lost family members and lost elections; worried over the future of their families, their communities, their planet; and experienced health setbacks, ability challenges, and the existential terror of getting through each day. Crafting these small bubbles of utopia offered them a blend of solace, release, and comfort—as well as a space to express uncomfortable truths.

Overwhelmingly, throughout my ethnography, I encountered individuals who focused on process as much as product. Most people told me not just about what they made but about how that making made them *feel*. Here, our understanding of the resilience generated through crafting benefits from recent work in religion, affect, and emotion.[60] Crafting resilience is not just about what people think but about what bodies do, and the sensations that intersect with those bodies. For the artists quoted above and many, many others, the embodied actions of knitting, sewing, carving, or sculpting provide soothing solace, or creative excitement, or other powerful feelings—craft reverberates in and around bodies, one of the "unspoken forces" that shape our being.[61]

What if this creative solace mattered as much as more popular ways of measuring Jewish communal strength, and how would that also change how Jews think about gender? Focusing on forces and feeling also gives us a way to conceptualize Jewish creation beyond a gendered binary of either male or female creators and beyond a focus on creation as tied to biologically male or female bodies. Creation as process, not product—and, according to some of my interlocutors, as itself a sacred action—resists the pronatalist imperative that has dominated so many Jewish American communal discussions over the past few decades, quite stridently since the 1990s.[62] So often, Jews, especially Jewish women, are told that their value for the community is in giving birth to its offspring. What if Jewish philanthropists cared as much about Jews creating new art and other forms of culture as they cared about Jews marrying other Jews and having Jewish babies? The emphasis on Jewish population size often leads Jewish communities to undervalue the creative forms and activities that can spiritually and artistically nourish Jews, whatever their numbers. When it comes to the process of crafting, we can move beyond an emphasis on the biological sex assignment of Jewish bodies, making room for broader notions of gender and for a vision of Judaism that is based, not on binaries and physical reproduction, but instead on more diverse fields of power and identity. Craft provides a more fluid way to consider Jewish genders or, as one of my survey respondents who identifies as genderqueer put it, "The space for fluidity in the art has helped me to accept the fluidity of my gender, in a way."[63]

Many of the people I met described how the skills and knowledge they had gained as artists had endured even when objects in their lives, or the lives of their companions, had been destroyed. Reflecting on the experiences of a friend who lost needlework in a natural disaster, Atlanta artist Flora Rosefsky told me, "Whether it's health or divorce or sickness or finances or . . . tornadoes or hurricanes or floods. But relationships and education in your brain and what you learn, that doesn't have to be destroyed."[64] In recent years, Flora has frequently deployed the image of the sukkah, the temporary shelter that Jews erect during their fall harvest festival—and an important metaphor for God's sheltering presence—in her art. Materiality matters, but so, too, does the survival of the social bonds that were created around and through that materiality, even as she emphasized impermanence. Objects are thus not only about their *own* materiality. If lost, though technically irreplaceable, the experiences that gave rise to such objects could be remembered, and the skills gained in making them retained.

Zelda told me that the crafting process was "like my meditation." She described how her experience of sewing changed when her sewing machine broke and, instead, she had to do the appliqué by hand: "I began to realize that I was in another world mentally. Not one problem went through my mind." She began to intentionally perform her work slowly, rather than by machine. Later in the conversation, she added: "It [sewing] means I could take what is part of life around me, which could be sterile to some people, and I could find something to create that is close to God."[65] Zelda's approach to crafting as spiritual resembles sentiments expressed by many Jewish artists, particularly in the Renewal movement.[66]

Here, the meaning-making of craft is once again about a process that transforms the everyday into the holy. Zelda used the term "sterility" to describe how some people encounter the material world that surrounds them, using examples, in our larger conversation, that ranged from the inanimate (cloth) to the living (plants, animals). I want to think with this notion of sterility in its medical, aesthetic, and biological valences. Medically speaking, something sterile is clean, untouched, cleansed of as many threatening visible and microscopic agents as possible, perhaps cut off from that which is not sterile by a boundary of some sort: a glove, a plastic package, an operating room door. Aesthetically, something sterile is a space or an object that is ordinary, blah, lacking in vigor, visual interest, or evidence of personality. Biologically speaking, to be sterile is the opposite of being fertile: it is to be unable to reproduce biologically, in a host of ways, ranging from natural circumstances to surgical interventions, both chosen and not chosen. Zelda contrasts what she does—creating holy feelings through stitching—with how a nonartistic soul might encounter fabric, needle, and thread.

One way to think about living bodies is as "nodes for the flow of power."[67] Zelda's body and so many others like it, bent carefully over needlework for decades, leverage an emotional religious power. So, too, do all of the artists in this chapter. From Robinson's rejection of empty spaces to the many abundant displays of stitching described above, these Jewish Americans, and, in this chapter, mostly Jewish American *women*, are unabashedly taking up space. They are also finding means of physical and emotional resilience, whether it is working through body shaming in a family altercation or knitting their way through upsetting political events, making meaning out of the challenges of parenthood or stitching their way back into the b'rit milah.

In terms of both the history and sociology of religions in the United States, these activities are not new. They do, however, refract our understanding of religion and gender, including both femininity and masculinity, in subtle ways. There were times in Jewish American history—particularly in the early twentieth century—when proving Jewish masculinity required an ethos of disciplining physically strong men who could also make things, who could till the land *and* build objects, who could produce, not just consume.[68] Jews do not always fit neatly into the dominant narratives of American religious history, and yet, of course, Jewish Americans have always also been a *part* of this history, shaping their lives in relation to popular cultural matrices with other populations on the land we now call the United States. After all, Jewish Americans did not invent quilting, embroidery, or knitting. But they made it their own.

Thinking with craft culture and generative resilience as lenses expands our conceptualization of Jewishness and gender within the broader field of scholarship on religions in North America. At first glance, many of the examples in this chapter would seem to fit the model of gender studies (then called Women's Studies) interventions that dominated the field in the 1970s.[69] The people discussed here are predominantly cisgender, middle- or upper-middle-class Ashkenazi Jewish women. Many, though not all, became mothers within heterosexual marriages. However, changing how we think about religions in America requires not just attention to the bodies and capsule identities of those we study but also careful readings of the rituals and discourses in which they take part, and what those processes signify.

Rereading notions of fecundity, sterility, and resilience in these examples demonstrates how the embrace of excess is itself a subversive act. Castigating Ashkenazi Jewish bodies, African American bodies, Latinx bodies, and a host of others as fat is a pattern with long legacies of racism and particular Christian notions of discipline and purity. Declaring, "Fat is good," or allowing Jewish art to take up space resists that history.[70] Likewise, we can find examples that disrupt the preponderance of fertility imagery in Jewish American imaginaries and arguments that challenge the unabashed pronatalism of Jewish American communities. Stoltz's *Hanging by a Thread* challenges a triumphalist narrative in which achieving parenthood means that one has arrived and fulfilled one's Jewish destiny. By literally fraying a symbol of prayer and adult Jewish commitment, she shows how maternal bodies, while prized rhetorically, can also be physically and spiritually marginalized in Jewish settings.

Looking at generative resilience through craft also attunes us to different narratives of American religious history. Historian Colleen McDannell reconceptualized Christian histories by focusing on shrines, clothing, kitsch, stores, and other sites of cultural formation, attending to how "Christians use goods and create religious landscapes to tell themselves and the world around them who they are."[71] Similarly, we can look to Jewish material cultures in order to see how Jews live their traditions in the everyday, how they embellish central life-cycle rituals, like circumcisions and baby naming, with colorfully decorated wimpels and pillows. For Zelda and Robin, "the cut that binds" was not a fully articulated ritual without these surrounding pieces.[72] To study Jews we also need to study their objects, and the co-constitution between people and possessions. These artifacts are technologies that forge new moments of Jewish community, some informed by the past, like circumcision, and some amplifying recent developments in the "spiritual marketplace," like New Age–inspired protection amulets, together.[73] In the next chapter, we turn more literally to this notion of technology and examine how modalities as ancient as the spindle and as contemporary as the World Wide Web all craft new models of Judaism.

## 2 : BLACK FIRE, WHITE PIXELS, AND GOLDEN THREADS

. . . . . . . . . . . . . . . . . . . . . . .

*Technology and Craft*

### WHEELS WITHIN WHEELS

On a brilliant, sunny, slightly chilly day in early May, I found myself on the Washington, D.C., metro. A cover of "All Along the Watchtower" blared on my headphones as the train lurched along through its square-patterned tunnels, then burst out above the Tidal Basin and across the Potomac. I saw the Jefferson Memorial, but mostly, I saw the afterimages of those domes of massive gray concrete squares, the ones that had been sliding by above me.

The wheels on the metro lurched onward, their rhythm matching the guitar chords in my ear canal. I thought of my conversation the day before with Amanda, who designed numerous Torah mantles for her synagogue in a Maryland suburb. I was interviewing her in person and saw several pieces in situ, but this one I glimpsed on the screen of her phone. She showed me the picture of a quilted, white-on-white High Holy Day Torah mantle. "The rabbi asked me to make a Torah cover for the new scroll," she said. "The theme of the yearlong event of writing this scroll was 'to turn it and turn it because everything is in it,'" she told me.[1] That phrase—"turn it and turn it"—is a talmudic reference to the Torah, not just as a physical scroll but as a symbol for all of Jewish teaching. Even the most wizened sage can find something new if they keep turning the words of Torah over and over again. Inspired by this theme, Amanda intentionally turned a traditional American quilt pattern—the log cabin square—onto a diagonal in order to evoke this idea. The technique of piecing a quilt met with a moment of textual interpretation: the result was something new. Twisting, turning, a distinctly American "handmade midrash."[2]

So much of the technology in the world of fiber arts involves circular motion. As the train rumbled on, I remembered that twisted cover and thought more about turning, and also about wheels: the wheels of the chariot vision in Ezekiel 1, the foundation of whole reams of Jewish mysticism. Often, technology is described in a language that we might call mystical or mystifying. Immersed in a bit of a numinous moment myself, I imagined the wheels and gears on a sewing machine that must spin to make the needle rise and fall; the circular whorls of drop spindles as they twirl in the air; the elegant wooden spinning wheels I had seen that week at the Maryland Sheep and Wool Festival. Do those wheels, I thought fancifully, have a spirit in them, like the spirit of the animals in the chariot wheels? Then I reconceived the spatiality of the metaphor: not everything involving wheels is circular. The train moved forward in a guided, fairly straight line, following the track, like the neat lines produced by a sewing machine or an artfully wielded tapestry needle. Lines and circles coexist.

The virtual and the material, the digital and the tactile, are symbiotic in the diverse world of Jewish crafts. Today's craft blogs have their roots in the sewing circles that go back for centuries. New digital tools are not separate from what we can touch; they are symbiotic with flesh and blood, steel needle and soft fabric. Furthermore, technology is not just instrumental. It is, itself, a practice and a way of knowing. It is also a bridge between humans and their objects. Hearing the stories of crafters and their technologies brings us to an intersection where the human and nonhuman are formed together.[3] In the early modern period, "for artisans, experience and the production of things were bound up with their own bodies."[4] For my crafting interlocutors, matter, practice, and selfhood are intimately connected.

Technology and Jewish fiber arts are not at odds; indeed, they "mingle promiscuously" in many of the cases I am studying, though not without moments of tension.[5] Such tensions are productive. As the sewers, knitters, weavers, and spinners all tell me, *tension* is not a bad thing: it is a necessary part of the physics of textile creation. Without some level of tension, or a tight pull, in one's knitting or sewing, the fabric will fall to pieces; the thread will come undone.

PLAITING TECHNOLOGY, CRAFT, AND RELIGION
Technology, or the practice of applying mental and physical machinations to a problem, has always been interwoven with religious practices. From the codex to the printing press to the World Wide Web, these two concepts have flowed in tandem. Technology and religion are not separate domains but, rather, phenomena that can be thought about together: "Technology—in the enlarged sense of materials, techniques, instruments, and expertise—forms the gridwork of orientations, operations, and em-

bedded and embodied knowledges and powers without which religious ideas, experiences, and actions could not exist."[6] All of the people in this book use technologies constantly. Some of those technologies are very, very old. The invention of string, created by plying together shorter fibers to form a long strand, goes all the way back to the Paleolithic period.[7] The drop spindle was an innovation in its day. Weaving, spinning, knitting, and embroidery are all mentioned in the Hebrew Bible and in rabbinic texts; the metaphors for these technologies are even reflected in some of the terms used for Jewish text study, like the *masseket*, or web of cloth on a loom, used to describe tractates of Talmud.[8] Hand needles, which today evoke a nostalgic feel, were once a tremendous innovation (particularly once they could be crafted from sharp metals). Much later mechanical technologies, like the sewing machine, the spinning jenny, and the automatic loom, helped to drive the Industrial Revolution—and they simultaneously provided employment, albeit in dangerous conditions, for many members of the generation of mass Ashkenazi immigration to the United States.[9]

Technologies suffuse every aspect of creation. However, there are generational, class-based, and minhag (tradition)-based divides on the role that technologies, particularly digital ones, can or should play in the creation of art and craft. Technologies radically enhance practices—but not without controversy or questions. At its root, the modern English word "technology" derives from the Latin *technologia* and, before that, from a Greek word intimately connected to the fiber arts: *techne*, which in its nominative form could mean craft, skill, trade, or art, cunning, wile, or means. In verbal constructions, it can also mean to plait (as well as to craft), a connotation that evokes binding, and thus, in turn, the Latin root for the English word "religion": "religion" is likely derived from the Latin *religare*, to bind. At their etymological core, technology and religion share this cognate shade of meaning.

Digital technologies are also a crucial creation tool for many of these artists. Some artists use computers to draw the designs they will embroider or special digital equipment to cut vinyl for their custom personalized wares. Crucially, computer-mediated communication—blogs, social media, apps, digitized patterns, and emails—forms its own web of connection and meaning-making for a number of crafters. It is important to resist the idea that the digital is somehow less authentic than the analog, somehow less real or tactile, while also considering the ways it changes practices and communities. The digital, which is often figured as virtual (though these are not the same thing), is intimately connected to the material, and not just because computers are made of copper and chrome, lithium ion batteries and metal wires. As we will see, digital tools are more than just assistants: they are a formative feature of religious craft practices.

## BLACK FIRE ON WHITE FIRE:
## JEWISH CRAFT BLOGS AND VISIBILITY

The sheer volume of craft blogs, Instagram feeds, and Pinterest boards by Jewish crafters is mind-boggling. Some have names that mark their affiliation—Cathy Perlmutter's *GefilteQuilt*—while others have names so oblique that you don't initially realize that they are a treasure trove of Jewish art and craft material until you read them, as is the case with *Sarah in NYC*.[10] Jewish craft blogs—like many other sorts of blogs—are a means of connecting across lines of distance, mobility, age, and, in some cases, ethnoreligious traditions, too. With their episodic nature and their details of everyday life, blogs inspire a sense of intimacy even if you have not met the author.

When I went to visit Sarah—the author of *Sarah in NYC*—in her Upper West Side apartment, I felt as if I were going to a friend's home, even though we had never met. Reading through her blog told me many things, but of course, I was also left with many gaps. Blogs elide as much as they show; digital narratives and social media are carefully curated. Sarah is a blogger, sewer, artist, cook, parent, and daughter of a rabbi. Her blog's tagline is: "a blog, mostly about my work making Jewish ritual objects, but with detours into garment making, living in New York City, cooking and other aspects of domestic life."[11] Through the blog, which began in 2009, I learned about her family, her synagogue community, her art, her cooking, the history of textiles, the garment industry, and much more.

"Black and White Fire" is the first in a series of posts describing Sarah's work on a custom prayer shawl for a rabbinical student. It includes descriptions of textile work but also of how her work combines text, prayer, practice, and her personal biography. She writes, "I was brought up in a tradition where the ecstatic and the spiritual are deeply private experiences. You are brought to those moments through the beauty of the texts. One's expression of that ecstatic moment is inward and private."[12] In our interview, she attributed this tendency to her ancestors' "Litvish" (as opposed to "Chassidish") origins. She then includes the entire Hebrew and English text of the *piyyut* (liturgical poem) that the student selected for his tallit. Part of her English translation reads: "*Now an angel of the Lord appeared to Moses in a blazing fire* . . . a fire that devours fire; a fire that burns in things dry and moist; a fire that glows amid snow and ice; a fire that is like a crouching lion; a fire that reveals itself in many forms; a fire that is, and never expires; a fire that shines and roars; a fire that blazes and sparkles."[13]

She describes painting the piyyut onto the silk: "Then as I copied the text, I paid attention to each word, to each letter of each word, each stroke of every letter."[14] Her blog shows images of the poem in a gleaming silvery white paint atop black silk. After painting it this way, she reproduced it in the reverse: black paint on white silk. Subsequent blog posts show the evolution of the tallit, often in combination with other activities, like celebrating the twenty-first birthday of her youngest child. (So, in this case, the picture of the calligraphy progress was juxtaposed with a shot of the birthday son and some scrumptious-looking hot dogs and meringue.) Other posts describe the technicalities of seaming, the "restraint" of working in black and white with minimal embellishment (that is, ribbons), with great care to explain things ("for those of you who don't sew, that's a heavy thread"). She brings the reader along with her on each step of the process, with captions like, "I love how the tiny stitches add a tiny sparkle of light to the black gros-grain ribbon.... It is in many ways a tiny detail that makes all the difference in the world. My stitches are small and neat and just slightly irregular. I think the irregularity is actually a good thing here."[15] Staring at the stitches on my computer screen, I felt a sense of hyperreality. Though I could not physically touch them, my office's immense digital monitor gave me a better view of the stitching than my eyes could have done in person. The digital does not completely displace the tactile; it also enhances how we come to know it. My sense of touch was truncated, but my sense of sight was augmented.

In Sarah's blog post about this tallit, there are layers upon layers of mediation. A prayer shawl, a ritual garment worn during morning prayers (and used on other key occasions), becomes an extension of multiple bodies, including both the creator and the wearer. A combination of machine technology (a sewing machine) and hand technologies (hand stitching and calligraphy) fold together numerous details in cloth. A digital communication technology—the blog—conveys both pictures and words to a readership beyond Sarah's warm, fiber-stuffed home, which smells of freshly baked bread and spices, a sensory experience from our interview that cannot be reproduced online.

The title for Sarah's first post about this prayer shawl is an allusion to a famous phrase that appears in multiple rabbinic and medieval sources: "The Torah given to Moses was written with black fire upon white fire, sealed with fire, and swathed with bands of fire."[16] The combination of Sarah's blog and her handmade creations forms a hybrid digital-material midrash (interpretation) that allows for a dramatic play of texts in a virtual world. Though midrash as a classical rabbinic form is now closed, some contemporary Jews use the idea of midrash as a verb, a way of re-imagining Jewish texts and finding new meaning within them; some Jews also produce "modern midrash."[17] In some interpretations, the "white fire" of this quotation—the space *between* the black letters—is associated with the oral Torah, while the "black fire" signifies the letters we can see, the written Torah. Classical Jewish textual interpretation has much in common with the world of digital texts: it links passages in an associative, often nonlinear manner.[18] As religion scholar Rachel Wagner writes, "The exploration of wired textuality invites us to consider texts *as* texts, and thus also as material objects transformed into information streams, with profound impacts for how they are used and treated. In the transformation of material books into information streams, we are witnessing also the transformation of sacred texts from a fixed series of words on a page—God's will typeset and printed—into fluid, shapeable and playable streams."[19]

Wagner's reading of sacred texts in the age of the Internet uses aquatic metaphors of fluid streams. On the blog and on fabric, Sarah's approach to texts has playfulness, but it is not, precisely, fluid. She is relocating the texts onto fabric; she is not rewriting them. Her work is moderately malleable, and in a signature move of both the mechanical and digital ages, it is *repeatable*. Of course, repetitions can also come from handwork—hence her design of repeating the piyyut on the material, once as white paint on black fabric, and once as black paint on white fabric. Here, we have a text transformed into a very particular type of material object: a fabric one to be worn—and then reproduced digitally in order to be shared with more of the world.

The "black fire on white fire" idea can be thought through in many ways. In one recent interpretation, the white space between the letters is feminized, standing in for the ways that women's experiences can add to the sacred.[20] As rabbi and author Malka Drucker writes, building upon that statement, "Overlooked and absent from half of the human narrative, women are like white fire, the element upon which black fire depends: without white, you cannot see anything. One day, when there is no injustice or oppression, we will be able to read the often ignored, invisible white language surrounding the black text."[21] While this particular interpretation has shades of essentialism and perhaps, though I don't think it was intended, passivity, the notion that is most helpful here is one of *visibility*. How can we make more experiences visible, comprehensible, thinkable?

Technologies like blogs make space, opening up new forums for interpretation; they may also make things more legible. Blogs like Sarah's make invisible labor visible. It's not just about the sewing. It *is*, of course, on its first level, about the sewing. But it is also about what she makes for dinner, the errands she runs, the laundry, the cleaning before Shabbat and holy days. The white fire of her blog is an insight into work that is typically coded as feminine and into labor, both paid and unpaid, that is not always apparent. This is something she conveys, at times quite consciously, in profoundly political ways. She shares her insights on the old linens that her friends donate to her, often from family members who are long deceased or who have recently died; she reflects on the twentieth-century home economics movement and her realization, as an adult, that this movement "was founded by feminists to elevate the position of women and to improve their education," eventually giving rise to things like the regulation of milk safety.[22] She reminds us that "just a few generations ago, table linens were household wealth that was owned by women. Those linens were expensive to produce. Women began producing and acquiring them as young girls and then built up their collections until they were married."[23] The text is always accompanied by full-color pictures, showing the warp and weave of the linens in question, the delicate lace of hand-tatted edges, the color of embroidery, the sometimes humorous images from old home economics books. The white pixels of Sarah's blog—and many others like it—reveal the vast amounts of work that keep a Jewish home functioning.

## MAGIC AND RITUAL TECHNOLOGIES
Kohenet Ketzirah Lesser is a Generation X digital marketing specialist in a major metro area. A *kohenet* is a Hebrew priestess. Ketzirah was ordained through the Kohenet Hebrew Princess Institute, cofounded by Rabbi Jill Hammer and Taya Shere; she was in the first cohort of women to complete this training in 2006.[24] I learned about her work through social media and sat down to speak with her one evening in May 2017. Ketzirah's blog, *devotaj*, provides "Sacred Arts for Spiritual Seekers and Bold Souls from Kohenet Ketzirah haMa-agelet." (*Ma'agelet* means circle maker and references the importance of circles in various traditions that have influenced her.) She creates "modern amulets, talismans, shiviti, shrines, travel altars, and spiritual tools that are handcrafted for those creating a vibrant spiritual practice that draws on past, present and future."[25]

I was particularly interested in Ketzirah's work because of the way it straddles the material and digital worlds. On the one hand, she is an artist, particularly of embroidery, and a creator of things whose power resides in their tactility and their sensory vibrations. Amulets, for example, are meant to be worn or to be hung in a significant location. At the same time, she was the founder of a virtual worship space called "OneShul," and at the time we met, she still led online Shabbat services and Rosh Hodesh ceremonies there. Her Tumblr, her Etsy store, and her Instagram feed all provide images of her material creations, as well as her creative writing, inspirational quotations, pictures of tarot cards, and other digital ephemera. What was it like to reside so deeply in both virtual and handcrafted worlds?

The most common type of item Ketzirah creates is the amulet. Online images of a healing amulet showed a delicate square of cream-colored fabric, with gleaming red spirals embroidered onto it. Like a fabric dumpling, the inside of the square was then filled with meaningful items, particularly herbs and crystals, then carefully folded and tied with red string. The Etsy description for this item read, "Ingredients: herbs, gem, crystal, cotton, embroidery floss, cord, prayer, blessing, kavanah, intention, magick."[26] In contrast, the amulet to ward off the evil eye was a vivid cobalt blue felt, stitched in white and black. It was "intended to hold you in the gaze of the Beloved Holy-one at all times, so there is no room for anything but love."[27] The cotton floss used for the stitching was "infused with salt and obsidian"; garlic, rue (from her garden), sea salt, a bit of afikomen (matzah from a part of the Passover seder), and eggshell, taken from an egg used in making challah (a special bread for Friday nights and holy days), were inside the wrap. In this process, not just the finished object, but the precise nature of its constituent parts is crucial, redolent with layers of spiritual significance.

For Ketzirah, rituals are a kind of technology, and technology can enhance ritual. I asked her about the process of making an amulet: where she makes it, how she thinks about it while working on it. She told me that the initial embroidery can take place anywhere, even on the bus. But then, she said,

When I reach the stage of assembling an amulet that's where it sort of starts to shift gears. For example, with a bundle-style amulet I'll pull all the ingredients together and place them into the center of a chalk circle that I've drawn onto my workspace. I pause to take a photograph each stage of the final assembly ... so its recipient can not only see the final result but also the intention of each part of the process. This allows me to also shift from maker mode to spiritual/ ceremonial mode as I finish the assembly and photography, before I start "bundling" it and performing the ceremonial aspects.[28]

*Black Fire, White Pixels, and Golden Threads* 57

Like Sarah, Ketzirah documents many substages of her creations. In this case, the digital illustration of each step is specifically geared toward education, with the goal of enhancing the spiritual experience of the amulet recipient—keeping them engaged with the process of creation and thus with the intentions behind the finished piece.

Ketzirah's amulet making is intimately engaged with many layers of technology. Crucially, there is no clear divide between what we might call secular and spiritual technologies. Consider, for example, the process by which an image gets onto fabric. Some skilled stitchers can sew elaborate designs straight onto the fabric without a guide, but it is more common to somehow place the lines of a pattern onto a different medium, then transfer it to the cloth, before sewing. "I don't hand draw well," she told me. "So my actual design process ends up being very digital," in what she described as "the greatest transfer process ever." She continued: "It's a water-soluble stabilizer that allows me to print the design, cut it out, attach it directly to the fabric, stitch right through it. After I've completed the stitching, I rinse the pattern away with water, which I also find adds a component of spiritual cleansing."[29]

In other words, the process of the project joins an extremely convenient form of image reproduction with an experience of water that is both practical and religiously meaningful. Pragmatically, it removes the sticky remnants of the stabilizer, leaving only the fabric and stitching behind. Yet water is also spiritually resonant. It is part of many Jewish rituals, ranging from uses of the *mikvah* (ritual bath), both old and new, to handwashing before meals. On her website, she illustrated this process, posting an image of the water pouring over an embroidered *hamsa* (hand) on a piece of blue felt—a ritual object in motion (fig. 2.1).[30] Ketzirah uses "the Jewish ritual toolbox" to make meaning on a variety of levels.[31] Though the selection of water is initially a pragmatic part of her assembly process, she *also* recognizes that soaking in water is a familiar move, one saturated with Jewish meanings, and interprets it as such. Though readers of the blog are not there to dip their hands into the water, they can follow this step in the amulet's layered journey from afar.

For Ketzirah, spiritual reverberations can be conveyed in either fabric or pixels (along with herbs, crystals, and a host of other transmission methods), which transitions us from water to electricity. I asked her about the interesting juxtaposition of her material amulets and the digital One-Shul services that she was still leading that year (as of the time of this writing, she no longer does so). "One of my Kohenet sisters called amulets 'post-it notes from God,'" she told me. "The most *p'shat* [plain] level of how they work to me is this thing reminds you. 'Right? It's a reminder, it's

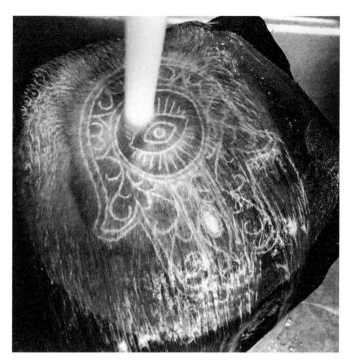

FIGURE 2.1.
*Ketzirah
Lesser, hanging
embroidery
with stabilizer
being washed
away. Used
with permission
of the artist.*

a physical thing that you touch.' ... It's another way of being Jewish every day." She said that in services, however, there are other ways of reaching people and of having something that mimics or even constitutes a physical connection. She explained that sometimes, during services: "I'll say, 'Okay, everyone. Hands on the keyboards. We're going to take a minute, and everyone is going to try to project their energy through the keyboard to each other.' ... It's very subtle, but I actually do pick up that type of energetic feedback that I get when I'm in person with somebody through the Internet. Not remotely at the level of being in physical contact, and it takes way more just to get it, but it's the people in the chatroom, are more than just words to me. They're very real as people."[32] In other words, physical distance does not negate the possibility of a material connection between bodies. Presences and human touch can be transmitted across the same wires that carry our digital data.[33]

In contrast with Ketzirah, who was discussing the ways that electrical conduits could also, literally, harness a kind of human energy, Sarah uses the *metaphor* of electricity to describe how she thinks about a tallit. As we looked at the tallit she had made for her own daughter, I admired the *pinnot*—the decorations at the four corners of the shawl where the tzitzit, ritual fringes, are inserted (fig. 2.2). She told me,

*Black Fire, White Pixels, and Golden Threads* 59

FIGURE 2.2. *Sarah Jacobs, corner of prayer shawl. Photograph by the author.*

The thought behind that is that you want the tzitzit to be not thought of as separate from the tallit but part of the whole thing. I think of the *pinah*, it's almost like the spiritual electrical socket. It's the thing that changes it from just being a beautiful shawl into being a tallit. I like to emphasize it. The other thing is that *davening* [praying] is hard, and sometimes it's hard for most people, and especially kids, to focus. Because the pinah is beautiful and pulls your eye in and because my clients have tied their tzitzit, it pulls them back.[34]

For both Sarah and Kezirah, objects are part of ritual technologies of self. A wide variety of factors—age, experience, location, what one is wearing, posture, natural inclinations, intentions—can all affect one's experience of being Jewish both in everyday moments (while wearing an amulet on a crowded subway car, for example) and in dedicated communal moments of prayer, whether those take part in a progressive Conservative synagogue like Sarah's or during an innovative kohenet ritual like Kezirah's. Prayer is enhanced by the "spiritual electrical socket" of the pinnot, and everyday activities—or extraordinary ones like attending protests—are made more Jewish by the presence of a protective amulet, a "post-it note from God."

In 2016, Samuel Barsky went viral. Over the coming years, his story spread. "This Man Who Knits Sweaters to Match Landmarks Is the Hero the Internet Needed," a headline in *Time* magazine proclaimed.[35] For approximately twenty years, Barsky has made sweaters of famous tourist locations—Niagara Falls, Stonehenge, the Hollywood sign—and then had his picture taken in front of the landmark, proudly wearing its depiction in yarn. When he started to post the pictures to Instagram, the Internet did indeed rejoice, and media outlets noticed. "It's always sweater weather for Samuel Barsky," Laura M. Holson wrote in the *New York Times*.[36] That feature also includes a quotation from Keren Ben-Horin, a fashion curator and writer on sweaters, who states that Samuel Barsky is "wearing them as works of art."[37] On his own website and Facebook pages, he identifies himself as "Samuel Barsky–artistic knitter." There, you can now buy mugs, tote bags, and other souvenirs with images from the sweaters emblazoned upon them. He code-switches elegantly, saying, "I knit jumpers," when speaking with the BBC. "I don't think I'll ever run out because I've come up with thousands of ideas in my life."[38] In Barsky's Internet fame, we see "the age of mechanical reproduction" triumphant. The sweater art is transmitted to the world in pixels, which, in turn, drives a demand for newly reproduced material items. When we look at Barsky's sweaters on our phones, we are embodying the predictions of philosopher Walter Benjamin, where "in permitting the reproduction to meet the beholder . . . in his own particular situation, it reactivates the object reproduced"; in turn, "every day, the urge grows stronger to get hold of an object at very close range by way of its likeness, its reproduction."[39] We long for something containing the aura of the original sweaters, even though we cannot hold them. The sweater print tote bag costs twenty-four dollars.

Barsky is also a Jew from Baltimore. In a *Times of Israel* profile, Rebecca Shimoni Stoil writes, "Sam Barsky is a modest Maryland man who knits improbable sweaters. But this Saturday evening, just following Shabbat, he turned on his computer to discover that he had become that rarest of 21st century unicorns—a human internet meme."[40] This piece pays detailed attention to the sweaters that stood out to me on Barsky's Instagram feed: sweaters for every Jewish holiday, a Western Wall sweater that is included in most of the professional media collages of his work, and other sweaters that detail his connection to both Jewish life and Israel. The photo of Barsky at the Western Wall is particularly striking. Taken on a clear day, the blue on the sky at the top of the photo matches the blue sky at the top of the sweater; the plaza behind him is sparsely populated, and the texture of the cracks in the soft yarn depiction of the wall really does evoke the ancient stones behind him. The excitement comes from the multiple levels of mediation, from the presence of a copy, in the form of a sweater, juxtaposed beside the original (except in the case of his Eiffel Tower sweater; because he has never been to Paris, the sweater is pictured in Las Vegas, a simulacrum next to another simulacrum—even more delightful). The article also features a picture of Barsky in his Yom Kippur sweater, a short sleeved white piece emblazoned with a replica of the High Priest's jeweled breastplate (one jewel for each of the twelve tribes); "Barsky is a proud Kohen," Stoil informs us, referring to the modern Jews popularly understood to be descended from part of the ancient priestly class.

In *The Forward*, in a piece titled "The Man Who Made Those Viral Sweaters Has One for Every Jewish Holiday," Talya Zax writes, "Sam Barsky came to knitting by chance, perhaps a divine one: it was 1999, he'd recently dropped out of nursing school due to medical issues, and he was searching for a new purpose." A few paragraphs in, Zax continues the play on divinity, writing that once the final stitch on an early elaborate sweater was in place, "he looked on his work and, like God on the seventh day, thought it good. Unlike God, it wasn't long until Barsky thought he might be able to do something better."[41] And thus, his self-designed landscape series was born. Obviously, this article is meant to be playful (and it, too, features a discussion of the Yom Kippur sweater). Barsky is not literally a god. It is striking, though, to see the connection between craftly creation and divine creation made so starkly, even in jest.

What does it mean to have an openly Jewish male Instagram knitting celebrity in the world? On some level, Barsky's global fame stems precisely from the perceived incongruity between his gender presentation and his hobby of choice. Though it emerged in medieval, male-dominated guilds, knitting is popularly depicted as an effeminate hobby (and not one for young people, either). In fact, the post that probably sparked Sam Barsky's viral turn came from an Imgur (online image-sharing site) user named "DesmondThePotato" and may have been intended in mockery: "This guy makes sweaters of places and then takes pictures of himself wearing the sweaters at those places," that user wrote, below a picture of Barsky at the Golden Gate Bridge.[42] The joke, however, was on Desmond the Potato, as Barsky's fame spread from continent to continent; he now travels to give invited talks at yarn stores and other venues. In his fame, though, I cannot help but also see an old historical pattern: that of the Jewish man constructed as effeminate, an idea we can trace back to medieval Europe and one with an ugly history. Yet this is an image that to some extent was then reclaimed and celebrated in America, particularly in the comedy of Woody Allen in the 1970s (although Allen was eventually accused of sexual assault, adding another layer to how his gender performance is perceived) and, later, in the work of Jerry Seinfeld. Part of Barsky's visual appeal is his mild schlemielness and the way he conforms to visual stereotypes associated with scholarly Ashkenazi Jewish men: flyaway brown curls, large glasses, loose-fitting clothing. There is an openness and friendliness to his gaze, too. The Internet loves an underdog, and Barsky fits that bill: nice, humble dude made good. On Jewish Instagram, of course, this played even more strongly: Nice Jewish Boy Makes Holiday Sweaters. I've followed Barsky on Instagram for years, and I, too, must admit to being charmed, especially by his Passover sweater picture, in which he holds a large round sheet of what looks to be *shumura matzah* (handmade matzah, one possible version of the unleavened bread eaten on that holiday).

Though he is clearly inspired and a strong artist, Barsky himself has admitted that he's not the most talented knitter from a technical standpoint. I can't help but think that a Jewish woman taking pictures of herself in landmark locations would not have gained this kind of Internet following; someone would surely have criticized her hair and asked if she had children. (Barsky does, of course, receive a fair amount of trolling, as does everyone, but he shrugs it off in interviews.) The incongruity of a man knitting—and also, in some cases, knitting about Jewish things—is part of what sparks the viewer's attention. It's as if the Jews finally have ugly Christmas sweaters, but even *better* because you can see the sweaters *in Bethlehem*.

If mid-twentieth-century Jewish Americans called their success stories "Only in America!" then Sam Barsky, Internet Everyman, is an "Only in America, via the Interwebs!" moment. "Your New Hero Knits Sweaters of Places and Then Goes to Those Places," reads the *Refinery 29* headline. "Hero," here, is served up with a side of irony—or is it? Barsky is popular because he is funny, turning hypermasculinized notions of the hero on their head in an age of comic book movies, but he is also earnest in a way that seems to resonate; lots of middle-class people want to see the world and to be so excited about the places they visit that they wear the appropriate gear. He just takes it up a notch by spending a whole month making the appropriate sweater. Six-year-olds wear Cinderella dresses to Disney World; Barsky wears a sweater with a waterfall on it to hike at Ein Gedi in Israel. Multiple technologies of place go into the making of this meme. The jet plane, allowing him to reach Israel, England, and Los Angeles; the advent of smartphones and Instagram; the comparative affordability of those technologies; and, of course, the knitting needle. Technologies of place change what we see and how we see it. They don't just bring us there or allow us to reproduce the scene; they alter how we collectively interact with locations. Having seen Barsky's New York skyline sweaters, I find the skyline changed, a new fuzziness to it, and his Instagram pictures have become part of how I imagine that iconic destination. Travel has long been intertwined with Jewish history, from pilgrimages and Holy Land tourism to the biblical stories of travel and flight that shape Jewish self-understanding. Just as there are "tours that bind," the objects that Jews associate with travel and with celebration are a form of material religion that links disparate individuals.[43] You don't have to be Jewish to appreciate the sweaters, and most of Barsky's followers are not ... but Jews displayed pride in the Jewish content of many of the sweaters.

Barsky's story is also a story of generative resilience. "Even though I have this neurological problem, I don't wake up every day thinking I'm someone with this neurological problem," he told Stoil.[44] At a time of crisis in his life—his departure from nursing school—knitting was an accessible hobby, one that also, ultimately, enriched his Jewish practice as well (for the longer festivals, he has made multiple sweaters). Now it is his livelihood .... But he was not the only Jewish knitter rocketing to Internet fame in 2017.

## A MEME MADE MATERIAL: THE PUSSYHAT PROJECT

Fiber art and resistance have a long history, from stories of knitters relaying messages to George Washington to the *arpilleras* (three-dimensional textile pictures) of Peru.[45] The Pussyhat Project, however, has a scope that may be unique to the viral capabilities of this particular digital age. A mere two weeks after Samuel Barsky went viral, real estate tycoon and reality television star Donald J. Trump was sworn in as the forty-fifth president of the United States. A few days later, on Saturday, January 22, 2017, millions of people took part in a major protest, the Women's March, in both Washington, D.C., and in cities across the United States and around the world. Many wore what became an icon of the march, a ribbed fuchsia cap with pointed cat ears: the Pussyhat. The hat made the cover of *Time*. It was an object that was at times adored and at others reviled (including among those who supported the goals of the march). It graced a statue of Eleanor Roosevelt. Someone at the Boston march made an entire tiny set of hats and placed them upon the *Make Way for Ducklings* statue in the Boston Public Garden.

The Pussyhat Project was cofounded by two Los Angeles women, Krista Suh and Jayna Zweiman; the hat itself was designed by a third friend, yarn store owner Kat Coyle. Zweiman is Jewish, a fact that came up in several interviews. She mentioned this background in one explanation of why she felt passionately about the project:

> I'm the granddaughter of four immigrants, and when I think about the Holocaust, I think, would I be one of those people who was sneaking people through the border? One of those people who was standing up and protesting? That's so much a part of my Jewish upbringing: understanding where my family came from, and so much of the luck that we had, that I even exist. I'm the product of the Jewish-American dream, and trying to extend that to other people is my responsibility.[46]

For Zweiman, being a Jewish American means protesting for justice and inclusion. I situate the Pussyhat Project in this research not just because one of the creators is Jewish but also because both she and many march participants explicitly framed their participation in the march in Jewish terms. To be clear, not all of the women I have encountered in this study are liberal politically (although, like most American Jews, they do trend that way), and Jews were obviously a minority of the participants present at the global marches. I discuss the hats in more detail in chapter 5, which focuses on ideas of tikkun olam, art, and activism. Here, however, the Pussyhat Project exemplifies another way that digital and material technologies jointly forge communities, meaning, and resilience.

Simply put, the Pussyhat Project is a product of the Internet age. It is a viral meme made material. The origin story for the hat has been told many times. At the time of the 2016 U.S. presidential election, Zweiman, an architect who was in a long recovery process after a severe concussion, could not travel as much as she used to or be in large crowds. That November, when Suh planned a trip to attend the Women's March, the pair started brainstorming ways for Zweiman to participate, too. They came up with the idea of the hat, which reclaimed the word "pussy," a euphemism for female genitalia that was used in a derogatory and violent manner by Trump in a recording that came to light during the campaign. The goal was to make a powerful visual statement, creating a sea of pink that would be glimpsed from above when news organizations photographed the crowds.

They circulated the pattern, which was extremely simple, via a wide array of social media outlets: Twitter, Facebook, Instagram, the popular knitting site Ravelry, and a host of other venues. The project's simple PDF gave a pattern for how to knit, crochet, or sew a hat, along with examples of notes that a creator could write to a hat recipient, and vice versa. The power of the Internet—along with networks of local yarn stores across the country, which became distribution nodes for completed hats—connected makers with those seeking headwear. The process linking the social media spread of the project, the brick-and-mortar physicality of the march in the streets, and the subsequent generation of millions of images from the marches is the kind of feedback loop that has occurred in the case of other twenty-first century protests, such as Occupy Wall Street and its iterations.[47]

Zweiman conceived of the project in both pragmatic and loftily aesthetic terms. On the one hand, themes of accessibility and access were paramount: "We also tapped into people who had never been knitters before. The idea was that anyone could participate, even people who couldn't attend marches for medical, financial or other reasons. You could be a knitter, a crocheter, a marcher, or none of that—you could just spread the word. Whatever skill you have, whatever you can give, you can be part of the project," she told Emily Cataneo in one interview.[48]

The addition of notes to the hats transformed the virtual into something that Zweiman described as particularly powerful, into the really "real" of a tactile gift, in her understanding: "I think that's really a beautiful thing, in this time of social media when we just forward articles. That feels very not real. Actually, making a hat is one of the most real things you can do."[49] *Making a hat is one of the most real things you can do.* In this statement, the older, tactile technology of needles and yarn is held up over the digital technologies that made the Pussyhat Project so popular. Touch triumphs. Even when separated by distance from particular marches, those who could not attend but sent forth pink hats were understood as sending forth a bit of themselves to the protests. Zweiman wanted the project to be understood as an inclusive one, one in which "every single person who participated in the project was a Pussyhat activist. Whether a crafter or a marcher, each participant made her own mark."[50]

When I spoke with Jennifer, a thirty-something mother and Hebrew school teacher in Pennsylvania, about her experience of making hats, her story confirmed this kind of proxy march participation. As a digital artist, rather than knitting, she added special vinyl letters to purchased hats in order to help local marchers represent their region in Washington. She could not attend the march because she was nursing her younger child and did not want to bring him into such a large crowd in midwinter. "Not being there, I felt like I was letting myself down, kind of. But one of the women who I made a hat for and mailed it to her, she sent me a picture of herself wearing a shirt and it said, 'also marching for' and it had names and she put my name on it ... and I started crying, it was so nice."[51] Jennifer's story fit in with Zweiman's emphasis on collective experience that included many possible roles. She told me that tikkun olam—repair of the world—was important to her sense of herself as a Jewish woman, but circumstances prevented her from being at the march itself. Through crafting and the feedback loop of her client's digital post, she was able to enact those values in a different way.

On the one hand, nondigital objects are what makes an experience more "real" in Zweiman's statement above—giving a hat is the "most real" thing. Yet such a project could not have existed without digital technology, a debt that its creators acknowledge. Zweiman applied the theoretical tools of her architecture and art backgrounds to its creation: "This project really brings in an understanding of architecture, how networks and spaces and people get brought together, as well as my art background. In some ways, this is a huge participatory art installation."[52] The power here is in the visual collective, and it is written in a language that is most legible from above, in the form of aerial photography of a large crowdscape. Here, it is helpful to think with what sociologist Courtney Bender calls "the skyscraper view" of American religion.[53] In the past few decades, the lived religions approach to studying religion has, quite helpfully, shifted our attention to what is on the ground, or, in an urban context, on the street in our study of both historical and contemporary religions in America.[54] This is a crucial perspective. However, stepping back to look at big-picture questions—the view from above—can be quite helpful when used in tandem with an on-the-ground view. Aerial photographs of the Women's March depict the sea of fuchsia that Zweiman and Suh had envisioned. In the same way, Jewish women's creations operate on both micro and macro levels. They may reach an immediate relative, or they may reach millions.

That the Women's March took place on a Saturday also provokes us to think about the relations among craft, technology, and observance of the Jewish Sabbath, which of course varies widely among Jewish crafters—as it has always varied among Jews. In one interview, Zweiman shared the fact that she spends Friday evenings at the Little Knittery in East Los Angeles, calling this "her own Shabbat."[55] This contrasts with Barsky's profiles in Jewish newspapers, which emphasized his more traditional Shabbat observance. The notion of Shabbat is a complex one when it comes to Jews, crafting, and technology. Most traditional halachic interpretations of the Sabbath laws forbid stitching on Shabbat, since it was one of the activities used in the building and decoration of the Tabernacle and since it is an act of creation. Just as God rests from creation on the seventh day, this reasoning goes, so, too, should humans. Thus, for some creative Jews, such activities are not a part of Shabbat. For others, it might depend upon the object in question. The majority of Jewish Americans do not identify as traditionally *shomer Shabbat* (those who literally "guard" the Sabbath laws). For them, knitting or sewing on Shabbat may be an entirely appropriate activity on that day, even keeping with the spirit of rest and being in community, as Zweiman described it. Throughout my research, I found that the range of Jewish practices around craft and Shabbat varied widely.

One respondent to my survey puts it this way:

I laughingly say that God is not a socialist, because talent is not distributed equally. I was allocated visual artistry and I'm okay with that. Musically I'm one step above tone deaf.... If I have a frustration, it's that it's easy to connect being musical with Jewish worship; it's less easy to do so with the visual arts. For one thing, we visual artists are required to shut it down on Shabbat, while the music just increases on Shabbat and holidays. One of the hardest things for me when I took on Shabbat observance was giving up the meditative stress release that for me comes from stitching. I mean meditative stress release is sort of the essence of what Shabbat should be, but if also I believe that making beautiful objects is an imitation/homage to God's work of creation, then there's no way around it: I'm required to set it aside for Shabbat, even though I find it calming and meditative.

For this woman, an activity she finds spiritually rewarding and relaxing—*restful*—is not an option on the holiest and most restorative day of her week. In contrast, another respondent to my survey wrote, "I love knitting on Shabbat. It's extremely mindful for me, and I can sit back and reflect on my week." I also spoke with a woman who attends a weeklong Jewish quilting retreat at a camp in Wisconsin and learned about the nuanced politics of who machine stitched on Shabbat, who hand stitched then (eschewing electricity), and who did not stitch at all.

The Women's March, which took place on Shabbat, also demonstrates the diverse ways that Jews approach their religious practices. For some, marching is work, knitting is relaxation; for others, knitting is work, marching is prayer; for others, all are acceptable Shabbat activities (at this and other marches, it was often possible to observe the boundaries of normative Jewish law while also attending the march, if one started from the right location). Other activists have argued that the mental exhaustion of constantly agitating leads them to need spiritual rest on Shabbat even if marching can fit within the letter of the law.[56]

The Pussyhat phenomenon is thus a small window into larger questions about what constitutes work, what constitutes rest, and where different modern technologies fit into that question, with answers that vary tremendously from person to person. Even this small sample demonstrates the wide variety of approaches to making Shabbat meaningful, either in concert with—or in the absence of—technology. What is at stake here is the entanglement of creation, work, observance, and rest and what it means to claim these categories as an authentic Jew. Although traditional Jewish law forbids taking part in the melakhot on Shabbat, a descriptive account of what Jews actually do on the Sabbath, and how they define work and rest, demonstrates that Jewish life on the ground is a nuanced phenomenon. Going to knit a Pussyhat in an intentional Friday night practice of rest, meditation, community, and tikkun olam is not a degradation of tradition but, instead, a new evolution of practice.

### COMMUNITY, CONNECTION, AND CONTENTION

The history of how gendered communities congregate around textiles is complicated. From medieval knitting guilds to Samuel Barsky's sweaters, knitting has been the province of people of many sexes. In the ancient Roman milieu out of which rabbinic literature emerged, for example, there is documentation of male weavers, sometimes working in the same shop as female spinners; but, at the same time, many rabbinic texts show a profound anxiety about men performing women's work (such as spinning) and an eagerness to differentiate labor into separately sexed spheres.[57]

Nonetheless, there is also a genuine history of women building community and resilience around the fiber arts, particularly in the United States, and there is a coinciding history of debates over attempts to revive and/or romanticize these associations, both literally and metaphorically, on- and offline.[58] Jewish craft blogs and other online extensions of this work operate within this discursive matrix, a broader social one in which "messages sent from hands that sew, knit, weave, or spin, sent from minds to hands to cloth in the past are now sent from hand to cloth to keys, continuing to build community and stretching the reach of the messages to global villages. The spinning bees and guilds of old are the netrings and knitting blogs of today."[59]

The notion of community manifests powerfully in some digital forms. Cathy Perlmutter's posts on her blog, *GefilteQuilt*, and a companion site, *JudaiQuilt*, connect women from all over the world, introducing them to new techniques. Along with several other quilters I have met, she also belongs to a Jewish quilting listserv. Sarah told me about the interfaith interactions that sometimes occur on a different list, *Quiltropolis*.[60]

Internet communication can be a means of reaching comrades you could not otherwise locate. Ketzirah told me, "When I started doing all of this, I didn't know anyone else who did anything I do. And technology gave me a way to put it out there and see if it resonated with anybody, and 'Did you do anything like this?' I found my tribe that way. My best friends in the whole world, I met first online."[61] Social networks and the web have all led her on various spiritual paths. In the 1990s, the digital world brought her to friends in the pagan community who, as she put it, supportively "kicked me back to Judaism." Later, she learned about the work of Rabbi Jill Hammer on the Internet, which was another major turning point in her spiritual journey.

Similarly, more on the sewing side of things than the Jewish side, Danielle, a lawyer in the D.C. area (and another Gen Xer), told me: "I have more online communities than in-real-life communities."[62] She also reported that it was her friends on an Internet board who finally gave her the "courage" to take her much-longed-for sewing machine out of the box and to begin using it. Thus, for those who are able to afford a reliable Internet connection, the Internet is a powerful space of access to a larger crafting community. This development is not confined to the fifty-and-under set. During the buildup to the Pomegranate Guild biennial convention, and in the weeks after I attended it, there was a major uptick in traffic on the guild email list and Facebook group—and the guild skews quite dramatically toward the baby boomers and older in its membership.

Digital spaces can connect; they can also be contentious. This is particularly clear in the case of the Pomegranate Guild. Cathy, who served a term as guild president, described one challenge of building the guild's Internet presence:

> There's such a concern for privacy and security. I think there's a real fear of being public. Now I have to say now it's how many years— it's fifteen years I've had the JudaiQuilt website—more—I've *never* received any kind of anti-Semitic anything. *Nothing.* But both the Jewish quilting listserv, and I think the Pomegranate Guild, too, are very cautious. The quilters do not want to go public! That's the way it was established. There's a fear that if we go public, messianic Christians might overwhelm us, or the anti-Semites. So they're concerned about both. And we have had—you know, there have been, from time to time—you know, I think, some messianic Christians,

there were some issues, in one chapter of the Pomegranate Guild, a long time ago. And the quilting listserv—there was one messianic Christian who was so low key that no one ever knew it.[63]

Thus, a fear of being the target of proselytization, anti-Semitic rhetoric, or other sorts of aggressions has led the guild to adopt a moderate—one might say ambivalent—attitude toward the Internet. The group has a website, some of which is public facing (this is how I discovered their existence), the rest of which is in a password-protected, members-only section. As part of my participant observation, I joined the guild. Patterns can be accessed there, and so can a historical treasure trove: over forty years of the Pomegranate Guild's quarterly newsletter, the *Paper Pomegranate*.[64] Similarly, the Pomegranate Guild email list and Facebook group may only be accessed by members in good standing. Worries about copyright, the sharing of images, and personal details online all drive these decisions. So does the fact that not all five hundred members of the guild use email or social media; several women at the convention told me things along the lines of "I'm not on email," but a number of members are quite active on the Facebook group.

Some accounts of the potentials of online community are utopic, while others stress how they can alter the universe, bending it toward new, imagined worlds. Many narratives of women's craft collectives have emphasized empowerment: "Women became a strong force as a community through the groups they formed to share in art, whether through quilting bees, [or] through art classes within the settlement houses."[65] Others note a wide variety of functions that online crafting communities create, including progressive, nostalgic, and ironic modes. One study of Stitch 'n Bitch groups and cyberfeminism found that some of the members of such movements demonstrate self-awareness of the impossibility of actually achieving the nostalgic themes they generate; as a result, they may deploy an ironic mode, where "the desire for a return to the past is parodied and presented as melancholic; a simulacrum of a past that never existed, rather than one to be re-created." Still, that phenomenon is "a new way of connecting, based on traditional craft skills and an entrenched gender divide"; it may be "a new form of craft; a form that is cognizant of the new circumstances of the Information Society and the alienation that can be experienced."[66]

Certainly, the digital connections in the virtual spaces I have described above—along with countless other blogs and groups, like *Knittishisms* and *Creative Jewish Mom*—provide vital connections for the women who take part in them. This is particularly true in the case of Jews who live in areas far from larger Jewish communities or those who have no nearby quilting or sewing friends. Even Cathy Perlmutter—who lives in Southern California, home to one of the largest Jewish communities in the United States—made many of her connections virtually, in part because she is often at her home computer (she works as a freelance writer) and in part because the L.A.-area traffic is so dense that it would take her more than an hour to reach the nearest face-to-face Pomegranate Guild meeting. Jewish craft blogs are a digital diaspora. Like the rabbinic responsa of past centuries, they link communities of craft across space and time: spaces that cannot be easily accessed, time that might not be in great supply for a face-to-face meeting but can be harnessed, here and there, to comment on a blog post or seek pattern advice online.

Social media scholars describe "the digital religious" as a "third space" between institutional and personal. They write of an "as-if-ness" in the digital, emphasizing the aesthetic, reflexive, and generative nature of these spaces.[67] These terms are all highly relevant for my craft bloggers—particularly the aesthetic cadence of as-if-ness. When crafters share their works-in-progress online, they are building up to a final big reveal: the unveiling of a finished object. Jewishness takes on a wide variety of inflections on these blogs, boards, and groups. The blogs and communities I have examined can be irreverent, earnest, celebratory, critical; interventionist, hortatory, sad. Furthermore, with powerful computers—also known as smartphones—in our pockets, the lines between the online and offline worlds have no neat boundaries. When I attended the Pomegranate Guild biennial convention, I lost track of the number of times someone pulled out their phone to show me (or another listener) a piece she had made. We are our digital and analog selves all at once, both together, much of the time.

## JEWISH CRAFTERS, AMERICAN RELIGIONS: FIRE, PIXELS, AND THREADS

What do the actions of Jews at the interstices of craft and technology tell us about Jewish life and about religions in America more generally? To think through the answer to this question, we return to the words of this chapter's title: black fire, white pixels, and golden threads.

First, the black fire. Here, I mean something akin to traditional interpretations of the "black fire on white fire" concept: I mean the black ink of Jewish texts—whether they are in a Torah scroll, a printed Talmud, a contemporary book of poetry, or the musings of a Jewish blogger. Jewish texts operate at myriad levels in the Jewish crafting world. Classical Jewish texts may inspire Ketzirah's designs. They may literally become a part of a textile, as they do when Sarah calligraphs them onto an object; they may be used in the blog post that explains a design. Further, *all* of these are Jewish texts, whatever their provenance. The musings on *GefilteQuilt* are a Jewish text as worthy of scholarly study as a tractate of Talmud. I realize that by emphasizing the importance of texts—in a project that is also about material culture—I may be continuing a text-centric approach. But, however the technologies of transmission might be changing—and those different mediations most certainly matter—we cannot entirely *escape* the study of texts among American Jews. The forms of mediation change, but new media is always, in part, also old media. The black fire of Jewish textual transmission lingers, strongly.

But we need more layers. Next, we have the pixel. A pixel—short for "picture element"—is the most basic unit of digital graphics. It is a tiny building block used, over and over and over, to compose an image. Each pixel, based on its geometric location on a display, can be programmed to shine in a particular way; pixels contain subpixels that can be told, by powerful processors, what color they should flash. They are the pointillist elements of our digital visual-scape. They make things visible. Just as the "white fire" of oral Torah (in one understanding) or of women's voices and experiences (in another) make what was once invisible evident, pixels quite literally allow us to see in the digital age.

Like the pixel, Jewish women's art and craft make new things visible through a wide variety of technologies. To return to the Pussyhat Project: one lone fuchsia hat in the crowd would not have made an impact, just as changing the color of only one pixel on a large monitor would not alter the image that you see. Putting thousands of hats together made a dramatic statement. Sometimes we attend to the pinpoint details of each tiny pixel. Sometimes, we need to step back and understand Jewish Americans in the aggregate. American religions may look different as composite mashups; they benefit both from nuanced, on-the-ground study and, sometimes, from a more distanced view.

Finally, we have the golden threads. Pixels—so tiny, controlled by binary-based programming—remind me of something else: the fine mesh squares that cover a needlepoint canvas, a vast white array with the faintest of black holes visible between the lines; into those, you must somehow fit a needle and thread, hundreds or even thousands of times. On my second day at the Pomegranate Guild of Judaic Needlework 2017 convention, I took a needlepoint workshop. Six women sat evenly spaced around three sides of a large table in a hotel suite. Our instructor, Randi, sat on the other side, showing us examples of the finished design: a red pomegranate on a field of taupe and pink, with flecks of gold upon its stem.

I had not done needlepoint since I was a child. My eyes blurred as I made my way through the beginning steps of the chart, placing pale pink silk thread into the "pith" of the pomegranate. In, out, on a slight diagonal, all of the way across the row. Then back, right to left (like Hebrew), on a different diagonal, creating tiny hexagonal boxes into which we would later thread beads. The canvas might as well have been microscopic (ruefully, I now viscerally understood the conventionwide registration instructions to bring "magnification and lighting as needed"). As we stitched, however, I gradually settled into the activity, starting to feel what both writers and computer programmers call "flow": the sense that your ideas are going somewhere, that you are engrossed in the activity, even though I was not *creating* the design itself, as I do when I write—I was implementing another designer's vision. Words, algorithms, stitches: they all entail a certain level of rhythm.

I am not the first person to make a connection between the needle arts and the binary language of computers. Ada Lovelace, the Englishwoman who was one of the pioneers of modern computing, was an avid knitter and weaver who apparently liked to work secret binary messages into pieces of cloth.[68] Still, this history is important. It is crucial to remember that fiber arts are not a nostalgic route of return to a predigital, halcyon age of glorious women's-only spaces that were somehow unsullied by future machines or virtual realities. Rather, they are, and always have been, a space of profound technological tinkering, pursued by people of many sexes.

At times, the sheer volume of Judaica, Jewish reflection, and Jewish creativity that I find available online feels overwhelming. Snowball sampling in the age of Web 2.0 has left me buried in an avalanche of objects, stories, and images. John Modern calls this "itematicity." Reflecting on the role of the historian in the age of eBay, he writes: "eBay is the ontology of the item. . . . Visceral loops between bodies, between bodies and imagined environment and imagined bodies. . . . There is desire and there is an object and there is the mediation of the bid. Call it *itematicity*. Digital life, days marked by their online intensities, a space into which everything—even the spirit of the collective—must pass."[69]

This is how I often feel as I scroll through the voluminous projections of Jewish craft blogs. The glowing white pixels overwhelm me, and yet the opiate effect of clicking on *just one more post* rushes through my brain. I am at sea in a field of white much like the needlepoint canvas. What do

I do? Sometimes, I turn to writing on a legal pad or on printouts of my sources, black rollerball ink scratching on white paper.[70] If I am feeling particularly indulgent, though, I do what I did in graduate school: I take out my knitting. The tactility brings me out of *itematicity* and into— what, precisely? My own material mystification? The literally weight of the yarn in my lap?

To understand Jews in America, we need to think on all of these levels: the textual, the visible (and invisible), and the material, in both macro and micro terms. We must also attend to the role desires play in creation and consumption, whether the item in question is an image, a ball of yarn, or an amulet. Technologies mediate those raw cravings. Digital technologies may accelerate them; hand technologies, through their weight and touch, may slow them down. Often, those crafts are transmitted, not just virtually, but materially, to gift recipients. It is to gifts that we now turn.

# 3 : THREADS
# BETWEEN PEOPLE

. . . . . . . . . . . . . . . . . . . . . . . . . . . .

*The Art of the Gift*

O n a Saturday morning in May 2017, I drove down I-75 to visit a small synagogue in Macon, Georgia, a town that was sleepy enough that day that I had to remind myself it was illegal to make a left on red. I was there to meet artist and art professor Laurel Robinson, and I had been invited to join her at services in order to see some of her work in situ. Though I arrived a bit after the service had begun, both Robinson and the rabbi, who went by Rabbi Aaron, came out to warmly greet me while a congregant led the chanting. I was ushered into a small, gray-carpeted chapel. In this egalitarian, welcoming space, every congregant sang along with gusto, even though there were only fifteen to twenty people present. When it came time for the Torah service, the *parochet*, a soft blue velvet curtain before the ark, was drawn back. A small Torah scroll in an elaborately carved, Sephardic-style silver case was removed from the ark for that day's reading. Its intricate design was Robinson's own.

Before the reading began, Rabbi Aaron came over to show me his *yad*. A *yad*, which in Hebrew means hand, is the pointer that a Torah reader uses to keep his or her place during the ritual reading. It had been a very special gift. It was carved from the ebony of a piano key—a tiny, elegant black hand at the end of a slender, brown wooden handle—and, as he told me, it was the first one Robinson had ever made. It was Robinson's yads that had brought me to Macon. Although she is trained as a professional painter, it was this craft—her voluminous production of yads, which she gives as gifts and does not sell—that had connected me to her work. I was struck, not just by how beautiful and innovative her yads were, but by the generosity with which she bestowed them upon those around her.

This chapter is about how gifts bridge lives. Gifts are a kind of ritual technology.[1] Like the spindle, which allows one to take loose fibers and ply them closely together, gifts, too, perform a kind of intertwining. They transmit sentiment and affection, but they are not simple. Sometimes, they are unwanted. Sometimes, they are returned. Gift giving—and receiving—creates an atmosphere laden with sentiment. Giving handmade gifts is a way of channeling excess into emotion. Ultimately, gift cultures reveal how we can bridge the gaps between our frail bodies, especially in times of suffering. I begin with gifts of yads in Macon, because this symbol of the hand brings a special kind of tactility into a central Jewish ritual, the act of reading from the Torah scroll in a communal setting.

GIFTS OF HANDMADE HANDS

One of the functions of handmade gifts is to cement the social bonds of friendship, which is what I encountered, in myriad ways, that day in Georgia. Robinson's *yads* were both an outgrowth of her lifelong journey through creative endeavors and a part of the material culture that brings this community together.

In a conversation that Shabbat afternoon, Robinson told me how she had gotten started creating things. "I've always been a kid that made things," she said, recalling how she would do art at home while her mother worked at household tasks. "You know, she'd be cooking and I'd be at the kitchen table and she would bring all kinds of junk for me to decorate. Quaker's Oats boxes, the cylindrical boxes." Later, she half joked, "I often think that I should do one big final exhibition and decorate oatmeal boxes. I always have this in the back of my mind that probably what I've done my whole life is just modify the notion of decorating an oatmeal box."[2]

She detailed an upbringing that was rich in art lessons, Hebrew school, Jewish summer camp, and an abiding interest in science, travel, and notions of geological time. She trained as a painter, became an art professor, and then traveled the world, from Australia to Spain to Israel. In the 1990s, the combination of some paintings she created about the Jewish expulsion from Spain and her budding friendship with Rabbi Aaron revived her interest in Jewish ritual and in exploring Jewish topics in her work.

The first yad that Robinson created came about by happenstance. Someone had scrapped an old piano and given her the keys. "So I had this big cardboard box full of piano keys, and I'm like, 'Okay, well, maybe I could carve a yad for Aaron out of a piano key. That seems like a good thing to do with a piano key for a keyboard player."[3] (Rabbi Aaron plays both piano and accordion.) Next, she carved a yad out of used chair rungs. Then her job as the art director of a Jewish summer camp in rural Georgia prompted her to make more. "Camp's insane and there's a service every five seconds," she explained. "There's different age groups and there's different Torahs, and so you can never have too many yads." Her words echoed those of Louise Silk, who observed that there is always space for another quilt. It seems that many kinds of Jewish objects are fruitful and multiply at the instigation of Jewish hands.

Thinking with the object of the yad evokes literal Jewish hands, what they do, and how they connect people. Robinson evinced a stance of largesse mixed with reward toward the yad recipients. At the camp, she explained, "I'd say, 'You're really a mensch, so here's a yad for you.'" Then, more generally, "I was sort of just giving them to people that I thought deserved them."[4] Here, the notion of gift meets the idea of being meritorious, hovering on the blurry line between gift and award. Gifts confer status, and they cement communities: "A gift that does nothing to enhance solidarity is a contradiction."[5] By distributing yads to the worthy among the summer campers, Robinson may have differentiated among campers, but she also built solidarity in the recipients, conferring a sense of belonging, both in the camp community writ large and at the Torah table. Solidarity exists among humans. It also describes the bonds between humans and their objects, and the ways that those objects promote connections among a cohort.

Robinson is not interested in making the yads commercially. She explained that it would not be financially beneficial to do so; one cannot pay the bills on yads alone. She is also not keen on making them for "collectors" and is hesitant about museum exhibitions, as well, although she has shown some of them with her paintings and she made a special "Purim set" of "mask, flask, grogger, and scroll" that resides in the permanent collection of the Jewish Museum in New York City.[6] Regarding yads on display in museums, she said, "Well, that's a stupid concept. It's a thing that reads Torah.... It's never read Torah and it's going in your museum? That doesn't make any sense to me."[7] "Museumification" unquestionably alters an object, though one can also argue that "museums are simply a medium."[8] Robinson is skeptical about the notion of putting this ritual object behind a glass, evincing concern over the kind of stasis this would imply. This is certainly one perspective on that process. When a ritual object is "gifted" to a museum, it does move out of one kind of communal circulation; a yad in a case or in a storeroom is no longer being handled by the Jews of a specific congregation for the weekly Torah readings. However, we should take those museums, community centers, and related venues seriously, as they increasingly become centers of Jewish American life.[9] If we consider the fact that a preponderance of Jewish Americans do not affiliate with a synagogue but that huge numbers of Jews and non-Jews visit Jewish museums and see ritual objects there, then a yad in a museum might—meaningfully—reach a large number of visitors, both

Jews and non-Jews. However, the sensory experience is different in each case: in a ritual Torah reading, a yad is grasped by the reader, entailing touch; in a museum case, a yad is examined visually, entailing sight. A ritual object in a case is different from a ritual object being used in a ritual. It retains strong cultural power, but it has been altered.

In my visit to Georgia, I saw evidence that the yads of this congregation were heavily used. Their recipients showed tremendous appreciation. After the morning service, a tall, silver-haired man in a Chagall tie, who had led some of the *davening* (praying), came over to show me his yad. It was in a worn leather case. Inside was a small brown and black yad, made of wood, on a hinge. It was a clever contraption that popped out of its own little storage box, sort of like the yad version of a Swiss Army knife. This yad has been all over the country with me, he explained. It had been held in his hand to read Torah in many states. Because I was in a synagogue on Shabbat, I couldn't record or write all of his words down as I heard them, but they were filled with warm regard for Robinson and a discussion of how she and her many creations are admired by the members of the synagogue.

At the kiddush (the lunchtime meal served after a Saturday morning service), the congregation continued to be very welcoming. A vocal six-year-old who talked a mile a minute kept trying to give me a pink and purple paper fan she had made, which she insisted she wanted me to have "because I just met you." At the time, my own daughter was six, so the vocal cadences were familiar to me, but I was also struck by the resemblance between her gesture and Robinson's gifts of the yads. Here, take this, I made it: a powerful mantra. We begin the act of giving when we are young.

After lunch, Robinson, Rabbi Aaron, and a few other congregants led me around the building and showed me more yads. In a classroom, beside a beautiful children's ark and a small Torah-reading table on which Robinson had painted jungle animals, they took out case after case after case. First there were two yads she had made for the rabbi's son, who was now a college student: one from when he was a small child, and another when he was thirteen. "A yad for a three-year-old," Robinson said, "Why not?" He had been "obsessed" with trains, and so she made him a train-shaped yad, in a box that had beautiful tracks at the bottom of its case. Then, when it became time for his bar mitzvah, she decided to make him something more mature, but since he had never ritually read from a Torah scroll with the childhood yad, during the service, he began chanting his Torah portion by using the train yad first, then made the transition to the new one. That bar mitzvah gift was also a gloriously personalized yad. By thirteen, they told me, he had gotten really into space and *Star Trek*, and so he said, "Make something techie," something that would look like it could fit that aesthetic. I opened the box to see it. This silvery yad incorporated shiny bits of metal upon the wood, with many other colors and an abstract design. These two yads, particularly the "techie" one, demonstrate how personalization is an important quality of hand-made ritual objects. The story of how they figured into a coming-of-age ceremony also exemplifies the many ways that Jewish Americans use material culture to signify both individual tastes and communal connections during rituals.

Robinson showed me a whole case of wooden yads that she had produced at camp, in a panoply of vivid colors. In a display case at the front of the synagogue, I saw a special yad for the fall harvest festival of Sukkot, where the handle resembled a *lulav* (palm, myrtle, and willow branches) and *etrog* (citron), containing the four species waved ritually on that holiday. Most astounding of all were the many special Purim yads. Purim is an early spring festival celebrating the events of the book of Esther, a biblical text that most scholars regard as a work of historical fiction set in the Persian empire.[10] On Purim, a yad is used to read from the *megillah*—the scroll of the book of Esther. Purim is a carnivalesque holiday, a raucous affair where everyone wears costumes, adults often imbibe alcohol, and participants are encouraged to make a lot of noise during the megillah reading, particularly when the name of Haman, the story's villain, is read. One yad case was covered with a painting of Haman wearing his stereotypical triangular hat. Inside, the yad could be flipped to face either way— it had two sculptured hands, pointing in both directions. "For when the holiday spins upside down," Robinson said. Another one was in a wooden box shaped like a mask—you opened up the mask like a puzzle to get to the yad inside. It was a yad, she said, that got bored reading and decided to take a drink—it split off, with a sort of extra stem that became a tiny— the tiniest!!—of shot glasses. Read—then drink!

Later in the day, Robinson and I talked some more about what the yads meant to her. She made it clear that painting is her main artistic vocation. She didn't "find herself" making a yad the way she does painting, but she was fascinated by the reactions of yad recipients. Laurel's yads are in synagogues all over the country and all over the world, including in Singapore and Romania. We also talked about prayer, life, the universe, and everything. She referred to the stuff of the universe as "cosmic jello": "I think that there is order and complexity in the universe and it's—$n$th dimensional. And I do think there's a big efficacy to prayer. I do think you can send a vibration of goodness through the jello and something can

80   *Threads between People*

happen.... Whether it does happen or not, who the hell knows? But it's worth giving it a shot. So, I think that for me, that's what making a yad is about. Giving somebody that something that wiggles in the jello when they read Torah."[11]

"Cosmic jello." It is a remarkable phrase. This framing conjures a world that is profoundly material, one in which prayer has a kind of heft to it and our prayer intentions can make that substance of the universe, that interconnected "jello," change. My visit with Laurel Robinson and the yads of Macon, Georgia, gave me the opportunity to see firsthand how gifts operate and circulate. My most vivid memory from the day comes from a moment during the Torah service. I had been asked to participate in the service and was standing on the bema at the front of the sanctuary during a portion of the Torah reading. Because the Torah stood upright in a case with its words facing the congregation, rather than flat on the table, as is more customary in Ashkenazi American synagogues, the Torah reader and the person who blessed the reading faced forward, toward the front of the sanctuary. They were also standing up tall, not bent over. I had the unusual vantage point of really seeing Rabbi Aaron's face as he chanted, using the ebony yad Robinson had made for him to keep his place in the reading. Robinson, who had given the blessing, stood beside him. The light streaming in through the stained-glass windows gave them both a gentle glow: old friends before the sacred open scroll. Because I knew the story of the yad, this particular moment of Torah reading felt hallowed by a surplus of affect: a gift of friendship made material. The cosmic jello vibrated with joyous camaraderie.

BETTER THAN SOMETHING YOU BUY IN A STORE:
NOSTALGIA AND HANDMADE GIFTS
Expressing nostalgia for previous ages of handmade simplicity is such a long-standing American pastime that such nostalgia itself has a history. Mid- to late nineteenth-century Americans, feeling adrift amid the forces of industrialization and urbanization, romanticized that which had been hand produced. Minister and theologian Horace Bushnell had coined the sentimental term "the age of homespun" in an 1851 sermon, but during the 1870s, which was a decade of expansion, industrial growth, and urban expositions that showcased new technologies, a longing for this bygone age of home production grew: "The mythology of household production gave something to everyone. For sentimentalists, spinning and weaving represented the centrality of home and family, for evolutionists the triumph of civilization over savagery, for craft revivalists the harmony of labor and art, and for antimodernists the virtues of a bygone age."[12]

Americans have often looked back to supposed halcyon eras of simplicity when there was a more direct connection between production and consumption. Jewish Americans can be contextualized in this trend, although their twentieth-century stories of upward mobility evince ambivalence about both wealth and objects.[13] Over time, gift giving, for example, became so central to ceremonies like the bar mitzvah that the gift itself became the chief subject of humor. In the mid-twentieth century, fancy pens and other signs of affluence had become such commonplace gifts that comics suggested Jewish boys should say, "Today, I Am a Fountain Pen," in lieu of "Today, I Am a Man."[14] While many Jewish Americans experienced upward mobility in postwar America and, as a result, paid more attention to synagogue architecture and other material accoutrements of worship, these developments also provoked criticism from many quarters.

Over time, Jews, like other Americans, developed a counterculture that attempted to reclaim Jewishness from its perceived classism, as youth movements in the late 1960s and 1970s "rejected the culture of affluence in which they had been raised and denied the possibility that a middle-class lifestyle could be compatible with an authentically Jewish one."[15] Out of this movement came 1973's *Jewish Catalog*. Richard Siegel, Michael Strassfeld, and Sharon Strassfeld modeled this handbook on *The Whole Earth Catalog*, and the series of Jewish catalogs would sell over two hundred thousand copies into the 1980s.[16] Doing things by hand was a crucial aspect of such guides, leading to a revival of interest in Jewish craft throughout the 1970s and 1980s. As Mae Rockland Tupa writes in *The Second Jewish Catalog*, "Whether it is clothes, candles, furniture, or jewelry, Americans are doing it for themselves again and finding it both rewarding and fun. Now is an ideal time to use the skills we have all been learning in our other craft classes and begin to make our own American Jewish folk art objects. We cheat ourselves if we don't invest something of ourselves in making beautiful things for everyday use. We lose the opportunity to elevate the ordinary to the spiritual."[17] Other, more recent explosions of DIY Judaism are pushed and pulled by broader American attitudes toward production, consumption, and doing things by hand. Gifts are a part of these cycles.

The power of trading that which is handmade is also powerfully religious, as "religious activity is at work in forming community, focusing desire, and facilitating exchange."[18] "Exchange" is the most crucial term here. In some framings, giving is connected with excess and also with loss, or "expenditure is premised on excess and extravagance, on loss and destruction, or, in a word, on the gift."[19] For the giver, a gift is a way of channeling a part of him- or herself. In giving, the giver experiences a loss—not a total loss of self, but a microsacrifice, an exchange of sentiment, money, and, especially in the case of handmade gifts, a loss of time: the time that it takes to craft a special object. Although giving entails loss, it also creates an excess of meaning, opening up new spaces for self-expression and the profusion of social bonds.[20] The gifts that I saw exchanged in my fieldwork were examples of loss and expenditure and of extravagance that forged threads between people.

A huge number of the participants in my study took part in handmade gift culture. In the ways that they discussed these gifts, my interlocutors often displayed the kind of nostalgia for the handmade that Americans have shown since "the age of homespun."[21] The hand itself was understood as conveying additional value to a gift made in that manner; the very body of the giver and the fact that it touched and forged an object mattered. Two subthemes I noticed in particular were the notion that handmade gifts were superior to purchased ones, and concern over whether or not handmade gifts were sufficiently appreciated by their recipients. In other words, were the hours of labor and concentration given over to the creation of the gift truly understood? Did the exchange make the abundance of sentiment that surrounds these objects apparent?

When recipients understood the value of such gifts, it clearly had a powerful effect on the maker. Dana, a crafter in her thirties who crocheted a king-size afghan for her friend's wedding present, told me, "I was very flattered when his husband emailed me to find out how to log it on their house insurance."[22] Similarly, Amanda, a quilter in Maryland, told me, "I like making things for people who appreciate them. There are some people that have no idea when they ask me to make something, how complicated it is. They figure, 'Oh, she knows how to sew, she can just whip it up.' Nothing is ever just whipped up. Making something like that is actually a lifetime of thought and process and love."[23]

Laura, a Generation X crafter who excelled at many fiber arts, as well as beading and painting, recalled making baby quilts for colleagues when she learned to quilt in her twenties. Two of her colleagues were pregnant at the same time. "I have always believed that something that comes from your heart and hand is better than something you buy in a store. Not everybody believes that. Sometimes, you give a gift and you say, 'And I made this,' and they go, 'Oh.' These women *did* appreciate it."[24] In her experience, a particular moment of life—the moment in adulthood when one's own generation becomes parents—catalyzed her lifelong investment in a multitude of crafting activities.

The gift holds multilayered powers. It is as if the gift object contains a bit of the giver herself. By taking hours, days, weeks, and even years to make an item, the creator invests a large portion of her selfhood into the object that is given. It is precisely the rarity and preciousness of gifts made with skill that endows them with power.[25] There is also a powerful emotional feedback loop in the giving of gifts, which is what Robin, one of the California crafters, described when she talked about the many items she has made over the years for both children and grandchildren. For Robin, giving gifts means evoking emotion and memory: "They're just fun little things, but these things just become family traditions. And like we said before, it's not the artistry, it's not that this is a gorgeous lace design, it's just the fact that it's something that we hope gets passed down." Robin was discussing the many items she has sewn for her family: pillows, prayer shawls, and elaborate felt flags to wave on Simchat Torah, the revelry-driven holiday where Jews complete the cycle of Torah reading and begin it again. She has made an individual flag for everyone in the family, but they signify more than just an adornment for a yearly celebration. Robin elaborated:

> You have to give them emotion. You have to give them memories. You have to make them have memories that they're not going to want to break.... But by the end I'm very pleased. I hope that the recipient is pleased. They always act like they're pleased when they get it, and like the kids with the flags, I always get a picture of them using it, at least the first year.... It may not mean anything when they're kids. A lot of times they're getting these things as kids, and you know yourself that it may not mean things to them as a kid, and years later, they [will] say, "Oh my God, my grandmother made this for me, and now that I'm an adult and a parent, this is really wonderful."

*You have to give them emotion.* Here, the gift is quite self-consciously described as a bearer of affect. The objects Robin gives to her family are made out of fabric, but they are also made out of feelings. They are meant to evoke further sentiment. She hopes that the knowledge of this hand-made gift will be associated with Simchat Torah far into her descendants' futures. The gift is also a kind of emotive glue, creating "memories they're not going to want to break," and thereby affixing the recipients more robustly into Jewish traditions. Robin also describes a kind of emotive feedback loop I have noticed in many of my conversations. Receiving the smiling pictures of the gift recipients with their flags is one step in the process of creation, an assurance that emotion was transmitted, an inspiration, perhaps, to produce more objects. This is particularly true in the age of the smartphone, where a recipient's gratitude for a new item can be rapidly conveyed via pixels and quick mobile connections, but it is not a new phenomenon. Since the age of painting and, later, formal photography, portraiture has often featured sitters holding sentimental objects produced by relatives, and portraits themselves—along with physical mementos like hair—became items of memory in the Victorian era.[26] The cell phone photo showing a gift recipient with gift in hand, received and perhaps in use, is just the newest version of that pattern.

Similarly, in her 1970s classic *The Work of Our Hands*, Mae Rockland Tupa describes how emotions were intertwined with the process of making a quilt as a gift for her young daughter:

> For me, the element of time sewn into an object enhances its value. The quilt in Figure 2 was made over a four-year period. A great many things happened to our family during that time, and as I worked on the quilt my emotions and thoughts were many and varied. When I look at it now, it seems like a parenthesis enclosing a chapter of my life. It is very precious to my family because they watched it grow and shared in the thrill of its completion in the frantic few days before the fifth birthday of my daughter.[27]

In this example, crafting has a mnemonic character. Tupa's observation reminds us that stitching is an embodied process, one that takes place in the context of a family's busy home life. Her deployment of the image of the parenthesis is particularly potent. A parenthesis holds something within it. The quilt is not just an object that keeps people warm; it is also a container for emotions and memories. Henri Bergson writes, "Does not the fiction of an isolated material object imply a kind of absurdity, since this object borrows its physical properties from the relations which it maintains with all others, and owes each of its determinations, and, consequently, its very existence, to the place which it occupies in the universe as a whole?"[28] Neither the quilt nor its maker nor her interactions with her family exist in isolation; rather, they are all co-constituted, objects in space that are also objects floating in a sea of affect.

Tupa's recollection connected gifts to time's passage and the growth of her daughter. Other objects gain their layers of sentiment because of their cyclical, repeated use over successive years. Few things make a creator happier than seeing her work in good use on holidays. In California, Zelda described how happy she was that a friend still used the tablecloth she had made for her and always explained its significance: "There's always a purpose to what I'm doing, a reason, and where it's going to go, if it's for me, or somebody else, always. And, you know, the fact that—it ends up in someone's home, like when I go to Honey on the second day

FIGURE 3.1. *Sandra Lachter, challah cover. Photograph by the author.*

of Rosh Hashanah, and she explains everything at her table—she's very good that way—and she comes to my cloth. And I feel good that this is going to be here, all this will be here, and it will remind them of the time that I did it."[29]

Thus, Zelda, like Robin, has a future-orientation in her description. Both women are trying to create emotional reverberations that will linger when they are personally not present. Zelda wants to be sure her table-cloth will "remind them of the time that I did it"; Robin looks forward to grandchildren holding on to an object that she made. In this way, generations are a powerful component of gift culture. Most of my interviewees made gifts for people who were younger than they were: nieces, nephews, children, grandchildren, younger friends. In her work on contemporary Christian pilgrimage culture, Hillary Kaell argues that gift giving is one of the "crucial ways in which older women navigate tensions specific to the consumer culture and religious patterns of the 21st-century US," a way in which "returned pilgrims both uphold the importance of individuality (as consumers and as believers), while also fulfilling what they believe is their special responsibility to bolster collective faith, particularly in the family."[30] Although Kaell spoke with women who were primarily consumers whereas my interviewees both consume craft supplies *and* produce finished objects, the pattern is similar, particularly if we substitute words like "practice" or "identity," which are more common among Jews, for the Christian emphasis on "faith." When Jewish matriarchs of the baby boomer generation and greatest generation craft objects for their descendants, they are carefully exercising their power, often otherwise circumscribed, in order to foster an attachment to both family and Jewishness among the recipients. I saw this clearly one day when I asked one interviewee if she had made any objects for her grandchildren. A few beats earlier in our conversation, she had been fretting a bit over their lack of participation in Jewish activities. "Maybe I should," she mused.

I also found many examples of gift giving in my online survey. There, respondents had a keen notion of how tightly object exchange is linked with emotional intent and community. One woman wrote, "I think a big part of Judaism is community based. I've given blankets as Jewish wedding gifts and kippot to friends. It's nice when I see the work in public. Even though I don't wear a kippah, it's nice to know I contributed to the kippot in synagogue on a particular day."[31] Similarly, another said that crafting "connects me to tradition and to other Jews—I took great pride in mindfully knitting a kippah for my nephew, focusing on him as I knit each stitch; I took great pride watching him wear it in synagogue."[32] (Figure 3.2 shows an example of a kippah.) Here, the action of knitting must be a mindful one, with a specific intention connected to the knitter's emotional state and focus. The act of crafting involves thinking actively about the intended recipient. Finally, another respondent brought in both notions of the divine and of community: "Exercising my creative abilities, when I can, connects me to God and gives me time to think by myself. When I give items to other people, it connects me to them, person to person."[33] This is powerful theological language. Here, the respondent moves quickly from language that connects her to divinity, in solitude, to language that connects her to community, through gifts. Creativity provides an outlet for spiritual solace in solitude but also an outward goal of sharing the products of that creativity with other people.

All of these examples feature a surplus of feeling that is transmitted materially. In thinking through the meaning of gifts, I keep returning to Robin's statement: "You have to give them emotion." That phrase, framed as an imperative, evokes many aspects of American religions and Jewish American life at the turn of the twenty-first century. The giving of gifts transforms individual practices of creation into an emblem of communal belonging. It also suggests how the language of gifts can overlap with the language of Jewish continuity. Robin and Zelda, like many Jews, were concerned with the legacy of their objects and with whether—or to what

FIGURE 3.2. *Sandra Lachter, kippah. Photograph by the author.*

extent—their descendants will identify as Jews. To give one's children and grandchildren emotions around Judaism is to hope that the feelings stirred by holiday celebrations and life-cycle rituals will prompt future returns to tradition: in other words, one hopes it will stick. For decades, worry over continuity has launched hundreds of think pieces, editorials, and philanthropic ventures throughout the Jewish American community. The importance of gifts and emotion is thus central not just to families but also to national and international philanthropies that seek to strengthen Jews' ties to their heritage. PJ Library, the arm of the Harold Grinspoon foundation that provides free children's books to Jewish children, calls its books "a gift."[34] Since 1999, the Taglit-Birthright Israel trips have quite intentionally used the emotions of storytelling to foster a connection between Jewish young adults and Israel.[35] Though the gifts I study here are not prompted by massive philanthropic donations, they sometimes operate on a similar principle: give the children Jewish emotions, and they will be Jews. On a familial level, Jewish crafters show similar concerns.

## TOUCHING IS BELIEVING:
### EXPENDITURE, RELATIONSHIPS, AND GIFTS

This chapter is populated by hands. It opened with yads, Torah pointers that often feature the shape of a hand at their end. In other cases, mystical meanings are endowed upon the hands of the makers. As religion scholar David Chidester writes, "If we want to get real, touching, not seeing, is believing."[36] It is the intimate touch of the giver that imbues these gifts with special emotional resonance. It is also loss that catapults an item into the category of "unproductive expenditures."[37] In this special kind of loss, the giver of the handmade gift distributes her very selfhood with the item in question. For my respondents, it is in part the hand that enacts this transformation, that produces this loss, this giving of selfhood. But giving has many meanings. In some ways, the handmade gift is simultaneously a loss and an amplification. My interlocutors understood handmade gifts as a giving of "heart and soul," but the gift, like the yad, is also a way of *extending* the self, and with it, one's emotions—a prosthesis. The gift is a technology that can be understood as either replacing or extending the body that made it, but, like a prosthetic limb, it is haunted by absence, too: by the echoes of the giver's presence even when she is not there.

In my survey, I asked two specific questions that resulted in a huge number of responses related to gifts. One was, "What do you do with the objects of your craft practice?" The overwhelming majority of participants essentially said they gave them away. I then asked, "Have you been the recipient of similar objects? What did that mean to you?" In that case, the majority of participants responded in the affirmative and shared stories of what receiving gifts meant to them. Overwhelmingly, they wrote of both comfort and love. The staggering volume and tenor of these responses demands that we take the intersection of religion and materiality quite seriously, attending to the thousands of handmade gift transactions that occur in North America each year. As people who make things, these Jews were particularly attuned to the time and care that goes into making objects. This means that they are not the average gift recipients. Still, their words bring many insights about how notions of expenditure, bodies, and selfhood contribute to our understanding of gift culture.

At times, respondents spoke of the creator's intent, but even more poignantly, they wrote of the individual's *hands*. One person wrote: "I always appreciate handmade objects that I receive far more than machine made ones, particularly since I know how much heart, soul, and hard work goes into making something by hand."[38] Similarly, another woman wrote, "It means so much to know that someone's hands were engaged in the creation of a gift. It represents an investment of time, raw materials, creative thought and energy that can't be replicated with something mass produced."[39] And another: "The things people make seem to be infused with, you know, something of *them*, and giving a handmade gift is a special act as a result."[40] These statements show that embodiment matters. Objects are not just objects; they are objects that have touched other hands, carrying with them the essence of another living being.

Some respondents understood the gifts they had received in ways that had metaphysical repercussions. One referred to receiving original art in this way: "They are pieces of the soul." Another wrote, "My grandmother knit for all of us—love made visible."[41] This statement reminds us of the power of visual culture in the twenty-first century; it could also have been phrased as "love made tangible." My survey informants, who were all, themselves, makers and creators in some fashion, were particularly attuned to the relations among selfhood, identity, and gifts. Several referred to handcrafted gifts as "precious" to them. In its English derivations from Old English and Latin, that which is precious is held dearly and is of great value.[42] In some cases, this goes well beyond a monetary value that can be rationally reckoned. In a Christian context, the term "precious" has also been used to refer to the body and blood of Jesus. Preciousness in a Western religions universe is thus already affiliated with sacrifice and with power. Even with other connotations, handcrafted gifts may hold us, ensnare us, even subjugate us. Or, if we are *not* attuned to them, we may bring them to Goodwill. Some of us, like the informants above, are hopelessly entwined in their embrace—a metaphor for the fact that, as humans, we are dependent, connected beings who do not exist outside of societies and communities. At certain times of our lives, such as infancy, old age, and illness, we are dependent upon others for our very survival. Gifts are an expression of our materially interconnected nature.

In family modes, gifts may reinforce kinship formations but also symbolize fault lines in those relationships. Gerry, one of my California interviewees, showed me pieces her mother-in-law had delicately embroidered by hand. "I knew that she accepted me when she started giving me her embroidered things," she said.[43] In other words, the transmission of handmade items is one that portends excess value. In this case, the giving of the items symbolized inclusion in the extended family unit. The loss of such items would be considered much greater than, say, the loss of a mass-produced chip-and-dip set, because of the hours of labor and care expended in their creation. This gift to Gerry sometime *after* her wedding, but still in the early years of her marriage, signified that she had been accepted into the family on a deeper level, that her home could become the repository of items of great value. Similarly, one of my survey respondents wrote, "When my mother-in-law knits me a sweater, I know that she genuinely sees me as part of her family." To create for others is to literally bind them into the family unit. Not everyone in the family gets a handmade sweater—it confers status and inclusion.

At other times, however, the circulation of gifts in a family context gets complicated. What happens when a gift returns to its maker? Gertrude, one of my octogenarian informants, told me that she had asked a young adult family member to return a Jewish baby gift. "I took it back, because listen, you're not going to be religious, you're twenty-nine years old, and you still don't go to temple—I'm taking this back!" she reported, laughing.[44] Although she was not angry, she expressed a sense of disappointment. She had labored on an intricate design for a baby who, as an adult, did not identify Jewishly. Such, of course, is the nature of all baby gifts—babies lack agency over religious symbols, while adults can take them or leave them. In this case, the creator repossessed her creation. It implied a binding and obligation the gift recipient could not meet, and so, it was rescinded. In this case, too much care had been lost, with too little received. The family bonds remained, but the Jewish bond was, in her view, broken.

In a similar vein, I saw a beautiful *ketubah* (Jewish marriage contract), made by one of my interviewees who was both a stitcher and a calligrapher. For this ketubah, she researched the history of many motifs and incorporated medieval practices, including some gold leaf; it's probably the most intricate modern ketubah I've ever seen. She had made it for a relative who later divorced; at that point, they felt this extraordinary piece should return to the person who made it. It hangs on her kitchen wall.

Sometimes, no matter how much emotion one gives, it isn't enough. I might personally be inclined to interpret objects as powerful because of the resonance they have had in my own life. "But she *made it*" was what swayed me, when my father suggested I discard Grandma Salle's needlepoint rabbi. A different person might have consigned that item to the donations pile. Bonnie, a stitcher in California who is married to a rabbi, sees these discards all the time: "We end up getting stuff from people whose parents or aunts or uncles have passed away and they don't know what to do with it. They don't necessarily want a Jewish thing. I mean, we have a Moses statue upstairs. I don't know what to do with it, but we're saving it there because there wasn't anybody to take it."[45] Barring fires or natural catastrophes, objects have long afterlives. Not all handcrafted gifts meet with sympathetic recipients.

At times of crisis, however, gifts can be particularly potent. We turn now to items offered in the spirit of healing or protection, to explore how tactility, prayer, and gifts are entangled.

In a small-town Pennsylvania coffee shop, Maya, a Gen X-er who describes herself as a "crusty Jewish atheist soul," discussed the ambivalent layers of meaning wound into her experience of knitting for a Christian friend who had recently been diagnosed with stage IV cancer. Efficacious healing prayers, she explained, are not her thing. She felt that "the *mi shebeirach* [Jewish prayer for healing] is a total piece of hooey, especially when sung to a Debbie Friedman tune."[46] What matters here, of course, is the question of what to do about—or instead of—prayer. Maya shared her visceral, somewhat alienated reaction to "watching all of these prayers" on a website set up to chronicle her friend's experiences. She knew that "the evangelical-inflected language of prayer" was not her own.

And yet, she was knitting. "So I'm knitting this chemo cap," she told me. Ironically, after spending forty dollars on new supplies, she learned that her friend's particular course of chemo would not result in hair loss. But Maya was still finishing the hat. "I told her I'm knitting it like sending her out with an umbrella so it doesn't rain. And I put her on the mi shebeirach Yom Kippur list so her name would be read out loud on the most crowded day of the year."[47] For Maya, knitting with intentions toward the object's recipient is a way she often "expresses love," and the chemo cap is an attempt to bridge cultural gaps through craft practice: "She is accepting the gift of my language of knitting, so I'm trying to give her a gift in her language of prayer."[48] Both the knitting and the prayer list constitute special "languages" for Maya and for her Christian friend. Maya's story of knitting the chemo cap bring us into the powerful ways that handmade gifts are a salve in times of trauma, a means of generating resilience that moves us beyond the world of straightforward exchange and into the murky realms of illness, healing, and broader hopes for protecting loved ones.

This story was not the only one I heard that touched upon notions of protection. Sandra, an active Pomegranate Guild member who had sewed since childhood and was deeply involved with her family, told me about an amulet she had made for her granddaughter around the time she became a bat mitzvah. It was a small hamsa, embellished with tiny pomegranates and beading. "I did it for Zoe with the idea that she would hang it over her bed.... I wrote a little note on the back that she can hang this over her bed and it will keep her safe through the night."[49] This gift made the bonds between grandmother and granddaughter tangible, encapsulated in fiber and ever present in that vulnerable time and space between sunset and sunrise.

The sheltering presence of handmade gifts is not just something I write about; it is also something with which I am viscerally familiar, a perspective that influences my analysis of the phenomenon. It is hard for me to write about gifts and gift culture without acknowledging how I personally became the recipient of gifts—including many handmade ones—while writing this book. In doing so, I have become intimately acquainted with the inequality of gifts, with the impossibility of ever truly reciprocating the exchange. I narrate this personal story because no ethnography is produced by an unbiased reliable narrator: we do our work in bodies, and the story of my body and the items I have received informs how I analyze gifts.

*Painted Pomegranates and Needlepoint Rabbis* had its genesis when I was a professor in Oshkosh, Wisconsin, but my research on it began in earnest in 2015, when I started working at Lehigh University. For years, I conducted interviews in person and online, and I spent a good deal of time doing participant observation, meaning that I learned by doing. I began writing the book as my interviews continued, a back-and-forth process that is not uncommon. Like many ethnographers, I got to know the people I was studying, and they, in turn, got to know me.

What happened next altered my relationship with those informants. In April 2018, scarcely a week before my fortieth birthday, I was diagnosed with cancer. We eventually learned that it was colon cancer that had metastasized to the ovaries, and my life as a stage IV cancer patient began. I decided to be transparent about my diagnosis and treatment, and I began writing about my experiences on a Caring Bridge blog. I also started to tell informants from my study what was going on, so that they wouldn't think I had simply bailed when I stopped attending knitting circle meetings and so that they would understand why the book, already slow in coming into shape, was taking even longer to appear. Some of them have since become active readers of my cancer blog. One alerted the members on the Pomegranate Guild Facebook page about my situation, and I received sympathetic messages from several women.

When one of my interviewees asked for my mailing address, I realized I was about to be interpolated into the patterns of exchange I had been pondering intellectually for years. Sure enough, less than two weeks later, I received a package from the regional knitting group where I had been sitting in, doing participant observation. Inside was a card signed by all

FIGURE 3.3. *Jodi Eichler-Levine, knit blanket for charity. Photograph by the author.*

of them—I could *hear* their voices, especially the steely imperative from one of their leaders in her underlined get well *soon*—and a handmade gift. It was a beautiful red crocheted shawl and matching head wrap. (The head wrap was extraneous, if still welcome; like Maya's friend, I got to keep some, though not all, of my hair during chemotherapy.) Overcome and drowning in a strange mix of gratitude and guilt, I cried a little bit. I wrapped myself up in the shawl and took a selfie to send to them (though it took me a long time to do so), deeply cognizant of the power of the gift feedback loop. I regarded the shawl with a mix of wonder and guilt. What had I done to deserve so many stitches, all sent to me?

This particular knitting group only exists, one could say, because of cancer. Their original mission was producing lap blankets for chemotherapy patients at a local hospital. In fact, at the time of my diagnosis, I was still working on the knit lap blanket I had cast on when I began sitting in with the group in 2017 (fig. 3.3). That blanket, made of a soft, variegated, fuzzy acrylic yarn, soon became a further mental puzzle for me. I continued to work on it, mystified and yet compelled by the strangeness of this process: I was making an object for an unknown, anonymous cancer patient while experiencing cancer myself and receiving similar items. It even became the knitting project that came with me to the hospital for my biggest surgery. There I sat, in the sunny recreation room on the fifteenth floor of Memorial Sloan Kettering, working on a charity blanket, a blanket that would become a gift for another cancer patient. The presence of the soft yarn in my lap, the clicking of my metal circular needles as I made it, comforted me. I do not know if it comforted its recipient.

In the fall of 2018, I had enough energy to visit the knitting group again. I had bound off the completed blanket, though I found it hard to let it go. I think of this as my "Linus from *Peanuts* without his security blanket" moment. Like Mae Rockland Tupa reflecting on her daughter's quilt, I realized that I had knitted so many of the emotions of my cancer journey into those yards of sunset-hued acrylic. Memories of doctors' waiting rooms, confessions of fear spilled out upon friend's couches, hours of recuperating on my living room couch with *The Golden Girls* in the background, careful but honest conversations about cancer with my then seven-year-old daughter: all of those were linked with this object that is no longer mine. It felt good to do something, though. I profoundly hope it is keeping someone warm. What I generated was, perhaps, useful, but for me, its power lay in how the act of twisting yarn around needles aided and abetted my mental and physical resilience.

Knitting for charity entails a different sort of gift from the sort I have discussed in most of this chapter. In this way, the red shawl I received from the knitting group is quite different from most of their productions, including my own contributions. I know from their accounts and from the speed with which the box arrived on my doorstep that the shawl was not cast on with me in mind; it was simply the most recently finished and aesthetically appropriate object, fitting for the occasion. Regardless of its origins, it *became* intended for me in a more direct manner as my circumstances arose. The path of giving is not always simple or straightforward.

I cannot repay the gift of this shawl or any of the other gifts—many of them lovingly handmade—that I received over the course of my cancer treatment. The shawl has created an imbalance between me and the fine women of this group. No ethnographer is ever a truly neutral observer, but now I am something else: I am a recipient of their care. All of the gifts I have received on account of my illness create this gap, and yet, they have sustained me. Unlike, say, a holiday gift exchange or a birthday present, I have nothing to give in return, except perhaps my continued existence on this planet, drawing breath, itself a strange and fragile gift and phenomenon that at many times has felt beyond my control. Though I am Jewish, I am reminded of a Christmas song, of the little drummer boy's plaintive statement: "I have no gift to bring (*pa rum pum pum*)." In return for the fearful status of having cancer, I received so many objects, and I was so fatigued that I could rarely express adequate thanks. Gifts received in a time of illness are qualitatively different from those received at a time of gladness.

Two images keep returning to me. One is Maya's notion of knitting as a parallel to prayer, her sending a chemo cap to her friend who still had hair like an "umbrella," just in case it rains. This imaginary umbrella and my actual shawl, spread protectively over their recipients, both evoke the sukkah, the temporary dwelling Jews set up during the fall harvest festival that bears its name. They are, emotionally, a sheltering, sustaining gift of presence. But of course, if these gifts could literally heal people, there would be no need for anyone to endure chemotherapy.

The other image comes from my visit with Heather Stoltz, a New York area–based fiber artist who also holds a master's degree in Jewish studies from the Jewish Theological Seminary. Stoltz told me about several pieces she had worked on that were inspired by interpretations of Hannah—the mother of the prophet Samuel, whose petition for a child is one of the most vivid biblical descriptions of prayer. As she told me,

> We studied this piece of the Talmud that talks about Hannah flinging her prayers at God.... That one line kind of stuck in my mind that she was flinging her prayers. It kind of felt aggressive to me. So, I made a few pieces about the prayers that I wanted to fling at God in that moment. One piece was called *Heal Her*, where I printed onto fabric "el na r'fa na lah" [please God, heal her] over and over again, and then put that on a pink piece of fabric and sculpted it into a three-dimensional pink ribbon, because in that year, several family members and friends of family had been diagnosed with breast cancer. So, that was one of those prayers to fling into the heavens.[50]

Stoltz also showed me a fascinating contraption she rigged up, based on this notion of "flinging prayers." She constructed a small catapult onto which participants could take a small fabric beanie, write a prayer on it in fabric marker, and then fling it toward a large black piece of fabric, where the cloth pieces stuck, creating a new, spontaneous artwork. Some people had decided to keep their beanies, while others had left them with her, and these were the ones I saw in her studio (fig. 3.4). One of the beanies, too, said, "el na r'fa na la." Others said, "slow calm," "Heal the Gulf (of MX)," and "Thank you, G—d, help me to encourage"; another asked, in Hebrew, "Who can heal me?"

The contraption was used at two workshops: "A Letter Unread: Drisha Arts Fellows Present a Year of Learning" (Drisha Institute is a progres-

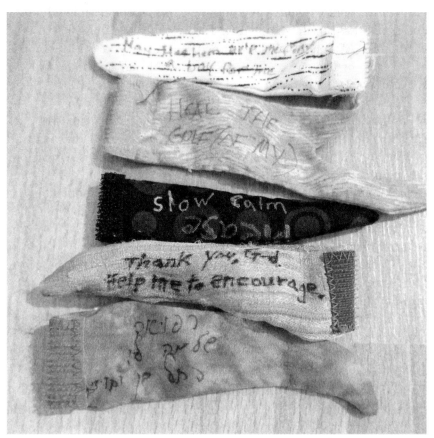

FIGURE 3.4. *Heather Stoltz, flung prayers. Photograph by the author.*

sive Manhattan space promoting classical Jewish text study, especially among women), and the Jewish Orthodox Feminist Alliance's "Putting Women Back in the Celebration." Stoltz's website includes a silent video of a series of women, and one young girl, taking part in this collaborative art-making venture. Some approach the table confidently, others hesitantly; most seem intent as they write their prayers. Then they place them on the catapult and let them fly at the black fabric, which gradually becomes more cluttered with prayers.[51]

This art installation is not a gift. It is, however, an example of prayers made material in a way that evokes Maya's comment about the "language of knitting" being adjacent to the language of prayer. Gifts perform a kind of enhancement that we should not take for granted. They make sentiment into something that can be grasped.

Gifts do not, precisely, heal. Neither, in many cases, do prayers. The biblical story that gives us the phrase "el na r'fa na la" is a troubling one for many readers, especially feminist ones. In it, both Miriam and Aaron question Moses's leadership, but God strikes only Miriam with a disease in response—Aaron remains unscathed. When Aaron begs Moses not to let Miriam "be like one stillborn, whose flesh is half consumed when it comes out of its mother's womb," and Moses, in turn, says to God, "Please heal her" (*el na r'fa na la*), the text says: "But the Lord said to Moses, 'If her father had but spit in her face, would she not bear her shame for seven days? Let her be shut out of the camp for seven days, and after that she may be brought in again" (Num. 12:11–14). Since Miriam is returned to the community after a seven-day isolation, most interpretations consider this prayer to have been successful. Yet this is also the last moment in the biblical narrative's final edited version where Miriam *does* anything; her next appearance is a single verse in Numbers 20, which reports her death. Perhaps Miriam was healed, and perhaps she was not; as is typical with biblical women, we don't get much of her story. In terms of later Jewish liturgy, the narrative setting ends up mattering much less than the striking phrasing of the ancient prayer itself.

I bring in this story not because I am concerned with its literal sense but because its attention to issues of touch, community, and healing are pertinent for closing this meditation on gifts. Part of what's so painful and so powerful for me, as I reread this text, is how Miriam cannot be touched, how contagion renders her body impermissible. This both contrasts and resonates with my experience as a cancer patient and recipient of gifts in ways that lead me to argue for the ongoing power of tangible exchanges. Being ill, especially during a health crisis that suggests your own mortality, makes you realize that your body is both tremendously isolated and frighteningly manipulable.

While undergoing cancer treatment, I felt ambivalence regarding the sense of touch. On the one hand, my body experienced many sensations, often in situations that were out of my control: the feeling of cold air on an operating room table, postoperative pain and staples in my skin, the sharpness of needles, the chill of chemotherapy infusions, the taste of saline whenever my chest port was flushed. On the other hand, I felt radically isolated within my body: I was frequently alone in a hospital bed or on my couch recuperating, humbled by the knowledge that no one else could take on these sensations for me, feeling trapped in this dangerous, faulty flesh.

The touch of handmade gifts bridged that gulf of somatic isolation. In fact, there was a day, as I worked on the notes to begin this chapter, that I sat in my living room, surrounded by such gifts. On my feet I wore pink cabled socks knit by a faraway old friend; on my lap was a special quilt pieced by another old friend's congregation; around my shoulders, I had draped the red shawl from the knitting circle. Though, unlike Miriam, I was not shunned by my community (or, as far as I know, cursed by God), I was feeling cut off from my usual networks, alone on my couch when I would normally have been at a weeklong seminar with colleagues. In that moment, the gifts worked their tactile power, their threads between people. In the softness of all that fiber, the warm brush of both smooth and bumpy fabrics on my skin, I literally felt less alone.

To be cut off from a community's touch, like Miriam in the book of Numbers, is to be cut off from humanity. Gift culture is the opposite of banishment. Praying "el na r'fa na la" is a way of generating hope when hope is hard to come by, of voicing powerful emotions about our lack of control over our bodies and those of our loved ones. Like the "flinging of prayers," the making of gifts channels emotions. In both their "excess and extravagance," these items sediment our sentiments.

Philosopher Pablo Maurette writes of the power of the "haptic," from the Greek verb *haptomai*, "to come into contact with," "to touch," "to grab": "The deponent character of the verb (active in meaning, but bearing the form of a verb in the passive or middle voice) reflects one of the most fundamental aspects of the haptic: its simultaneity. To touch is to be touched. To feel something is to feel oneself."[52] On the couch, surrounded by stitches, I was briefly reassured of my own existence and the reality of other humans' care. The simultaneity of touch in the form of gifted fabrics replaced the simultaneity of having those people in the room with me. Such is the power of gifts.

Touch helps us to keep our place. Gifts orient us. This returns us to the gifts of yads with which I began this chapter. There are multiple reasons that Torah readers use a yad as they make their way through long columns of Hebrew text. Touching the scroll with one's bare hands would damage this sacred object: the oil on our skin would degrade the parchment, the hand-scribed ink might smudge. But if one tries to chant Torah without a physical guide, it is easy to become lost in that sea of letters that lack punctuation; one would be more likely to make errors during this ritual, a ritual where the pronunciation of each word must be precisely correct. Torah reading is thus something one does by feel as much as by sight and sound. The yads that Robinson crafts, with their tiny hands, are like virtual limbs, extensions of the self where one's physical skin cannot venture.

Like the yad, gifts orient both givers and recipients. They provide signposts of who matters, and how. Who is in the family? The one who receives a gift. They protect, and they transmit emotion: "You have to give them emotion." Gifts connect human beings across the boundaries that separate our fragile, disease-prone bodies. Gifts are vectors of "fellowship, power, and presence."[53] In this chapter, we have seen how these items bind friends and families in times of worship and memory, prayer and illness. We now broaden our portrait of objects and the people who make them by examining how crafting creates whole communities and how those communities strengthen those who populate them.

# 4 : BEZALEL'S HEIRS

. . . . . . . . . . . . . . . . . . . . . . . . . . . . . . . . . . . . . . .

*Crafting in Community*

"**S**omething magical happens when women sit and stitch together." So said one of my fellow participants at the 2017 biennial convention of the Pomegranate Guild of Judaic Needlework. This statement encapsulates how I had landed in a posh suburban Atlanta hotel with approximately eighty Jewish women for three intense days of stitching, learning, and catered kosher meals. What is this magic, and how does crafting in community generate resilience?

That morning, at the jingle of a tambourine, a hotel ballroom filled with Jewish needleworkers settled slowly into a low hum. It was time for the official opening of the biennial convention of the Pomegranate Guild. Jewish women from all over North America, from Idaho to Massachusetts and Calgary to Fort Lauderdale, had gathered for sewing, knitting, crochet, quilting, food, tours, and, above all, camaraderie. The ballroom's twelve tables were covered with black cloths. Each one had a handmade centerpiece, a basket featuring a sewn, crocheted, or knit peach and pomegranate clustered together, uniting the symbol of Georgia with the symbol of the guild (fig. 4.1). Guild president Cathy Perlmutter called the convention to order, and Rabbi Dr. Avi Kuperberg, the husband of incoming guild president Adrienne Kuperberg, gave a short sermon, or *d'var torah* (word of Torah), on the convention's theme: "I Have a Dream," an homage to the U.S. civil rights movement in which the citizens of Atlanta played such a crucial role. One wall of the ballroom was adorned with handmade banners, one representing each regional chapter of the guild (fig. 4.2). After lunch, we would return to workshops on everything from knitting a "scrumble" to the "Zentangle" method of doodling a needlework design.

The Pomegranate Guild of Judaic Needlework is just one example of the many spaces where craft happens in community. Creation is a dialectic between self and surroundings; an organization founded in the late 1970s simultaneously encapsulates trends from the religious history of that time and presages twenty-first-century developments. Through a study of the Pomegranate Guild, as well as a Pennsylvania knitting circle in which I

FIGURE 4.1. *Peach State Stitchers, centerpiece, Pomegranate Guild of Judaic Needlework Biennial Convention, Atlanta, Georgia, May 2017. Photograph by the author.*

FIGURE 4.2. *Peach State Stitchers, Pomegranate Guild banner, detail, Pomegranate Guild of Judaic Needlework Biennial Convention, Atlanta, Georgia, May 2017. Photograph by the author.*

did participant observation for over two years, we see how communities of feeling gather around objects and the process of making them. Jewish crafting groups enact a culture of teaching, learning, and collective identification. This culture has historical roots in American feminist and countercultural movements from the 1960s and 1970s, as well as consonance with older Jewish traditions, and analogies with Christian crafting circles. The magic of such groups is found in the ways they generate resilience by providing a "third space" where participants can "make homes" and "confront suffering," generating meaning and forging bonds of friendship around needlework.[1]

POMEGRANATES, PEACHES, AND COMMUNITY

The Pomegranate Guild of Judaic Needlework was founded in January 1977 when a small group of women, and one man, met in the greater New York City and Long Island area in order to begin an organization dedicated to "synagogue decoration, Judaic symbolism, Jewish art or Judaic embroidery."[2] The guild's early years were marked by a mix of formality and professionalism. Initially, it held yearly juried shows. To qualify as a guild member, one's needlework had to be exhibited in one of those shows and judged on the following five criteria: "symbolism, use of symbols, design and color, needlework, and use of materials."[3] "Friends" of the guild, whose work was not ready for showing or did not receive adequate marks, could be affiliates but not, technically, members. In its earliest days, the guild members were particularly concerned with skill level and the quality of the works they produced.

The earliest guild members worked primarily in embroidery and identified the need for a group that was specifically "Judaic": "We are few in number and need each other very much."[4] An account of the first group exhibition, held on June 6, 1977, is described in that fall's edition of the *Paper Pomegranate*: "The judging, like other standards defined by the Guild, was hardly a casual affair. The Guild believes that embroidery is a fine art form.... It was therefore imperative that the judges be professionals in their respective areas of expertise, but it was not necessary that they all be embroiderers."[5] Thirty-one embroiderers submitted works to be judged on that date. This language shows that, in its initial incarnation, the guild identified more strongly on the art than craft side of the art–craft continuum. This is not surprising. Many of the founders were members of existing embroidery guilds, which included technical judging of this sort. The goal was for the Pomegranate Guild to be a home for specifically *Jewish* needlework, in order to safeguard the community's history while also maintaining a high level of artistic achievement. What was

"Jewish" could vary and was not strictly delimited. Some of the objects in the early guild newsletters are ritual items or decorations for Hanukkah. Judaic "symbols," such as lions or the menorah (multibranched candelabra), were discussed, as were needlework techniques from different global Jewish communities. Early members frequently used the term "art," which fits with the broader 1970s enterprise of encouraging critics and historians to understand that the media in which women had often worked, like embroidery, must be recognized as fine arts alongside painting and other male-dominated fields.

The guild's early activities were busy and extremely varied. They included lecture series, trips to local museums, the maintenance of a slide library and reference books, and the sharing of design ideas and skilled techniques. Early newsletters include a mix of reports on activities, histories, member news, judging criteria, book reviews, and articles, each carefully researched, about different historical Jewish arts—for example, a "Spanier Arbeit Atarah." An *atarah* is the neck edging of a tallit, or prayer shawl; in this case, it was done with a special kind of "Spanish work" embroidery.[6] In 1980, the guild experienced tragedy when their newsletter editor, Binyamina Silverman, was murdered in her New York City apartment. In a memorial speech quoted in the *Paper Pomegranate*, President Rita Drucker memorialized Silverman's educational accomplishments, her public exhibitions, and her warmth, even across distance: "Many members of the Guild never knew Binyamina personally; they only came to know her through her work on the *Paper Pomegranate*. From scores of these women I have received notes of condolence written as if she were a personal friend, for that was the spirit in which she edited our paper. We have all lost a good friend, an artistic companion, and an inspiration."[7] Some members still remembered this occurrence when I interviewed them in 2017.

As the guild developed and grew, it began to take on different shapes depending upon the region. The earliest guild newsletters indicate connections between New York and California, as workers at the Los Angeles Skirball Cultural Center corresponded with East Coast fiber artisans and curators. One of the most interesting things about the Pomegranate Guild is how it spread nationally—and ultimately, internationally—at a time well before the Internet enabled rapid networking across great distances. The Los Angeles chapters were seeded through communications sent from New York to the Skirball Cultural Center. Ita Aber, an early guild president and author of *The Art of Judaic Needlework*, visited Los Angeles in person. Gerry, one of the founding members of the Los Angeles chapters, described how she made contacts in cities across the country when she accompanied her husband on business trips. While he attended conventions, she struck out on her own, contacting local embroidery guilds and synagogues, conducting seminars, and spreading word of the guild's activities. "When my husband traveled and lectured, I got in touch with someone, whatever city we were going into, and I showed them my stuff and they showed me their stuff," she explained.[8] In this way, Gerry made contacts in Chicago, Atlanta, and other locations.

Because the group's self-understanding often rests on ideas about ancient Israelites, a brief detour into biblical texts sheds light on the group's foundation and the narratives that drove it. The story of the Pomegranate Guild cannot be told without also telling the story of Bezalel, the mythical chief artisan of the tabernacle in the Hebrew Bible. The "About the Guild" webpage of the group's website opens with the following quotation: "And they made upon the hem of the robe pomegranates of blue and purple and scarlet and twined linen. And they made bells of pure gold and put the bells between the pomegranates upon the hem of the robe, round about the pomegranate" (Exod. 39:24–25).[9] In this section of Exodus, we read about how Bezalel and his assistant, Oholiab, made the *mishkan* (Tabernacle), or tent of meeting, to house the tablets of the covenant. They also make the priestly vestments, which are described in great detail, including the quotations above, using silver, gold, and other items given by the community as a whole. Why so much detail? This is, perhaps, because the Torah as we know it today was influenced and, in some cases, edited by a much later priestly class—the priests of the second temple in the years from the late sixth century B.C.E. to its fall in 70 C.E.—as the texts of the Torah were brought together and redacted into a larger, aggregate shape. The temple was a place of rich and complicated materiality, of messy, bloody sacrifices and shining riches. Bezalel is often invoked by contemporary Jews when they talk about the arts; indeed, the most famous art school in modern Israel is the Bezalel Academy of Arts and Design. For Jewish artists, Bezalel looms large as an emblem, a way of saying that Jews, too, have a long history of art and craft.

The work of these biblical male artisans became foundational images for a group composed primarily—but not entirely—of women. The past is made present in their current mission: "When members of the Pomegranate Guild sit down to stitch, they are making more than just table linens and wall hangings. They are reviving Jewish traditions through their work with textiles."[10] In this way, they construct themselves as Bezalel's heirs, linking their contemporary actions with tradition, that evergreen motif of Jewish identity.

Although in its early days the guild emphasized juried approval for full membership, it eventually evolved to welcoming all who were interested, regardless of their level of skill—to wit, this statement on the current website: "In the Jewish tradition, an item created by an unrecognized stitcher is as esteemed as one created by a master artisan."[11] Bezalel might be the archetypical leader of the pack, but all of Israel is included in the notion of hiddur mitzvah, or the adornment and enhancement of a commandment. Just as the Israelites are said to have given of their own gold, silver, and skills to aid in the creation of the Tabernacle, the members of the Pomegranate Guild believe in giving of themselves to create a greater whole. Today, its members include many everyday crafters who would never aspire to juried shows alongside skilled needleworkers who do pursue those avenues, in addition to many stitchers who occupy a middle ground.

I was privileged to meet with members of the Pomegranate Guild in multiple settings. This included interviews with several California members and attendance at a Los Angeles chapter meeting in April 2017; participant observation and many interviews at the May 2017 biennial convention in Atlanta; a visit to an exhibit put on jointly by the Philadelphia chapter of the guild and Congregation Keneseth Israel of Elkins Park, Pennsylvania, in the winter of 2018; and many regional interviews and electronic communications. It is difficult to put the warmth I observed among Pomegranate Guild members into words. My ethnography showed me the centrality of making emotional connections and the importance of interpersonal relationships for every person with whom I spoke.

Bonnie Vorspan, an early member of the San Fernando Valley chapter, told me how overjoyed she was when a night group of that chapter started in 1983. At the time, her children were young and her social contacts were limited: "I thought I died and went to stitchers' heaven. It was absolutely amazing, the stitches that opened up for me, the projects. I was like a sponge."[12] For Bonnie, connecting with other crafters was a way of unleashing and enhancing her own skills. Finally, she had met other people as devoted to the needle arts as she was, providing her with enormous opportunities for learning, as well as a warm community environment.

Sandra Lachter, who came from a southwestern region of the guild, was a lifelong sewer and knitter who first came into contact with other crafters through shared adversity. It turned out that she and the president of her local chapter were both breast cancer survivors in the same support group, which paved her entryway into joining meetings. "They were mainly doing things I didn't have a skillset in, they were doing needlepoint at that point, never done it. But you sit around with a group of ten or fifteen women, and she will show you a few tips, and the next thing you know, I'm enjoying it, I'm loving it. I can't get enough of it."[13]

She also shared how important the group had been to her after her husband's death: "They were all there for shiva. They just showed up magically at the funeral. I just felt like, yes, this is a core group of my friends. … Our friendship really is around our love of doing needlecrafts."[14] Shiva is the seven-day mourning period that Jews observe after the death and burial of a close family member, during which friends and other community members come to their home. Here, a group that developed around one set of Jewish practices—crafting—translated itself into the performance of another Jewish action—that of comforting the bereaved in a time of mourning. Generative resilience on the collective level comes from the meeting of creation and community.

In California, Gerry conveyed a great deal of the guild's meaning to me throughout our conversations. One phrase of Gerry's stuck with me for months after our interview and inspired this chapter. "They're just the best gals," she told me, over lunch at a country club near her home. "The important thing was that we helped each other, and the groups just grew by leaps and bounds." She added, "The interesting thing was that these women were all of different levels of ability. Different ages, different observance of the Judaic way. Didn't make any difference. We just had a great time doing things together."[15]

In this way, the Pomegranate Guild is a prime example of postdenominational Judaism.[16] The emergence of separate Jewish denominations— for example, Reform, Conservative, Reconstructionist, and Orthodox, each with its own seminaries, prayer books, and legal bodies—is a phenomenon that was particularly pronounced in the United States, one that reached its heights in the early post–World War II period, when many of my informants were children.[17] By the 1970s and 1980s, the differences between the movements were becoming less rigid. Today, despite the continued existence of the movements and their institutions, we see much more blurring of the lines between them and even the merging of synagogues across denominations as overall synagogue affiliation declines.[18] Though the Pomegranate Guild was founded at a time of higher synagogue membership, it was doing something rather different from synagogues, focusing on material culture rather than doctrine, prayer, or youth education; it was also different from activist groups. In some ways, its development is akin to the *havurah* movement, which also grew as a home-based network of circles, though its aims are different.[19] (The havurah movement, which, like the Pomegranate Guild, flourished in the 1970s and 1980s, involved small groups of Jews—friendship circles—meeting in members' homes, rather than a large synagogue, for services and other activities; it provided an intimate, member-driven approach to Jewish communal practice, and its reverberations are still felt among Jewish Americans). In the contemporary moment, the Pomegranate Guild shares much in common with other Jewish-identified organizations that focus on a particular activity or affinity, such as the environment (Hazon), urban agriculture (Jewish Farm School), or genealogy (Jewish Gen).[20]

The healthy coexistence of Jews with varying modes of observance was in clear evidence at the 2017 convention in Atlanta. During the breakfast hour, some members opted in for a glatt kosher catered breakfast, while others dined on bacon—the ultimate *treif,* or nonkosher, food—at the hotel restaurant. Some were keenly aware that the fiftieth anniversary of Israel's victory in the Six-Day War was coming up that week; others were not. There were women in *sheitels* (wigs), hats, or scarves typical of those who observe certain modesty provisions in Jewish law, and women with uncovered hair wearing shorts, and everything in between. I was witnessing a microcosm of Jewish American religious diversity, and it seemed to be going swimmingly (though I know that as a relative outsider, I was not privy to any logistical dramas during the conference's planning phase).

In other ways, however, the rooms in which we stitched and ate and talked were not diverse. For one thing, as noted above, the convention was primarily composed of women (with a few husbands in tow, mostly heading off to golf during the day). More significantly, I saw overwhelmingly Ashkenazi women, those descended from central and eastern European immigrants—meaning, they were mostly white (or white enough), particularly in the context of the American South. Ashkenazi Jewish racial assignment has varied across American history.[21] Jews, like other so-called white ethnic groups such as Irish and Italian Americans, have not always been considered white, depending upon the context. However, in the American South, eastern European–descended Jews have certainly been considered much whit*er* than African Americans and were treated as such during slavery and segregation. Even though most Jewish Americans are descended from European Jews who immigrated to the United States between 1880 and 1924, today's Jewish American community is diverse. According to one recent study, Jews of color comprise 12 to 15 percent of American Jews.[22] Other Jews come from Sephardic communities, groups that fled the Spanish expulsion in 1492 and spread out across the Middle East, North Africa, Latin America, and other regions. Jews also have long histories throughout India, the Middle East, and China, and scholars of Judaism in Africa continue to find Jewish communities, not just in Ethiopia, but in several other countries as well.[23]

In Atlanta, the irony was striking. The convention's theme of "I Have a Dream" evoked the city's role in the history of the Civil Rights movement, and yet I did not see a single African American Jew in the room. There are, of course, many likely reasons for this. For one thing, this was not the whole guild; only a small percentage of the membership traveled to Atlanta. The guild is certainly not intentionally exclusive. Yet, despite its innovations, the Pomegranate Guild has much in common with other mainstream Jewish organizations, including those stemming from the late nineteenth and early to mid-twentieth centuries, such as Hadassah, the Women's Zionist Organization of America, which was founded in 1912 but remained a popular social network among middle-class Jewish women well into the 1970s and 1980s.[24] Though the Pomegranate Guild is a child of the 1970s, it initially developed along the backbones of existing, older networks of synagogue sisterhoods, museums, and JCCs (Jewish community centers): all institutions of Jewish American life that are typically dominated by Ashkenazi Jews. Thus, the guild began among primarily Ashkenazim and has attracted more of them. There is internal diversity to be found along various axes of difference—for example, the keynote speaker in May 2017 hailed from Latin America—but it is, by American standards, a predominantly white space. The "I Have a Dream" theme had an accompanying contest. Individuals and chapter members were asked to use that idea in pillow creations they brought to display at the convention. Several members of the local chapter, the Peach State Stitchers, interpreted the idea globally, creating a group display, "We Have a Dream . . . for Peace."

Today, the Pomegranate Guild encompasses several hundred members, primarily in the United States and Canada but with at least one member as far away as Australia. At the time of this writing, thriving chapters exist in Atlanta, northern New Jersey, Philadelphia, the Pioneer Valley of Massachusetts, Connecticut, Los Angeles, Arizona, and several other locations; a Yellow Rose chapter was recently founded in Texas. At the same time, a large number of the group's members are "Independents," stitchers who either don't live near an active group or who can't attend local meetings but who share in the guild's mission and ethos through newsletters, online groups, and national conventions. The past decade has seen a compression in the size of the guild, with a few chapters folding, and continuity and legacy were concerns in most of the interviews I conducted.

## "THE CHRISTMAS CRAFTS ARE JUST OUT OF CONTROL": POMEGRANATE GUILD AS JEWISH SPACE

The Pomegranate Guild functions as a Jewish haven in the typically Christian-dominated American craft world. This came up in many casual conversations during my convention fieldwork and also, frequently, during formal interviews. As Bonnie told me: "I found other Jewish women who were doing Jewish things, because the world is not Jewish.... There's huge Christmas stuff, there's huge Halloween stuff, there's huge Easter stuff. If we don't do Jewish things, who's going to do them?"[25] She explained how she would "take non-Jewish designs and make them Jewish."[26] A pattern for a fabric Christmas wreath, for example, was transformed, in her capable hands, into an autumn wreath to decorate her sukkah, the temporary dwelling Jews erect during the fall harvest festival of Sukkot.

Similarly, Cathy Perlmutter, who served as the national president of the Pomegranate Guild from 2015 to 2017, explained how her sense of alienation in local, non-Jewish craft settings drove her to seek out Jewish venues. "So, I joined the quilt guild, and of course they had their new member tea on Yom Kippur," she said. "And I tried to talk to them about it, and they just didn't want to talk about it. They just didn't get it."[27] For both of these women, and many others, the Pomegranate Guild became a safe space where Jewish traditions could be not only recognized but celebrated.

As Stacey, a New England member, told me, "I think there's so much in the crafting world that's not Jewish, particularly around Christmas. I mean, the Christmas crafts are just out of control. So it's nice to have a group where you can celebrate your own traditions and celebrate your religion without feeling like you're the only one making a dreidel while everyone else is making ornaments."[28] I encountered similar conversations throughout the 2017 biennial convention. At one embroidery workshop, participants bemoaned the dominance of Christmas crafts and enjoyed the fact that we were making tea towels that celebrated iconic biblical heroines instead. Over dinner one evening, a woman who had lived in both the Midwest and the South told me that in the non-Pomegranate craft groups, everyone bonded over their Christmas crafts, leaving her to feel excluded. In the Pomegranate Guild, she said, everyone bonded over their tallit bags and challah covers instead, and she got to be a part of it. It became clear to me that part of the Pomegranate Guild members' resilience came from the group's function as an alternative crafting space where Jewish objects, stories, and rituals were at the center, not in the margin.

For women who lived in areas with few other Jews, the Guild was a particularly valuable link to other Jews. At the biennial convention, I spoke with Lindi, who hailed from Wisconsin. As an independent member, Lindi had come upon the guild in a story that echoed Gerry's stories of early guild connections: she was accompanying her spouse on a business trip and reached out electronically to learn about fabric shops in the city they were visiting. She connected with an active guild member, and the rest was history. Lindi really enjoyed the convention atmosphere. "I love the people, the Jewish women that are here. I like the fact that it's Jewish, it's creative, it's fiber, and that there's a connection among the women that are here. Especially, coming from a smaller community, I don't always have that connection. I have to seek it out. And I always feel that it's as much a part of our responsibility to seek out things as other people to seek you out."[29] Lindi had strong connections with non-Jewish quilters in her hometown, but incorporated Jewish symbolism into a great deal of her work and found meaning in connecting with other Jewish quilters.

Being proud of Jewishness in mainstream craft spaces was also important. Arlene Diane Spector, a past president of the national guild and frequent regional officer, told me the story of how a group of guild members had made it their goal to get Jewish pieces recognized at the Woodlawn Plantation Needlecraft Exhibition, in Mount Vernon, Virginia, which, at the time, often featured a large number of Christmas decorations. One of Arlene's friends said she wanted them to make "a Judaic statement, because we're Jewish and we should be acknowledged." Arlene added, "Our goal was not to get ribbons, our goal was to make a Jewish statement in an area where there were not a lot of Jews."[30] Despite this humble aside, one of her submitted pieces, an intricate black-work depiction of Naomi and Ruth, received an honorable mention one year (fig. 4.3). I viewed the piece in her home, where it is displayed on a living room wall with other framed needlework, its ribbon still affixed.

This delicate piece shows two women, one facing forward, the other pictured in turned profile, her long braid spreading down toward the bottom of the canvas. Ruth's famous speech, including the phrase, "For wither thou goest, I will go, and whither thou lodgest, I will lodge; your people shall be my people," is inscribed around the border of the image. Although this Jewish piece is most definitely not a Christmas craft, it was inspired by a Hebrew Bible passage that is common to both Christians and Jews, one that is popular in both traditions as a story of conversion; it is also important because Ruth ultimately holds a place in the genealogical tree for King David and, in the Christian tradition, Jesus. Thus, while this Jewish statement was certainly no Christmas ornament, it was

also not as ethnoreligiously particularistic as, say, a challah cover or Torah mantle, objects specific to Jewish rituals and only Jewish rituals, would have been.

To be clear, Jewish crafting is not always "anti-Christmas." Among the roughly 50 percent of Jewish Americans who marry non-Jews, including Christians, we see ever more fluid and nuanced revalorizations of both Christianity and Judaism as "cultures" that can be blended without offending the Jewish spouse; "Chrismukkah" crafts abound on Etsy and elsewhere.[31] For the women of the Pomegranate Guild, however, identification of Jewish crafts over and against Christian ones is still an important dividing line. Due to the current length of the commercial season, "for both celebrant and noncelebrant alike, there is no escaping Christmas"; furthermore, "American Jewry's success in challenging Christmas's vaunted status rests upon forging an identity that is at once separate from the religious and historical dimensions of Christmas, yet convergent with its underlying spirit."[32] Even though the Jewish women of the Pomegranate Guild were internally diverse in their Jewish practice, they agreed on what they were *not*: they were not Christian. Thus, on one level, the Pomegranate Guild functioned as a space where members of a minority culture could congregate and fully be themselves. Not every member of the Pomegranate Guild necessarily observes Yom Kippur, but all agree that the guild would never hold the new members' tea then. Even more critically, they helped one another to learn more about both the fiber arts and Jewish traditions, with a particular focus on how these two overlapped. This leads us to an examination of the Pomegranate Guild as a teaching space.

## TYING TZITZIT, TEACHING, AND LEADERSHIP

Teaching and learning were central to many members' narration of what the guild meant to them. Many of the earliest guild chapters were in fact known as "study groups." Before widespread home computer use changed how we approach images, many chapters maintained slide carousels with examples of Jewish textiles, symbols, and other art, as well as reference books and pattern libraries. (Newsletters continue to include patterns today, which is why on the Pomegranate Guild website they are accessible only to dues-paying members.) The Pomegranate Guild is a place of strong fellowship and pride in both artistic skill and the act of teaching. Part of being a Jewish organization means studying and learning together.

Stacey explained to me how important it is that everyone take turns teaching the others a skill. "We also think that it's really important for everyone in our chapter to teach something because the full exercise of prepping for a class and structuring your technique so that you can teach it is a very different experience than doing it yourself. So, we try to encourage everyone to take a class that they want to teach."[33] In this way, the Pomegranate Guild is not meant to be a passive space. Rather, the idea that everyone has something to teach to the group, whatever her level of skill, suggests a strong sense of engagement and expresses a more generalized way that classical Jewish values, such as group study, influence the guild's ethos.

This emphasis on the collective also has roots in the fact that the Pomegranate Guild was born out of various Jewish and feminist (and Jewish feminist) aspects of the 1970s countercultural stew. Although the Pomegranate Guild members are keen to pass on traditions, they also owe their origins to movements that challenged the social status quo. Peachy Levy, who is an internationally renowned fiber artist and was a key member during the early years of the Los Angeles chapters, told me how she first became a fiber artist. It is a story that emerges from both crafting and feminist matrices of the late 1960s and 1970s. Levy first learned how to make a challah cover at a workshop at her synagogue. "When we joined the synagogue there was a class offered to learn to embroider a challah cover. I wanted to do that, so I took the class, learned from an excellent and talented teacher. We made a sampler, I made the challah cover, and discovered that I had the talent to satisfy the urge that I had to make Judaic objects. That was the beginning of my art career in the field of Judaic textiles. It was a way that I could artistically comment on the beauty and values of Jewish tradition."[34] She also described art classes at Everywoman's Village, a popular Los Angeles-area venue during this time period. Today, Levy has produced hundreds of commissioned pieces, particularly Torah covers, including one that is the first item you see when entering the permanent collection of the Skirball Cultural Center in Los Angeles.[35] Her story was one of many I heard that began at that historical seam.

In this way, what would become the Pomegranate Guild was an extension of other democratizing, collectivist movements in the Jewish world and in the United States writ large during that era. The Pomegranate Guild began in the period that gave us the havurah movement and *The Jewish Catalog* in Jewish circles and that gave us *Our Bodies, Ourselves*, the campaign for the Equal Rights Amendment, and *Ms.* magazine in broader progressive circles—with significant overlaps, given the widespread presence of Jewish women in those American movements.[36] What all of these endeavors have in common is the notion that everyday people do not always need experts to tell them how to do things or to lead them in all matters. All of these movements emphasized the collaborative, the cooperative, the ability to do it yourself. Crucially, however, these movements were not just the story of individuals. They were about practices happening in groups, with people—often women—teaching one another new techniques and sharing from their experiences. The creators of *The Jewish Catalog* were deeply influenced by the counterculture and very interested in enabling Jews to do Jewish things in a tactile way, though book sales did not necessarily translate into book *use*. In an oft-cited passage, the authors wanted to "transcend supermarket challah and factory made talleism" for something more personal, more "authentic."[37] This was in part about giving power back to "the Jewish individual." On the ground, however, DIY Judaism also empowered individuals *within* collectives like the Pomegranate Guild.

An artifact from the West Los Angeles chapter of the Pomegranate

FIGURE 4.4. *West Los Angeles chapter, Pomegranate Guild of Judaic Needlework, pomegranate display. Photograph by the author.*

Guild illustrates this point. When I attended one of their meetings, Gerry and several other members showed me items they would use as displays when spreading word of the guild to others. The one I found most fascinating served as a teaching piece not just for outsiders but for group members. It dated back to the early 1980s. On large pieces of poster board taped together to form an enormous trifold, the chapter's founders had mounted over a dozen squares, each depicting the same pair of pomegranates on a vine (fig. 4.4). Every square, however, was done in a different style of needlework: cross-stitch, crewel, weaving, needlepoint, quilting, appliqué, crochet, Swedish huck (a special type of embroidery), and more. Each one also featured the name of the woman who had created it. The poster board showed the yellowing of age, and many of the names were familiar to me from my perusal of the guild's early newsletters. The techniques showcased here were traditional, each executed to perfection. But I cannot help seeing the object itself as a radical piece. At a time when women in the Reform and Reconstructionist movements were just beginning to become rabbis and women in the Conservative movement still could not quite do so, the women of the Pomegranate Guild were taking on their own mantles of leadership, study, and teaching, in their own newly created, cooperative world.

The trifold display also reminded me of a conversation I had had the previous day with Bonnie. Bonnie, who is married to a congregational rabbi, was very proud of a particular moment from her son's upbringing. She told the story in this way. When her son was in Hebrew high school, he participated in a tallit-making workshop, which included the process of tying the tzitzit (fringes) onto the corner of the tallit—a very involved process that requires careful counting, wrapping, and manual dexterity. "He did it very ably, he was very quick, and they said to him, 'Could you tie the tzitzit because your father is a rabbi?' He said, 'No, it's because my mother was in the Pomegranate Guild.' Now, that certainly wasn't why. He was just able to do it, but how neat, that that was his response, that it was hand stuff.... I thought it was a very cool thing for him to say."[38]

In this anecdote, we can see how much pride Bonnie took in having her accomplishments recognized by a family member. The heritage and leadership that matter here are not the traditional mode of rabbinic authority (rabbinic power itself has waxed and waned over the course of Jewish history). Rather, in this story, it is a feminized domain of handcrafts that is held up as a sign of Jewish skill and authenticity. The Pomegranate Guild is a form of "everyday religion" that makes space for alternate ways of creating Jewish community and expressing pride in Jewish identities.[39] It is a "third place," a space for gathering outside of either home or work where group members form bonds around a shared interest and activity.[40] Although the women of the Pomegranate Guild did not always explicitly identify with the women's movement of the 1970s or 1980s, those feminist waves among Jews and other Americans made room for these kinds of groups. While some women were becoming rabbis—Sally Priesand became the first ordained Reform woman rabbi in 1972, with other women following close behind her—the Pomegranate Guild members were making leadership inroads in a different way by reviving Jewish textile traditions in rooms of their own.[41]

"WOMEN WHO MAKE A TZIMMES":
A PORTRAIT OF A KNITTING CIRCLE

The Pomegranate Guild is not the only setting in which Jewish creativity takes place in community. Many other, less formalized networks of Jewish crafters are found throughout the country. Another way I learned firsthand about this phenomenon was by sitting in with some Pennsylvania-based synagogue knitting circles and interviewing their members. Over time, I grew to know the women of one circle particularly well.

Like the Pomegranate Guild, this group consisted primarily of Ashkenazi Jewish women from the baby boomer generation. They formed around the year 2009, incorporating members from two synagogues in the same town, along with some unaffiliated folks. Initially, they made lap blankets for chemotherapy patients at a local hospital; over time, their reach expanded to homeless shelters and other charities. Unlike the

Pomegranate Guild, they were not particularly concerned with aesthetics or fine needlework. Though many of the blankets they produced were beautiful, the characteristics that mattered to them most were warmth and washability.

The nature of conversation that happens while members of this circle knit and crochet is an embodied, meandering experience that evokes sociologist Courtney Bender's notion of "kitchen talk," which she derived from her work at a nonprofit devoted to preparing meals for AIDS patients.[42] In a similar vein, I observed the ways that both quotidian and extraordinary topics came and went in these interactions over the click-clack of needles. Like Bender in the nonprofit kitchen, I typically had my hands full—of yarn—during this fieldwork and had to take notes in my head as best I could, writing down my memories after the fact.

Is there always, as the opening quotation to this chapter suggested, magic present when women gather together around needlework? I can't answer that question in any meaningful way, but I *can* say that there is a uniquely mesmerizing, warm sense of camaraderie in these spaces and try to characterize what I observed and experienced. Just as the term "magic" implies a technique for altering the universe in some way, the act of being in these rooms felt like participating in a craft (pun intended) that transformed my sense of self during the hours I was there. This knitting group met monthly in different members' homes, gathering for two or three hours of work, always followed by lunch ("There are cardiac Jews and gastric Jews," one of the founders told me, implying that this was an example of gastric Jewish identity). The first time I attended a meeting, it was a hot summer day in 2017. I was welcomed into an immaculate home where a group of six women sat and stitched and talked and ate tuna on crackers and delicate, lacey cookies. At some other meetings, as many as eighteen or as few as four women were in attendance. By the summer of 2017, they had donated a grand total of over 875 blankets to local charities since their founding.

At the group's meetings, conversation would ebb and flow among its members. There is a kind of companionable quiet that comes as the women sit together on couches and in armchairs, each absorbed in the knit or crochet stitches on her lap, a languid sense of heaviness as they talk while the stitches multiply.

"Are you going to write about women who make a tzimmes?" Joan, one of the group's founders, asked me one day. I had disclosed the topic of this book project to the group, emphasizing my interest in women's lives. Tzimmes is a sweet, stewed carrot dish served on many Jewish holidays, but she did not mean this literally. "To make a tzimmes," in her construction, meant to stir things up, to be willing to stick one's neck out and make a bit of a mess. Even though each home I visited seemed even tidier than the last, these were indeed women "who made a tzimmes." They were passionate about their various causes, taking on cancer and homelessness armed only with size 9 knitting needles and giant skeins of Red Heart yarn.

The topics of conversation at each meeting varied widely. Health—the health of those in the group itself, their families, and the local synagogue community—was a particularly pronounced theme, as various members and their loved ones battled everything from minor joint pain to major surgeries. Travel also came up frequently, as did the arrival and welfare of assorted grandchildren, childhood memories, car troubles, current movies, local yarn stores, synagogue politics, and a host of other issues. National politics came up rarely; I had a sense that the group was politically heterogeneous and chose to avoid the sticky situations that might arise from such discussions. Explicit discussions of Jewish topics waxed and waned; talk about upcoming holidays and life-cycle rituals, such as the naming of a new grandchild, were most common.

Some of the knitters had a prodigious output of blankets, producing several a year; others labored over the same project for months. I fell into the latter category, for several reasons—I am a slow knitter, and I work on too many projects simultaneously. One woman who was legally blind was part of the core of the group, able to knit by feel even with limited vision, producing prodigiously. Another woman told me she took knitting with her everywhere she went, even in the dark of the movie theater.

The women of the group were eager to welcome me into the "knit club" even though, hovering on the cusp of forty when I first joined, I was decades younger than most of them. Though I tried to be relatively quiet in order to better follow their topics of choice, I often did take part in conversations, and as I wrote above, they were very concerned when I was diagnosed with cancer and missed several months of meetings.

As with the "best gals" of the Pomegranate Guild, friendship and social bonding were a major aspect of the knitting circle's success and continuity. "I've just met the loveliest women, unique in that they are very helpful to one another. It's not like any competition. It's a community effort," Jan, a long-standing member of the group told me. "They're just a bunch of warm, kind, helpful, considerate people and delightful to be with. So I've really looked forward to it every month, and I think everybody in the group feels that way."[43] Some of the women had been present for the entire decade of the group's existence; others were newcomers. All of them expressed similar sentiments.

In what ways is this knitting group a Jewish space? I want to think with the frame of what is Jewish expansively, as a critical construction, not just a function of Jewish-affiliated bodies. I want to "approach Jewishness as an interpretive mode," to make our attention "move from identifying the bodies, objects, and territories of the Jewish people to interpreting the ideas, politics, and material resources that structured bodies, objects, and territories as operating in Jewish frames."[44] Thinking about what it means to interpret a gathering like this through Jewish frames helps to expand what we talk about when we talk about Jewish studies. It also allays the concerns of some of my interviewees, throughout the project as a whole, about who counted as Jewish and what kinds of Jews I was looking to study. In the meetings of the knitting circle, different small details called for interpretation from the vantage point of Jewish studies. There was the use of occasional Yiddish phrases; the mentions of synagogue politics; the memories of family members who worked in the garment industry; reflections on the history of the region's Jewish community; the family heirlooms from the age of mass immigration on the wall of one home; and the day we ate baked ziti at a table resplendently set over a tablecloth that had been embroidered by the hostess's mother. Like many of the other people quoted throughout this book, the women of the knitting circle varied heavily in their ideas of what it meant to be Jewish, but aspects of things that I would identify with Jewish culture, history, and ideas wended their way into many conversations. Yet when one group member waxed poetic about patriotism and the beauty of seeing America from an RV—was this a Jewish expression? When we met at the home of a member who lives in a renovated church, and saw how she had filled the former confessional with cloth storage, were we engaged in a subversively Jewish act? The irony was certainly discussed by those present. The women of the knitting circle were not just Jewish people, although they all identified as Jewish. The knitting circle was a site of everyday Judaism, one where Jewish *currents*, more than Jewish frames, irrupted into the conversation. The discussion of driving off to look for America (to paraphrase Paul Simon) was, in this context, overlaid with ideas about belonging and contributing to a greater whole that, for this speaker, came from her own status as a pillar of the local Jewish community. The laughter over congregating in a former church came from a deep-seated awareness that the women did not fit a Christian mold. These are not the kind of Jewish activities that demographers ask about in a questionnaire, but they are, nonetheless, Jewish ones.

The group members also identified the group as Jewish in its mission. Jan explained it to me in this way: "A basic tenet of Judaism is *tzedakah*, which is really more than charity but more like an obligation to do for others, and *tikkun olam*, which is the repair of the world. So whatever you can do to make others comfortable falls under that category. So it really has Jewish values." At one larger, particularly well-attended meeting, Joan showed a picture from back when the group had completed fifty-five blankets; the number was now closer to one thousand. "So my kudos to all of you for your nimble fingers and your active minds and your generous hearts," she said proudly.

The charitable work of this knitting circle was both continuous with and a departure from the gift and consumer cultures we have seen in other examples. The blankets all receive a sewn-on label proclaiming that they are "a gift from" the knitters of these synagogues. Here, the specialness of the blankets is directly connected with the activity of hand-knitting and crochet. It would be more efficacious simply to take the money that these knitters and various supportive donors spend on yarn, use it to purchase affordable blankets, and hand them out at shelters and hospitals. This, however, is most assuredly not the point. In order for the blankets to be truly special, and perhaps, on some level in the creators' minds, for them to be an adequate mitzvah (good deed, literally "commandment"), they must be the work of the knitters' hands. To be a proper gift, the mode of creation matters. It matters as much for those making the blankets as it does for the recipients, if not more so. In this, both the women of the Pomegranate Guild and the ladies of the Pennsylvania knitting circle have much in common with the Christian shawl ministries that became immensely popular in the late 1990s and early 2000s, and to which we now turn.

## JEWISH CRAFTERS AND CHRISTIAN SHAWL MINISTRIES: A COMPARISON

Jewish women are not the first or only ones to find camaraderie in gathering to stitch in groups. As Rozsika Parker observes in her history of embroidery, "Sewing allowed women to sit together without feeling they were neglecting their families, wasting time or betraying their husbands by maintaining independent social bonds."[45] In particular, both the synagogue knitting circle and the Pomegranate Guild resemble the prayer shawl ministries described by Donna Bowman in *Prayer Shawl Ministries and Women's Theological Imagination*. A comparison with this mostly Christian group helps us to understand Jewish charity crafting in sharper relief.

The Prayer Shawl Ministry was founded in 1998 by Janet Severi Bristow and Victoria Galo, both graduates of Hartford Seminary's Women's

Leadership program. It has since become an international phenomenon, with ministries across the globe (albeit concentrated in the United States), books, prayers, special patterns, and hashtags.[46] The original prayer shawl pattern was worked in a design based on knitting and purling in threes, representing the holy trinity. The shawls are typically given to people in times of need, such as illness or grief, although sometimes they are distributed at times of joyous transitions, such as the birth of a baby. Bowman's rich study includes interviews with eighty-three prayer shawl makers across the United States, and it is primarily from here that I draw my comparisons.[47]

Bowman found that prayer shawl makers were overwhelmingly retired, like many of the people I interviewed.[48] For the prayer shawl makers as for the Jewish needleworkers, intention and the intended shawl recipients take on an enormous role: "As a response not just to a single person in need, but to a needy world, the shawl is elevated out of the strictly personal."[49] This notion is akin to tikkun olam, the idea of repairing the world that Jan invoked in our interview.

Though at first glance both the Pomegranate Guild and the synagogue knitting circle might seem to have much in common with the shawl ministry, in tone and in practice they also have a wide array of differences. The Prayer Shawl Ministry is more obviously religious in the ways that Americans have been taught to recognize religion. With its Protestant origins and emphasis on the power of prayer, the prayer shawl movement, heterogeneous as it might be, has hallmarks of the Christian norms that have come to define religion in the United States. In their manual to the ministry, Susan Jorgenson and Susan Izard encourage knitters, if they are working in a solitary mode, to "become inwardly still and wait into the silence for the presence of God."[50] In some church-based shawl ministries, the congregation as a whole blesses and prays over the shawls before they are distributed to recipients. Some shawl ministry members see these objects as a way of spreading the gospel, hoping that in some way the shawls will inspire others toward a life of faith. That proposition raises ethical dilemmas—are these gifts given freely, or is there a string of evangelizing attached?—which Bowman richly explores in her ethnography of these ministries.[51]

At the Jewish knitting circle in which I participated, prayer is not a common topic of conversation, nor are there special services dedicating the lap blankets before they are donated. Unlike Christians, Jews do not typically use the language of ministry around their charitable donations, and contemporary Jewish Americans do not generally seek converts. Rather, the language of repair—tikkun olam, as Jan invoked it—or the use of the phrase "social justice" is much more common. The Jewish women who make blankets for those who are ill, homeless, or the victims of domestic violence are not hoping that the blankets will inspire anyone to convert to Judaism. The Pomegranate Guild members have a shade more of what I might call zeal in their desire to spread the good news that, yes, Virginia, there *is* Jewish visual art, but, in like fashion, they are not seeking higher levels of Jewish observance or belief from their members or potential members.

There are also, however, ways that the Jewish crafting groups I observed are quite similar to Christian ones. Both groups are dedicated to charity work. (Though the Pomegranate Guild began as an art organization, most chapters complete regular "mitzvah projects," like the creation of knit hats for newborns.) The Jewish women are more apt to use terms like *mitzvot* (commandments) and "tikkun olam," while the Christian women tend to use words like "charity" and "grace," but both evince a strong desire to do good in the world. Both Jewish and Christian women find a strong sense of fellowship in their activity as part of a group, even if such groups also include tensions. As Bowman puts it, "One of the most basic and pervasive reasons that prayer shawl makers gave for their involvement in the ministry was the idea of connection."[52] Crafting, here, is a way out of isolation. "Women who make a tzimmes" are in good company—for one thing (and this is not a small thing!), the other women around them know the meaning of the word "tzimmes."

Is there cross-pollination between Christian and Jewish crafting circles? Sometimes, yes, especially when it comes to inspiration. The prayer shawl of the ministry is quite different from the Jewish tallit, which is a shawl with fringes on each corner that must meet Jewish legal specifications and is most typically worn by men and now, many women, during morning prayers. In the Jewish case, it is a shawl to wear while praying; in the Christian case, it is a shawl that has been *prayed over*. In contrast with the average Jewish prayer shawl, which tends to be of refined tailoring even when it is humble (or colorful!), the ministry shawls look more like the large cozy triangles or rectangles worn by American women to stay warm or as a fashion accessory. However, one of Bowman's interviewees specifically mentioned the Jewish example in deciding whether to send prayer shawls, which she perceived as feminine, to men. At first, she was quite hesitant about this notion. "But then you get to thinking about it and the Jewish men wear shawls, so what's wrong with a guy having a shawl?"[53] This is a fascinating statement when thought through in terms of the history of gendering Jews. In both European and American contexts, Jewish men were often gendered as effeminate, too scholarly, and lacking in so-called masculine strength.[54] Here, in a reversal of sorts, the fact that Jewish men wear shawls to pray rendered other shawls sufficiently masculine for Christian men to don them.

Jewish and Christian crafters inspire and interact with one another in other ways, too. Flora Rosefsky told me how some non-Jewish women have been involved in the creation of the community quilts she designs and oversees, including her very first such project at a JCC in Upstate New York.[55] Jewish and Christian women trade ideas on Pinterest boards and craft blogs, and sometimes participate together in "craftivism," discussed below. The Prayer Shawl Ministry itself includes mentions of ceremonies that incorporated people of different traditions, as do stories in the group's published books.[56] The overwhelming number of prayer shawl knitters are Christian, but the phenomenon has broader repercussions.

Aside from their differences around notions of ministry and prayer, Jewish and Christian crafting groups seem to be two flavors of a similar phenomenon. Both inherit notions of needlework as women's work that have origins in the ancient, medieval, and early modern periods but that flourished in the Victorian age and the decades that followed it.[57] In their more recent incarnations, both are also heirs to the women's movements of the 1970s and the second DIY revival of the late 1990s and early 2000s. Both signify ways that laypersons have reclaimed autonomous authority at a time of increasing professionalization among religious groups in America. Both are mildly countercultural movements that also trade heavily in the commerce of the day: buying yarn, fabric, and embellishments are all consumer habits. Both are, ultimately, alternative ways of finding ethnic and religious bonds in a collective setting that is different from a traditional prayer service.

## GATHERING AROUND THE SIGNS OF THE NEEDLE AND THE POMEGRANATE

Thinking with Jewish crafting groups helps us to reassess how we understand collectives in the study of religion. The women I conversed with gather around the sign of the needle, a technology that yields many kinds of products, and around the image of the pomegranate, a potent ancient Near Eastern symbol given new life here in North America. Artist Louise Bourgeoise ascribes "magic" to the needle in a manner very similar to the women I sat beside at the biennial: "When I was growing up, all the women in my house were using needles. I have always had a fascination with the needle, the magic power of the needle. The needle is used to repair damage. It's a claim to forgiveness. It's not aggressive, it's not a pin," she writes.[58]

I want to think seriously with what it might mean to bring together notions of magic and community around the signs of the needle and the pomegranate. In the history of anthropology and religious studies, the idea of magic is a loaded term.[59] At times, it was used to denote (and denigrate) so-called primitive religions, to demarcate outsiders. In more recent years, particularly since the rise of women's spirituality movements in the 1970s, we have seen a rise in on-the-ground reclamations of magic, both literally and metaphorically, from flourishing neopagan groups to the infusion of magiclike practices in mainstream traditions.[60]

Jews, who have their own traditions of magic (see: ancient curse bowls, amulets) and their own biblical and rabbinic histories of denigrating such magic, are not immune to these cultural currents. In invoking magic, I don't mean to suggest that the women of the Pomegranate Guild or the synagogue knitting circle are literally trying to do magic, and they would probably not want to be characterized in that way. But I want to consider the notion of the needle and, in a different way, the pomegranate as magical for several reasons. Aside from the invocation of magic in the conversation with which I opened this chapter, taking magic seriously gives us a new frame for the ways that communal formations function in terms of space, energy, and the power of creation. Ultimately, magic in community is another mode of generative resilience.

Magic is a kind of ritual technology. Through magic, spaces can be set aside, marked as special, or, to use phrasing native to Jewish tradition, made holy. The spaces of the Pomegranate Guild are carefully marked and set aside, especially at the biennial convention. Just as Hebrew Bible narratives include a calling together of many distinct tribes and clans into an Israelite whole, the international Pomegranate Guild convention is a space where regional chapters proudly proclaim their unique presence through brightly colored chapter banners. The women of the Pomegranate guild are not drawing chalk circles to contain the sacred, but they are creating holy boundaries in a different way. One day after lunch, I walked the wall of banners, marveling at the way each represented a region and, within it, a great mix of individuality and community. The Connecticut chapter banner included a host of different finely stitched, bright red pomegranates. The Desert Cactus Chapter banner included not just pomegranates but also green cacti (of course), desert flowers, and an armadillo (fig. 4.5). The Long Island Study Group—the first chapter to form—had a banner that featured an enormous image of a threaded needle poised above a pomegranate (fig. 4.6). Some banners had intricate beading worked into the fibers. All of the banners had images of pomegranates. There was a pseudotheurgic power to the repetition of this tal-

FIGURE 4.5. *Desert Cactus chapter, Pomegranate Guild of Judaic Needlework, banner. Photograph by the author.*

FIGURE 4.6. *Long Island Study Group chapter, Pomegranate Guild of Judaic Needlework, banner. Photograph by the author.*

isman, as if the pomegranate were not just the symbol of the guild but a living part of it.

In all the spaces where I have sat and crafted with these various groups, there has been a charged sense to the air, an energy flow that I struggle to write about in nonmystical terms. Have I fallen under the spell, so to speak, of the crafters I have encountered? There is a kind of soporific effect that comes with the calm of being surrounded by other stitchers, particularly knitters, a feeling of serenity in this terrain. Is this spiritual? Is this magic? I may not know how one can quantify feeling magic, but I can, assuredly, say that I took comfort in these homosocial spaces of stitching.

This comfort is one of the ways that crafting communities generate resilience, an intersection where craft circles provide a new vantage point on community and American religions. In recent years, other scholars have attended to how parody and activism are inflected by religious ideas; how ideas from the age of the transcendentalists and New Thought resurface in New Age practices; how communities of religious and interreligious feeling form around military chaplaincies, gay martyrs, and interfaith celebrations, to name just a few sites.[61] Thinking with the communal generative resilience of the Pomegranate Guild and cognate groups opens up a new vista for understanding how ethnoreligious communities operate in the United States. The Pomegranate Guild and the knitting circle are catalyzed by objects: the making, sharing, and giving of material items. Even though many Jewish stories focus on themes of descent, these communities are framed as ones of common consent.

Through the "transmission of affect," crafting groups are a vital and lively site where makers forge social bonds that are just as valuable as the objects that prompted their gathering together.[62] Over and over, members of the Pomegranate Guild told me that what keeps them coming back is the people. The communities of feeling formed around the needle and the pomegranate are lifted up as the group's sine qua non, that without which it would have no meaning, no purpose, no foundation. Months after I met with Gerry, she mailed me a copy of a letter she had described during our interview. After the death of a longtime Pomegranate Guild member in a different state, the woman's husband wrote to Gerry, conveying, in great detail and with great feeling, how much her local guild chapter had meant to her. The combination of friendships with the sense of also advancing a greater purpose—of putting more beautiful Jewish things in the world and making items that could be of use to those in need—transcended even death. The power of the Pomegranate Guild had been evident even to the spouse of a member. The memory of those sentiments and bonds lingered on.

We can link this bonding around the act of creation with some of the biblical accounts that the Pomegranate Guild members consider foundational texts. Near the start of this chapter, I described stories of Bezalel, the master biblical artisan, and his apprentice. In Exodus 35, there is an account where Bezalel does not create alone or even with just one assistant; instead, he needs the entire Israelite community. In this unit, Moses says, "Let all among you who are skilled come and make all that the Lord has commanded" (Exod. 35:10). We read long, itemized lists of the treasures the Israelites brought to this construction project. The text says that "everyone who excelled in ability and everyone whose spirit moved him came" (Exod. 35:21), that "all the skilled women spun with their own hands, and brought what they had spun, in blue, purple, and crimson yarns, and in fine linen" (Exod. 35:25). Eventually, the text does single out Bezalel, and Moses says that God has "endowed him with a divine spirit of skill, ability, and knowledge in every kind of craft" (Exod. 35:31). But in his labors, Bezalel is joined by "every skilled person whom the Lord had endowed with skill, everyone who excelled in ability" (Exod. 36:2).[63] You could say that this is a story about taxes and conscripted labor (and on some level, it is). Or you could say that it is one about access and community building. All members of the community work together to make a sacred space.

Though Bezalel is a legend, the women of the Pomegranate Guild and groups like it are Bezalel's radical heirs. They take this notion of creating in community and extend it farther, for, though skill is still treasured, it is no longer requisite. All who are hungry to come and create can come and create. Inheriting both the countercultural collectivist tendencies of the 1970s and this older biblical notion of communal fabrication, my interlocutors have forged spaces of teaching, learning, and fellowship through compassionate conversations that unspool around threads, buttons, and needles. It may or may not be magic, but it is a social alchemy that produces a quiet yet potent euphoria.

# 5 : TIKKUN OLAM
# TO THE MAX

............................

*Activism and Resistance*

I f there is a phrase I encountered in writing this book even more frequently than "community" or "friends," it was this one: "tikkun olam." *Tikkun olam* is the pair of Hebrew words typically translated as "repair of the world" ("repairing the world" more accurately reflects its grammar). In some usages, it stands in for a Jewish notion of social justice. In myriad contexts, both online and in person, crafters said that they did their work to make the world a better place, whether they were knitting breast prosthetics for cancer patients, creating art pieces about school shootings, or taking part in collective "craftivist" movements in response to national and international political events and crises. The nature of these activities varied widely, but the theme—of repair and of mitzvot (commandments)—remained consistent. Craft activism may or may not be efficacious in causing societal change, but it provokes strong feelings and does powerful cultural and political work. Such actions generate resilience, yet they also project an aura of domesticity that can unwittingly reinforce traditional gender values. Craft activism blurs the boundaries of public and private. It heals, but it also divides.

Craft activism is not new, and it is not unique to Jews. During the American Revolution, women formed the backbone of an effort to clothe the new nation in as many homespuns, hand-knits, and domestically woven American garments as possible. In Philadelphia, they referred to their efforts as "George Washington's Sewing Circle."[1] Even in this era, personalization was a method of connecting giver and recipient. When these women sewed 2,200 shirts for Washington's army, they "attached the sewer's name to cement some personal bond with the wearer."[2] Here, though the women initially hoped to simply send along money to the troops, Martha and George Washington wanted them to make something instead (this may have been prompted by concerns about troops imbibing alcohol). The women's response interwove the personal and the political almost two centuries before that phrase became a mainstay of feminist theory. Giving something tactile and sharing names with a stranger are practices that remain a core part of craft actions. In this colonial iteration and in many wars that followed, the notion of sacrifice through manual labor loomed large as an appropriate way for noncombatants to contribute to the war effort.

Over two hundred years later, craft actions took on a new dimension in the form of the NAMES Project Foundation's AIDS Memorial Quilt. In 1986, San Francisco activist Cleve Jones, inspired by the visual collage of names of AIDS victims at a yearly memorial vigil for Harvey Milk and George Moscone, created the first panel of the quilt in memory of his friend Marvin Felman.[3] The project consists of large, three-by-six-foot coffin-size quilt panels, displayed on the ground side by side. Each panel typically commemorates someone who has died of AIDS. At its first exhibition, in October 1987, it contained 1,920 panels. To date, more than 48,000 panels have been completed (still only a tiny fraction of global deaths from AIDS), and sections of the quilt have toured internationally. The AIDS quilt is an icon of contemporary large-scale memorial efforts and a watershed moment of using a domestic textile form for activism.

Ultimately, in the early twenty-first century, the discourse of craftivism emerged. The term's first use, in 2003, is attributed to writer and maker Betsy Greer.[4] She writes that "craftivism is a way of looking at life where voicing opinions through creativity makes your voice stronger, your compassion deeper, and your quest for justice more infinite."[5] Craftivist practices have ranged from "yarn bombing," which is the act of knitting or crocheting around large public structures to draw attention to a cause, to charity donations, to groups like the Social Justice Sewing Academy that attempt to promote empowerment, community, and education through crafting.[6] Although not all of the makers I have met would describe their work as "craftivist," many would, and others engage with these movements and historical currents in more oblique ways.

TETHERED TO A SEA OF PINK
When Pussyhats went viral, a small number of publications highlighted the Jewish identity of Jayna Zweiman, who, along with Krista Suh, created the hat. These pink hats with cat ears were meant to be an empowered response to President Trump's crude statements about women's bodies during the 2016 campaign. Many Jews took part in making and/or wearing hats. Notions of Jewishness, collective action, what makes for efficacious activism, and the emotional tenor of that activism all varied among both media portrayals of these protests and among my informants. Although all of my interlocutors found the creation of these objects to be

meaningful on some level, not all of them believed that these moments of craftivism would have political consequences. In other words, repair is sometimes elusive. The hats operate on several levels. Feminist theologian Anna Fisk writes that "the knitting circle may be like a twenty-first century version of the consciousness-raising group."[7] For a few weeks, the Pussyhats brought a community together beyond physical boundaries. They were also, however, an imperfect and divisive symbol.

For Zweiman and Suh, the creation of the hats was not just about the visual statement at the Women's March itself. It was also about accessibility and broad participation that linked those who could attend a physical march with those who, for many reasons, could not. The hats were also a means of forging a tactile connection to a handmade item whether one could or could not knit. As they told *Teen Vogue* in the days before the march, one goal was: "To give an outlet for people who won't be at the march to support the marchers. When a marcher marches, she or he will be representing not only themselves, but also the maker of their hat. Also, with each hat that a knitter knits, we ask that she includes a note to connect with the marcher and share her perspectives on women's rights issues. Imagine a sea of pink where each pixel represents both a marcher and her hat maker!"[8] Like the AIDS Memorial Quilt, the Pussyhat Project bridged presence and absence, tethering those who could not physically march with those who could via strands of fuchsia yarn sent through the United States Postal Service or distributed via networks of local yarn stores. The intention of including a note to buttress a personal connection between maker and wearer is strikingly similar to the way that colonial women included their names as they sewed shirts for soldiers.

The category of ability also looms large here. Zweiman's experience recovering from a concussion made it unsafe for her to travel and to stand in large crowds for a long time. This caused her to think about the many reasons why individuals might not be able to attend the marches and to consider ways of overcoming this gap. "I am currently unable to be in large crowds, a limitation that inspired the project's framework allowing everyone to take part and be visible. There are so many reasons why a person may not be able to be on the frontlines—it could be because of health, finances, or scheduling. Through Pussyhat Project, a person could be a knitter, marcher, both, or neither and find a way to be part of the project."[9] This statement fits in with a social understanding of disability, in which disability does not reside just in a body but, rather, in the societal structures around bodies and the ways that social formations can exclude and marginalize many people. The Pussyhat Project is an example that unites Jewish ideas about repair of the world with activism around ability, a crucial intersection.[10]

Other interviews and blog posts emphasize the ways that Zweiman's Jewish background inspired her work on the Pussyhat Project. "I think at the heart of the pussy hat, it's my *tikkun olam* to the max project. How can we make the world a little bit better?" Zweiman, who was thirty-eight at the time of the 2017 marches, says in one interview.[11] In the *Forward*, an article titled "The Secret Jewish History of the Pussyhat" discusses the challenges Zweiman's grandparents had faced as immigrants; her grandmother was a World War I refugee. It also mentions her childhood town of Newton, Massachusetts, her attendance at a Solomon Schechter school, and her matriculation at Brown University, as well as her adult work on various political projects. In that piece, Zweiman says, "We want to create a movement, not a moment. There's been such a strong sense of isolation throughout the election cycle. This moment is about bringing people together."[12] Perhaps not surprisingly, various alt-right websites picked up on this article as proof that there was a Jewish conspiracy behind both feminism writ large and, by extension, opposition to President Trump. Although there is no way to count precisely how many Jews attended marches or knit Pussyhats, theologian Donna Bowman conducted a survey of just over eight hundred hat creators in the months after the march. She cautions that her sample is not representative, but 6.5 percent of her respondents identified as Jewish—more than triple the Jewish percentage of the U.S. population. Bowman found many themes related to explicit religious action (prayer while knitting the hats) and implicit theology (discussions of love and connection) in her published work on this phenomenon but did not quote any Jewish respondents directly, at least not in a way that makes their identities clear.[13]

For some of the Jewish women that I interviewed, marching, knitting, and receiving a knitted hat were all explicitly understood in Jewish terms. One woman from Milwaukee told me how she had received her hat as both the yarn and hat traveled through networks of friends across the Midwest. She continued,

> Many of the political positions that I hold (about caring for those who have less, about religious pluralism in the United States and the safety of minority faith communities, about the equality of the individual, and the protection of our civil liberties and civil rights) have come to me through a Jewish lens. These are many of the same issues that my grandmother and my mother and my father and my

cousins and aunts and uncles have long advocated, and they marched for them in the past. While they are political issues in the United States, they are also important to the lives of my family and have been since my family came to this country.[14]

Knitting hats in abundance and handing them out to both friends and strangers was another theme. Some of the women I interviewed for this book had piles of pussy hats sitting in their homes. One New York City march participant wrote: "I managed to dig up a bunch of pink yarns that other people had given to me. I knitted three of them for a friend, her sister, and a friend of her sister, who were all going down to D.C. I knitted for the two people that walked with me, and since I had a few left over, I gave them away. One was to a photographer on the Metro North train we were on—she was thrilled to have a hat, and another to a particularly vocal woman we passed as we were walking to 2nd Ave." She characterized her Jewish connection to the march in this way: "I don't think we felt that threatened as Jews during the planning stages of the march, but the more we saw signs that people were holding, the more Jewish we felt. We were all raised knowing what happened when no one spoke up. So we needed to speak up."[15] In this statement, Jewishness is also connected with an implicit reference to the Holocaust, to the kinds of horrors that minorities might endure "if no one spoke up." As she put it, "I saw a lot of my peers at this march—i.e., a lot of women with long gray hair!" Attending to the Pussyhats means attending, in part, to the Jewish activism of older women, an often-overlooked segment of activists.[16] She had learned the Civil Rights anthem "We Shall Overcome" on the bus to a JCC-sponsored summer camp as a child. In this way, Jewishness was also connected with the history of U.S. activism.

Although many Jewish women were enthusiastic about the hats, others, even those who had knit many hats, were skeptical about their impact. Dana, a thirty-something knitter, told me, "I don't know if I buy knitting as an act of resistance. Like, quite frankly, I think that we could spend a lot of time deluding ourselves that knitting is an act of resistance, and we could knit a pink Pussyhat for every single Democrat in the country, and there could still never be another free election." She did acknowledge that "I think that it was an amazing unifier," adding, "I want knitting to be part of the revolution, I think it's important that protest be fun so that people don't burn out." She elaborated further, thinking through both the politics and economics of the march:

> The artisanal craze is fundamentally a bourgeois craze, right? Like yes, it is a resistance, there's also I think an important resistance to

neoliberalism in knitting because it is never the most efficient way to get what you want and it is never the most effective way to use your time. And so, yes, it's an amazing organizing strategy and it was wonderful and it united knitting groups and it made me, it made that march feel like my own. I'd had some horrible racial incidents in D.C. over inauguration time and election time, and as a friend pointed out, as we marched in a sea of people in hand-knit hats, it was a reclaiming of the city that I'm currently living in and that was absolutely the God's honest truth. But I'm hesitant about the idea of knitting for the revolution because in the end knitting needles are not—for all I've given myself puncture wounds with them—they are not, in the end, bayonets.[17]

This observation speaks to both the affective power of the march and its potential political limits. It also provides an important reminder of the internal diversity of the Jewish community. As a Jewish woman with brown skin, Dana had experienced every day, face-to-face racism, amplified by the election atmosphere, in a way that most white Jewish women had not. As a result, her perspective on the state of U.S. politics, on physical safety in winter 2017, and on the urgency of the need for social change was different from that of many other informants, and it provides an important reminder that the Jewish American community is heterogeneous.

Dana was not the only interviewee who was ambivalent about the hats. In Washington, D.C., another interviewee told me, "I freaking hate the Pussyhats. I mean, I hate them. They're not me . . . it's totally a personal thing. I love how empowering they are to the women who dig them. It's a total 'good for you, not for me' thing." However, she had crafted around political events in a different way: she made protective talismans for protesters, including herself. "The idea there was empower and protect. It was to make you feel safe enough and to actually hopefully protect you in the process."[18]

On a national level, the hats met with important criticism on various fronts, including criticisms around race, transsensitivity, class, and more.[19] Some women of color took the color pink to refer literally to light-colored genital flesh among white women, thus occluding women of other races. Transgender women challenged the focus on the vagina as a sign of womanhood, calling attention to the different kinds of bodies inhabited by those who identify as—and are persecuted as—women. These are all important criticisms. Suh and Zweiman have said that their intention was to undercut the objectifying language used by President Trump as a form of sexism, rather than to fetishize anatomy. This was a way of reclaiming the word "pussy," so often seen as dirty or shameful in some way, and to celebrate all bodies. More broadly—beyond the Pussyhats—the strong, national coalition of activists that had come together at the first march gradually atrophied as internal divisions emerged among Women's March leaders. There were also much-publicized conflicts and controversies over statements made by some national leaders, as well as controversy over some leaders' attendance at events with Louis Farrakhan. All of this resulted in an atrophy of support for the official National Women's March organization.[20] The Pussyhats, of course, were not the work of those leaders—they were their own parallel craftivist movement. Still, writing from 2019, more than two years after the initial protests, I have found it strange to reread the glowing accounts of solidarity and camaraderie that accompanied the 2017 protests. They seem like relics from a time that is already quite distant.

Back in 2017, however, the Pussyhat, despite its flaws, was an icon of generative resilience for millions of people. Even my interlocutors who disliked the hats or questioned their political efficacy acknowledged the fact that the hats had transmitted a sense of camaraderie. The Pussyhats also remind us that to understand Jewish American lives, we need to look beyond the pews and consider many other modes of communal and spiritual participation. Jewish and radical feminist identities intermingled in various ways from the 1960s through the 1980s, as "Jewish backgrounds, ethical imperatives, and networks and associations played a major part in shaping the contributions of Jewish women's liberationists and Jewish feminists."[21] As the creation of a Jewish woman and her non-Jewish friends, the Pussyhats continue that tradition. Abraham Joshua Heschel's famous statement after the 1965 Selma-Montgomery march is also frequently cited by Jews and other contemporary religious activists: "Even without words our march was worship. I felt my legs were praying."[22] To understand Jews, gender, and the Pussyhat phenomenon, we need to take that sentiment seriously, not just for its fame but also for its claim. For many Jewish Americans, pursuing social justice is a genuinely Jewish and, at times, a spiritual practice—perhaps even the most Jewish thing they do. As Nat Bernstein writes in the online magazine *Jewcy*, networks of Jews gathered together both before and during the march, sometimes combining the march activities with Shabbat activities. This included observant Jews like her who found ways to march within Jewish law's limitations for activity on Shabbat. Bernstein writes: "'This makes me proud to be a Jew'—my father, who insisted on wearing his own hot pink pussy hat the whole day—said quietly as we set out . . . beaming at the signs quoting the Talmud, Deuteronomy, Abraham Joshua Heschel, Emma Goldman, Hillel, and other seminal Jewish texts."[23]

For one day, despite the hats' controversial imperfections, Zweiman's "tikkun olam to the max" project forged an emotional community of collective protest that powerfully linked the public and private realms for a large number of marchers, both those on the streets and those who made hats at home. On the material creation level, the making of the Pussyhats was a widespread, tactile means of coping with the depression many liberal Americans experienced after the 2016 election. These small domestic gestures buttress individual and collective resilience. As cultural critic Ann Cvetkovitch writes, "Those humble material locations are also the spaces in which depression can be transformed through practices that can become the microclimate of hope."[24] In her discussion of crafting and the "utopia of ordinary habit," she writes:

> Unlike forms of sovereignty that depend on a rational self, crafting is a form of body politics where agency takes a different form than application of the will. It fosters ways of being in the world in which the body moves the mind rather than the other way around, or in which, echoing neurobiological views in another register, body and mind was deeply enmeshed or holistically connected.... Crafting emerges from the domestic spaces that are at the heart of women's culture to provide a model for ways of living that acknowledge forms of structural inequality while also practicing modes of bodily and sensory life that incorporate or weave them into the fabric of a daily life that literally includes texture, color, and sensory pleasure. Crafting is about a way of being in the world that requires not just knowledge but practice.[25]

Although it is difficult to judge the political efficacy of the Pussyhats or the Women's March, on a material level, they did, indeed, evoke a "utopia of ordinary habit." Craftivism did not begin or end with the Pussyhat on the cover of *Time* magazine. Jayna Zweiman went on to found a new craftivist project, "The Welcome Blanket," which focuses on migration and has toured several small art museums. Scholars are noticing an ongoing uptick in post-2016 craftivism.[26] The Pussyhats were not perfect, but they give us a snapshot of craft activism that many participants understood through a Jewish lens, one that continued a long trend of craftivism and pushed many new waves of craft activism onward. What could be more utopian, in spirit, than hoping to repair the world with needles and yarn? The Pussyhats took the metaphorical notion of mending inherent in the notion of tikkun olam and brought it out into the streets to accompany overt political action. Cvetkovitch, too, writes that her examples "are reparative ones."[27] The seduction of repair is strong. What happens when repair seems inaccessible? Can there be mending not just after political loss but after lives have been lost to acts of violence?

## JEWISH HEARTS FOR PITTSBURGH

On October 27, 2018, a gunman opened fire during Saturday morning services at the Tree of Life synagogue in Pittsburgh, Pennsylvania, killing eleven people and injuring six more. It was the deadliest attack on Jewish Americans in U.S. history. The shooting took place amid rising anti-Semitic speech and anti-immigrant sentiment. Amid other forms of hatred, the gunman's online writing revealed that he was angry with the Hebrew Immigrant Aid Society for bringing "invaders" into the United States.[28] The U.S. Jewish community reacted with grief, fear, and a great sense of unease. Prayer vigils, including interfaith ones, were held nationwide, and the predictable "We Stand with Pittsburgh" memes appeared on social media soon after the Sabbath had ended. The fears that many Jewish Americans had expressed during the 2016 election cycle—"we've seen this before"—had come true.[29]

Out of the myriad responses to this anti-Semitic mass shooting, Jewish Hearts for Pittsburgh—a craftivist movement that I learned about from one of my Pomegranate Guild contacts—arose, quickly gaining over one thousand members in a Facebook group. Their initial goal was to send knit, crocheted, or otherwise crafted hearts melded with Jewish stars to Pittsburgh as a way of showing support to the Jewish community of Squirrel Hill, the neighborhood where the shooting took place. Intrigued, I joined the group and sent in a heart. Later, I conducted phone interviews with the group's founders and corresponded with several participants by email and Facebook message. Like the Pussyhats, Jewish Hearts for Pittsburgh was a digitally born craftivist action that resulted in material items traveling across the country. In contrast to the Pussyhats, here crafters responded to a concrete act of violence that occurred in a Jewish space and was directed against Jews. At the same time, they were reacting to a global increase in white supremacy, which threatens many constituencies. Over time, the group, which was interfaith, also created hearts for the victims of other mass shootings, which continued to happen with alarming regularity.

The hearts were the brainchild of Hinda Mandell, associate professor in the School of Communication at the Rochester Institute of Technology, and Ellen Dominus Broude, a media executive. Mandell's first forays into

FIGURE 5.1. *Abbie Van Wely, Jewish hearts, 2018. Photographer unknown.*

craft activism centered around yarn bombings during the 2016 election. Then, when a Jewish cemetery in Rochester, New York, was desecrated, she crocheted "what would become the template for the Jewish Hearts for Pittsburgh. I crocheted a blue star of David, and I crocheted a little red heart that I sewed in the center. Then I also crocheted a pink heart and added a blue star of David in the center" (fig. 5.1).[30] She brought these to an evergreen tree at the cemetery and snapped some photographs, adding, "One of the things that I believe strongly about when putting yarn in public is to be a steward of that craft and not just let it become litter." When she returned to the cemetery a week later, the hearts had been removed, presumably by the space's caretakers.

Then, over a year later, the Pittsburgh shooting happened. Mandell posted a picture of her previous hearts and some skeins of yarn in a Facebook "Craftivist" group, where it caught the attention of Broude, who became her partner in the project. Broude, who is from New York, was planning a trip to Pittsburgh, where her daughter lived, in late November. She would transport the hearts there. As the daughter of a yarn store owner, Broude had both craft and craftivism experience. She had picked up her knitting needles for the first time in many years to make Pussyhats and had participated in a project called "Hearts for C-Ville" after the 2017 white supremacist demonstrations that led to the death of a counterprotester in Charlottesville, Virginia. The two women started an administered Facebook group called "Jewish Hearts for Pittsburgh." Mandell hoped to get two hundred members. Broude, with her media expertise, suspected it would draw more. By the time of the first installation of hearts, the group had over 1,000 members; at the time of this writing, it has 1,260 members. The idea was simple, as Mandell explained: "We had a couple of basic rules. We wanted people to create what we call a 'Jewish heart,' which could be a Jewish star with a heart inside or a heart with a Jewish star inside.... Our only no-no was we didn't want to include the color yellow because of course the historical ties to stars of David during the Nazi reign. That was really the only no-no."[31] Although most hearts were knit or crochet, they came in myriad media forms: popsicle sticks, paint, quilt, needlepoint, cross-stitch, hand and machine sewn, ceramic, fashioned from twigs, "shrinky dink," framed mason jar tops, origami, paper cuts, and more. Contributions came from Oregon, Wyoming, New York, Nebraska, Colorado, Florida, Arizona, Massachusetts, Virginia, Hawaii, Ohio, and other states, and more than a dozen countries.[32]

Many themes emerged in my conversations with Mandell and Broude, and in my interactions with the online group as a whole, as well as the attendant media coverage after the hearts were installed. These included the diversity of the participants, the notion of handcrafters as givers and doers, the absence of political discussions among group members, language around healing, and the notion of reclamation.

Mandell phrased it this way:

> At this point my connection to craft and activism is really like a higher calling. I'm not religious. I identify very strongly as culturally Jewish, but I imagine that this is what it's like when one is called from a higher order to do something. It's just simply something that I feel compelled to do, and I cannot shake it. When that attack in Pittsburgh happened ... and I don't have a personal connection to Pittsburgh, I've actually never been there ... but for me, the answer in terms of a community response is something I see in terms of yarn, because the symbolism is just so powerful when we think about the fabric of life.[33]

For Mandell, as for many Jews, the notion of activism and, in this case, specifically *craft*-driven activism, is given a vocational (in the original sense) overlay: to create in response to destruction is understood as a necessary, powerful emotional response, and the metaphor of a "fabric of life" is also the way to memorialize literal lives. Indeed, many contributors sent in eleven hearts to commemorate the eleven lives lost; others sent their batches in multiples of eighteen, the number that in Jewish tradition numerically symbolizes the Hebrew word for "life."

For all of those involved, the possibility of *doing* something—and doing something *active and material*—in the face of tragedy seemed to have a tremendous appeal. Mandell connected this to the innate nature of crafters: "I think there's also a long history of yarn workers that is connected to charity and to goodwill. People who create stuff with yarn. . . . I mean, show me one person who has a yarn fetish who hasn't made something for someone. Then there's also people who donate chemo caps or baby blankets or baby caps, and these are not . . . they're truly acts of goodwill. I think that yarn folks are active by nature. They're giving by nature, and they want to engage in their craft by nature."[34]

Similarly, Broude reflected, "Crafters are givers, because they often make for themselves, they make for others, and this was just such a hideous, ugly act of such epic proportions that people really felt moved to show love and support. These were good people who participated. . . . This is what crafters do. They make. They create. They comfort. They channel their efforts."[35] Here, the nature of crafting is contrasted with the nature of violence. Crafters are "good," there to provide comfort in times of trial. The act of giving is not just a form of exchange on a personal level; it is transformative on a societal level, meant to repair, to collect, to combat hatred.

Although the project was not conceived in an explicitly religious vein— it was meant, primarily, as a gesture of support in which anyone could participate, regardless of personal identity or convictions—many contributors talked explicitly about religious symbolism, practice, or belief in their posts and in the notes they included with their donations. They came from many traditions: "These were people of faith. Pick a faith, any faith, and an assault against one is an assault against all. I heard that over and over and over again. We had all colors of the rainbow crafting with us," Broude said.[36] The group included people who identified with many traditions: Jews, Muslims, Catholics, Quakers, Assemblies of God, nondenominational Protestant, and more. Because the attack took place in a religious space, during a prayer service, many religious people seemed compelled to do something in response, and many consciously framed their crafting as having a spiritual meaning.

Sometimes, this was reflected in how they created the hearts. In the Facebook group, one Jewish participant wrote: "I stitched the felt heart, eleven times. With each time I went around, I recited Kaddish [the Jewish memorial prayer] for each victim. The shadow behind the star represents our support for Pittsburgh, the denim is fraying at the edge, because as this tragedy reminds us, life can be unraveled at a moment's notice ... so remember to live your life to the fullest."[37] This participant intentionally connected the number eleven, for the eleven victims, and linked them with the action of stitching. She combined a traditional prayer act with a new craftivist act, ritually innovating as she went along. The Kaddish is a particularly fascinating, and central, Jewish prayer. Written in Aramaic, portions of its text are repeated at various times throughout most Jewish liturgies, but when it is recited in memory of those who have died, it takes on different qualities and even different rules around its recitation (who recites it, when, how often, if they stand or sit, and how many people must be present), depending upon one's particular minhag, or communal tradition. The Kaddish does not contain any words about death; rather, it contains words of exaltation for God and closes with a prayer for peace (*Kaddish* is typically translated as sanctification). The act of saying Kaddish is a practice of discipline and consolation for the mourner. Thus, in this example, the acts of stitching and prayer are both linked together quite powerfully in a reaffirmation of life.

Based on her readings of the notes that accompanied the hearts, Broude said, "For a lot of people, it was a very contemplative, meditative, prayerful experience." For her personally, the act of making the hearts was less spiritual, but it was definitely mindful: "So you get to a state of flow and your mind has gone blank. . . . That was, for me, as I was making these, learning this crochet pattern that my friend designed for the project, and it just ... it helped me stop thinking about the evil. It helped me focus on my thinking.... You know, for me as an American Jew, this is getting very, very, very, very, very scary."[38] In these examples, we see how the action of making was what mattered. Process was a resilient means of coping with tragedy.

Other stitchers wanted to transmit prayers *through* these objects *to* the mourning Pittsburgh community. Metaphysically, this idea closely resembles the language of the prayer shawl ministries. One woman wrote, "I wanted the grieving community to know that not everyone is hateful and hopefully they would feel some of the love and prayers for them that went into the making of the stars."[39] Several interlocutors, as well as some Pittsburgh residents who helped to spread the hearts around the city, used the word "therapeutic."[40] Another member wrote, "While crocheting, I've been thinking how making connections together is how faithful love overcomes hateful terror. Peace."[41] Craft is a transmission beacon and a metaphysical suture. The idea that material objects can contain and transfer sentiment and healing is an old one. The notions of flow and the idea that communities are interconnected—that everything is significant on a cosmic level—resembles the nineteenth-century notions of groups like transcendentalists, Swedenborgians, and spiritualists, as well as contemporary New Age practitioners. Though the rhetorical framings are a bit subtler, the refrains of "therapy" and "healing" among Jewish Hearts for Pittsburgh crafters resemble notions of healing energy in the language of those other movements, giving us a new example of these modalities.[42]

Some of the most evocative stories came from connections with other mass shootings. Jewish Hearts for Pittsburgh received hearts from Parkland, Florida, where seventeen students (some of them Jewish) were killed in a school shooting in February 2018.[43] Similarly, the following note in the Facebook group drew strong reactions: "As I made my heart, I had a lot of memories come to my mind. It will be twenty years in April since my life changed. I was a junior at Columbine High School sitting in a cafeteria one moment and running for my life the next. My life changed in an instant. Soon cards and little tokens of love started pouring in. Each one helped me find a little strength to get through the hardest trial of my life. With my heart I am sending out my love and my strength. Thank you for organizing this."[44]

Mandell, Broude, other participants, and national reporters were deeply affected by this particular donation. "Exactly twenty years later, now she is trying to create a small bit of comfort," Mandell said.[45] "It gives me chills," Broude reflected.[46] It is, indeed, a powerful and sobering generational transition. A student survivor of the 1999 Columbine shootings was now in her late thirties and passing on hopes for healing to a community attacked in a house of worship, a similarly vulnerable space.

This juxtaposition suggests the policy implications—and attendant activism—that could be incorporated into this installation. Mandell and Broude, however, both insisted that the project's goal was not political, and my own observations of the posts in the Facebook group bear this out. Mandell said:

No matter one's political views in terms of being part of the right or the left, what happened in Pittsburgh is horrifying. People were gunned down in a house of worship. That act seemed to transcend political divisiveness. There is no talk of politics in this group. There are indicators of people's political views, but it's kind of like a politics-free zone. By that I mean, Democrat- or Republican-free zone. I think that allowed people to feel comfortable to come to this place because we're not going to talk politics. We're just really here to try to bring love in the world, to be supportive, to be community based, and to be kind to one another, and to raise each other up.... I'm happy to be corrected, but I view the Pussyhats as more political because that's more about taking action and making change and putting our bodies on the street to show that we will stand up for women's rights. This is more ... it's quieter, because a number of volunteers put their bodies in the community, but they were just agents to hang the stars, and then they left. The Jewish hearts were intended to speak for themselves. I don't view it so much as political as more of a cultural movement aimed at social justice.[47]

As both Mandell and Broude noted and as I observed, the membership of the group was politically diverse. As Broude and Mandell approved requests to join, they saw that some included #teamTrump and other politically conservative hashtags on their Facebook profiles. Lobbying against gun violence is (currently) characterized as a liberal position in U.S. politics. When it comes to comforting the bereaved, however, it appears that political boundaries do not always apply. This is particularly complex in a country where, on the one hand, the years 2015–19 have been years of rising anti-Jewish incidents.[48] At the same time, however, the United States also has a history of evangelical Christian philo-Semitism, which can stem from well-intentioned interfaith dialogue movements that began in the twentieth century but can also—in other cases—incorporate Jews instrumentally into end-time millennial salvation schemes. (This final trend is certainly a reality, but I did not witness it, in any way, shape, or form, among the Jewish Hearts for Pittsburgh community.) A good descriptor for this action might be nonpartisan rather than nonpolitical. There certainly are significant differences between the Pussyhats and Jewish Hearts for Pittsburgh. Mandell's use of the word "quieter" is telling. Though the hearts would indeed be displayed in public, they *were* "quiet"—unaccompanied by masses of people, chants, and signs, these craftivist items would instead "speak for themselves," with materiality constituting its own potent discourse.

One member of the Facebook group, who wrote to me from New York City, did see her Jewish Heart for Pittsburgh as another link in a chain of political activism:

I learned about Jewish Hearts from my knitting store in NYC, Knitty City. I made knit hearts with charms and ribbons. I started knitting pussy hats as an activism project against the Trump administration, then hand warmers for the gun march with an embroidered eye, to say, "Congress we are watching you." With the Pittsburgh, Christchurch & Poway shootings it was the only way I felt I could let these communities know how terribly sad I felt! It meant, I could send love in a way that would be lasting and a reminder of my solidarity with this community. My only other thought is that I know we can conquer this hate by doing acts of kindness and it has to be an everyday act in our own community.[49]

For this woman, there was a clear through line from one collective craftivist action to the next one. Other members of the group, in contrast, may have knit a Jewish Heart for Pittsburgh but no Pussyhat. I certainly saw many Pomegranate Guild members' names listed and recalled from conversations over stitching there that the guild is a politically diverse space (at the biennial convention, I did some embroidery next to an avid supporter of President Trump). In a nonsystematic study such as this one, it is impossible for me to separate out Democrat from Republican from Independent hearts, nor would that be in keeping with the self-stated goals of the action. I am fascinated, however, by the very strong difference between the tactics of the Pussyhat Project and of Jewish Hearts for Pittsburgh. Both consider themselves craftivist. For the Pussyhat makers, the hats symbolized a definitive call for action. In contrast, the Jewish Hearts for Pittsburgh, in bridging political divides, took a more general stand against hate; even the obviously liberal statement above says, "We can conquer this hate by doing acts of kindness." It appeals to the everyday, rather than the extraordinary.

At the end of November 2018, Broude drove over two thousand hearts to Pittsburgh. News reports said that forty volunteers took on the task of installing the hearts, often in bunches, all over the city, with a concentration in Squirrel Hill, the neighborhood near the synagogue that is home to many Jews. Images of the hearts in situ filled the Facebook group for weeks and appeared in numerous news reports. A friend who is a professor in Pittsburgh sent me several of her own images of the hearts and wrote about the interesting juxtapositions of the hearts and everyday businesses and symbols, including a neon beer sign (fig. 5.2).[50] The hearts were hung near a mural of Gandhi, in front of the residence of the late Fred Rogers of *Mister Roger's Neighborhood*, in the windows of local business, near synagogues and the JCC, and elsewhere across the entire city.[51] Jewish hearts were also hung on myriad fir trees. Some were simply outdoor plantings, but others were Christmas trees, sending a message of cross-religious solidarity. In one television news report, an anchor said:

FIGURE 5.2. *Jewish Hearts for Pittsburgh in situ, Pittsburgh, Pennsylvania, 2018. Photograph by Rachel Kranson.*

"It represents the Jewish concept of repairing the world by bringing symbols of love to the Pittsburgh community." In the same story, Broude said, "There is more love than in evil in this world. That people are good, no matter what their religion, no matter what their race, what their creed, that there is love and support. What we heard from the members of our group was gratitude for being able to do something."[52]

Jewish Hearts for Pittsburgh operated as a reclamation on multiple levels. For both Broude and Mandell, it was a way of recasting social media—digital spaces in which they both said they had seen a great deal of hatred. Instead, this group brought strangers together across the Internet for something *good*. Broude said, "Social media is the root of all evil, for sure, but it was very nice to be able to harness social media for good, not for evil, and to build positive community. And it became like a little bit of a therapy session in that group, you saw."[53] One of the group participants told me that making a heart "was an opportunity to show love when there is so much division and hatred."[54]

Ultimately, the Jewish Hearts for Pittsburgh project was a redemptively framed one. Its organizers and participants fully recognized that the violent rending that occurred when eleven Jews were murdered in cold blood could not be undone. Nonetheless, they sought healing and a way to bridge cultural divides after a shooting driven by ethnoreligious hatred. The word I saw most frequently in the group's posts and my emails with participants was "love."

Sadly, the group has had more occasions to send love to places touched by violence. Members and their friends sent over five thousand hearts—often incorporating the color green to honor Muslim traditions—to Christchurch, New Zealand, after the mass shooting that killed more than fifty people at worship in a mosque there. The day that a shooter killed one woman at a Chabad center in Poway, California, a feeling of déjà vu overcame the group. "Are we making hearts for San Diego?" one poster asked two days later. (Hearts were, indeed, sent to Poway.) When I started to study Jewish Hearts for Pittsburgh, the project interested me because so much of what it was doing seemed religious: confronting suffering and tragedy through collective meaning making and material culture; making new meaning during a troubled time. Now, several shootings later, I see a new way that Jewish Hearts for Pittsburgh is functioning religiously: it has become a repetitive action, a cyclical response. Like many religious rituals, the making of the hearts has become routinized. Though different individuals have taken on the role of point person for each round, this grief response now has a cycle to it. Shootings keep occurring, so hearts keep flying off of needles and crochet hooks, scissors and blocks of clay.

The message of Jewish Hearts for Pittsburgh is an overwhelmingly one of healing and repair. What about works that respond to gun violence and hatred by dwelling in their pain, tearing open the wound, rather than healing it? For that, we turn to works by fiber artist Heather Stoltz and ceramicist Linda Schwartz.

## SEWING STORIES, SOWING SOCIAL JUSTICE

On Heather Stoltz's fiber art blog, *Sewing Stories*, there is an image of a bright orange quilt, bisected by purple triangles, and almost entirely covered in small black satin ribbons. These are not ordinary ribbons. Rather, they would be familiar to many people who have attended a Jewish funeral. Traditional Jewish mourning practice entails the rending of the mourners' garments as a visual sign of the loss they have experienced, the broken incompleteness of their world without their loved one. Some contemporary Jews still do this literally, wearing a shirt or other item of clothing they have torn. Among other Jewish Americans, however, a different practice has evolved. Instead of ripping a piece of clothing, these mourners pin a small black satin ribbon (called a *k'riah*, for "rending," ribbon) to their lapel or dress. The ribbon is then torn, sometimes in a formal ceremony, other times in a quiet moment. Stoltz used more than a hundred of these black ribbons in her quilt *Dark Days: Where Does It End?* She explained her piece in this way: "In the three years since the shooting at Sandy Hook Elementary School, there have been approximately 150 school shootings—that's almost one each week. The number is hard to imagine, as are the tragic deaths that resulted. This piece marks each shooting with a black k'riah ribbon with the date, town, and name of the school written on it."[55]

For Stoltz, school shootings are deeply personal. "When the Sandy Hook shooting happened, my nephew actually was in the school at the time," she told me in her suburban New York living room.[56] Her nephew was six in 2012—in the same grade as most of the victims—and lost one of his best friends in the shooting. "I had to react to that," she said. On the blog, she describes the first quilt she created in this series on school shootings and gun violence. Titled *Shattered Childhood*, it depicts a large silhouette image of her nephew standing beside his friend. The text of a news article about the shooting is superimposed over the silhouette, but it is fragmented, literally *shattered*, "cut into 26 pieces to represent the 26 victims and to resemble broken glass." In the upper left-hand corner of the quilt, five colorful balloons drift up and away toward the edge of the scene. They commemorate a memorial balloon release initiated by her nephew, in which he and other surviving classmates took part. Stoltz writes that they are "a symbol of hope that the community rise from this tragedy, carrying with it the memory of those lost."[57]

Both *Dark Days: Where Does It End?* and *Shattered Childhood* constitute Jewish responses to America's gun violence epidemic. *Dark Days* takes the k'riah ribbon, which is usually an ephemeral piece of Jewish ritual material culture, and renders it permanent, a sign of mourning in the aggregate that is unending, affixed against a vivid orange background that suggests fire and danger. Less directly but no less evocatively, the panels in *Shattered Childhood* that "resemble broken glass" evoke Kristallnacht, the night of broken glass, of widespread violence carried out against German Jews on November 9–10, 1938, an event that looms large in histories of the Holocaust.

The idea of shattering also suggests the *kelipot* (literally "shells" or "husks"), which are the containers that held divinity then broke, in the mystical Lurianic creation myth. That narrative is also the story from which the notion of tikkun olam emerges. In *Dark Days: Where Does It End?* sewing does not heal. Instead, the viewer of this piece is affixed to the repetitions of near-permanent violence. Through this quilt, Stoltz demands that we confront pain and that we dwell in it, that we mourn, rather than leaving it behind. *Shattered Childhood* simultaneously heals and retains a sense of brokenness. The balloons do evoke hope, but the "shattered" panels of the news story remind us that we cannot undo the loss of life, and in particular young life, that has occurred. Reparative as sewing might be, there are things that it cannot mend. Stoltz's work confronts us with this existential imperfection. The quilts are aesthetically beautiful. They are also steeped in horror.

"Fiber art in particular has this history of talking about social justice issues," Stoltz told me.[58] When she makes commissioned pieces, as she often does, those are about what a client wants aesthetically, but when she makes an art piece for herself, she confronts a problem or tells a story. For her, art is often not playful (a theme that came up in many interviews) but quite serious. "I feel like what I create for my own work is something that I have this need to tell a message. All of them tell a story in some way. Whether that'd be trying to give people a new interpretation of a Jewish text or expressing some of the joys and difficulties of parenthood or trying to say something about a social justice issue, it's always a message for them. So, it doesn't feel so playful."[59] She pointed both to historic examples and to the work of artists in various New York collectives, such as Jewish Art Salon, as examples of art that makes a statement. Stoltz also described how her upbringing taught her to be actively involved in working toward social justice. "Both of my parents volunteered for all kinds of things. My brother has type 1 diabetes, so we were always involved in the juvenile diabetes research foundation. I don't even remember how old I was, probably four or five the first time we went to our first walk and I held a handout." She added that her parents "made sure that we knew we lived in a place of privilege. We traveled a lot.... Wherever we were, I remember it wouldn't just be that we would be on vacation on the beach. They would make sure to drive through the poor area of the town and remember."[60]

Social justice intersects with Jewish themes in nonfiber media, too. In December 2016, I was browsing the items at a Pennsylvania JCC craft fair when I came across a ceramic plate with a quotation from the book of Amos: "Let justice well up like water and righteousness like a mighty stream" (Amos 5:24). I was struck by the use of this quotation, which was frequently deployed by Martin Luther King Jr. and other Civil Rights leaders, but also by a note next to the plate, which stated that a portion of the proceeds from its sale would be donated to the Southern Poverty Law Center. Here amid the holiday merriment was a small, stark moment of activism.

Two months later, I interviewed Linda Schwartz, the creator of that plate, as well as numerous other items of Judaica and social justice art. During our conversation, which took place just a month after President Trump's inauguration, Schwartz shared how her Jewish upbringing had been intertwined with political and ethical concerns: "Even though I wasn't raised very religious, I was raised in a very moral way, with my father really big on social conscience. We were really raised with social justice in mind.... I felt a real empathy for the Civil Rights movement because I saw it as an extension of the Jews fleeing Egypt, just like at the end of our seders. Even though we didn't go to synagogue and we didn't go to Hebrew school, my mother drummed into me the golden rule."[61]

Schwartz told me about the origin of the plate bearing the quotation from Amos. She had gone to a program at a synagogue in Philadelphia and saw the text on one of its stained-glass windows. She was moved by it and, in particular, by its association with Martin Luther King Jr.'s speeches, and then she learned that it was "etched into the wall of the Southern Poverty Law Center's building." So she decided to make the plate with the center in mind. Schwartz had longed to be a freedom rider in the 1960s but was too young to do so. Now she was finding ways to protest during another political moment that she found profoundly frightening.[62] Linda's identification of Jewishness with the pursuit of social justice express a theme that was present in abundance throughout my interviews, surveys, and online correspondence, in so many more examples than those I have summarized in this chapter.

In my conversation with Peachy Levy, she, too, identified this as a central motivator in all that she does Jewishly, in both her fiber art and her philanthropy. As she spoke about how she begins each piece, she said, "I like to work from text. Jewish values are high on my list. That comes from the concept of tikkun olam, repairing the needy world."[63] This is encapsulated in her fiber piece *Tikun Olam*, which appeared in exhibitions and is reproduced in a printed catalog of her work. The main portion of the piece is round like the earth with different colored fabrics seamed together, tattered and torn with ragged edges, yet with some golden fabric showing through, "symbolizing God's presence," according to Levy. The words "Tikun Olam" stretch across this circle in a vivid, contrasting deep blue with golden threads binding the letters. "These threads are a symbol of God needing us to mend what has been broken," she explained.

The threads are beautiful, but it is the ragged edges that speak to me most as I reflect upon the projects featured in this chapter. From Pussyhats to ceramic plates, all of these efforts attempt to cope with profound brokenness. In doing so, the many crafters who took part in these efforts added a new chapter to the history of religious activism in America. In bringing these examples to light as religious ones, I want to broaden the range of protests we see as religious.[64]

The intersection of Jewish activism and craftivism in these recent examples is continuous with many themes in the history of U.S. activism and can be compared with protests that use the symbolic vernaculars of other religious traditions. The AIDS Quilt is a particularly crucial antecedent in terms of how protest is gendered. In interviews, AIDS Quilt founder Cleve Jones said that one of the reasons for choosing a quilt was its "warm" domesticity: "As I said the word quilt, I was flooded with memories of home and family and the warmth of a quilt when it was cold on a winter night."[65] Part of the quilt's remarkable success at "normalizing" AIDS victims comes from this imagery of nostalgic domesticity, although many quilt panels also engage in practices of camp.[66] Gendered dynamics are a powerful aspect of how public protests are understood. The AIDS Quilt has succeeded as a public memorial in part because the American folk form of the quilt is an accessible, recognizable vernacular that can also be structured subversively. Recent fiber arts activism is similarly malleable. The Pussyhats had a pattern, but it was a simple one, open to embellishment and personalization, although the goal of a "sea of pink" did put some limits on individuality. The Jewish Hearts for Pittsburgh pattern provided a great deal of room for individual expression. Like the AIDS Quilt, both projects deployed the imagery of a craft that is now coded feminine in order to raise awareness or provide comfort.

In her groundbreaking work on the Sisters of Perpetual Indulgence, sociologist Melissa M. Wilcox writes about the expectations that surround protesters' gender presentations: "Feminine people are expected to provide community service and to perform emotional labor, whereas masculine people are not."[67] For Wilcox's informants from the sisters—a group of predominantly gay men who dress parodically as nuns, evoking Catholic visual forms while engaging in acts of parody and protest—taking on the symbols of Catholicism and engaging in this ministry provides for a "resacralization" of queer bodies that have been castigated, particularly during the AIDS epidemic.[68] Though few have called them "camp," the Pussyhats engage in a similar kind of subversive public reclamation, rendering the feminine bodies so degraded by President Trump's statements into powerful protesters who would not be silenced. They were not a perfect unifier. Nonetheless, the "tikkun olam to the max" project did max out: it became an icon. Interestingly, though criticisms of the hats in terms of their cisgender and white privilege abounded, few people criticized the gendered dynamics of having knitting become a major symbol of the march. Perhaps this was because knitting has been sufficiently trendy since the early 2000s (and taken up by enough hipster men) that it has already moved beyond feminine stereotypes, but I doubt that this is the case. By having a textile symbolize a movement, the Pussyhat continues a process that began in the 1980s with the AIDS Quilt. Harnessing feminized craft imagery makes a protest more palatable, substituting one stereotype about feminine caring and nurturing in order to temper other stereotypes about angry women.

Along a different axis, both the AIDS Quilt and Jewish Hearts for Pittsburgh bring together acts of mourning and counting. The AIDS Quilt made the gravity and scope of the AIDS crisis palpable. By creating coffin-size panels to represent thousands of individual victims—making the quilt so large that it would first cover and then exceed the size of the National Mall—the AIDS Quilt activists were making a policy point about the immense need for research and changes in public health policy. It was also a moment where counting was a way to recognize the humanity of each victim. In the case of the Jewish Hearts for Pittsburgh project, though the scale was smaller, the effect was similar. Without being prompted to do so by anyone, many creators chose to craft eleven hearts in memory of the eleven victims, in some cases, as we saw, linking the counting with prayer. They were schooled in a memorial culture

FIGURE 5.3. *Jewish Hearts for Pittsburgh with explanatory flyer, 2018. Photograph by Rachel Kranson.*

that numbers its dead, from the names engraved on the Vietnam Veterans Memorial wall to the AIDS Quilt and to the empty chairs of the Oklahoma City National Memorial. The work of memorializing is also the work of quantifying. In American memorial culture, counting and naming are religious acts.

In small and large ways, contemporary Jewish craftivism continues activist legacies that Jews and, particularly, Jewish women have fostered since the 1960s. One of the photos that my friend sent from Pittsburgh illustrates this well. In it, a blue and white crocheted heart containing a star hangs from a tree branch. The early winter setting is evident, with many bare branches; on others, the remaining leaves are brown. To the right of the heart, there is an immaculate, carefully designed, full-color flyer that says, "Jewish Hearts for Pittsburgh." It details the project and includes images of other hearts (fig. 5.3). The photo reminds me that organizing is an infinite task, that revolutions begin in living rooms. This flyer evokes the photocopied "zines" of earlier feminists. Volunteers didn't just take the time to stitch hearts and to hang them, already a major task; they were also educators who explained their work. Most of all, Jewish craftivism remakes space. The Pussyhats, like the AIDS Quilt, covered the National Mall. The Jewish Hearts were sprinkled all over Pittsburgh like the divine sparks of Lurianic legend. Both projects altered the affect and meaning of wounded spaces, reclaiming them for people who were experiencing alienation. Craftivism may not always lead to policy change, and textiles "live at the edge of crisis, often creating conflicts or tensions as much as assuaging them."[69] Today's Jewish crafters and artists continue this imperfect, unending work. In doing so, they confront the past, the future, and the nature of generational connections, to which we now turn.

# 6 : GENERATING
# THE GENERATIONS

. . . . . . . . . . . . . . . . . . . . . . . . . . . . . . . . . . . . .

## *Crafting Memory in a Fragile World*

I am in Los Angeles, having lunch on a typically sunny April day as children frolic nearby in their Easter finery. It is one of the middle days of Passover 2017—and Gerry, one of the founders of the West Los Angeles chapter of the Pomegranate Guild of Judaic Needlework, is telling me why she creates. Gerry became invested in the creation of new Jewish textiles while she worked to preserve old ones at the Skirball Cultural Center in the 1970s. "A lot of Jews and their pieces were burned out during the Holocaust. It was time for us to make more pieces, the contemporary ones," she explains.[1] Over just a few days, Gerry was one of three women who told me that the Holocaust was a motivation for creating new Jewish art. Creation, they argued, was the best way to respond to genocide and the legacy of trauma that catastrophe left behind for modern Jews.

Thinking about how the Holocaust motivates crafting also raises broader questions about Judaism, memory, and descendants. To create objects is to engage in a quest for continuity. How do objects generate the generations? The Pomegranate Guild in particular struggles with issues of declining membership; other crafters also wonder how their own Jewish crafting traditions will be passed down. In my participant observation for this project as a whole—but especially in interactions with women who were my senior—I was keenly aware of my doubled role as not just an ethnographer but also a younger Jewish woman who does needlework (albeit not with the skill of most of these women). I am thus, potentially, not just a bearer of memory in words but also in thread, a daunting responsibility. In this book *and* in my knitting basket, I am a custodian of memories.

Material memories matter. As a practice, crafting solidifies sentiment, but it also reveals the limits and gaps of transmitting skills, values, and heritage. To understand Jewish crafting, we need to think deeply about how it connects with major nodes of Jewish memory like the Holocaust, as well as how, more broadly, it is linked with heirlooms and generational connections.

## "WE HAD NO HEIRLOOMS":
## CRAFTING AFTER THE HOLOCAUST

The Holocaust looms large in Jewish American life—particularly for Jews who lived through the post–World War II decades. What we now call the Holocaust would rapidly become a major part of Jewish American identity-making; by the late 1970s, it was well established as a major aspect of collective memory for Jews and many other Americans.[2] By the mid-1990s, which saw the opening of the U.S. Holocaust Memorial Museum and the immense box office success of Steven Spielberg's film *Schindler's List*, it had become a fixture in not just Jewish American culture but American popular culture more generally.[3] Despite my knowledge of this history, I was still surprised when discussions of the Holocaust featured prominently in several interviews. I did not begin my work by looking for the Holocaust, but inevitably, it found me. Most important, in each conversation, the Holocaust was not just an item of reflection but also a central motivation for crafting.

The first such conversation was with Gerry. Like most Jewish Americans today, Gerry is not related to any Holocaust survivors; most contemporary Ashkenazi American Jews are the descendants of immigrants who arrived here before 1924, when new immigration laws restricted arrivals from southern and eastern Europe. Gerry became interested in creating Jewish objects because of the textile preservation work she was doing at the Skirball. One day, a newsletter from the newly formed, East Coast–based Pomegranate Guild arrived. Gerry, Peachy Levy, and several other women formed the initial nucleus of the Los Angeles "study group." Although there was already a general embroiderers' guild in Los Angeles, Gerry emphasized that the group "was not creating the Judaic textile, which needed to be created to add into the world for all of the pieces that were destroyed during the Holocaust."[4] Her logic was both impeccable and heartrending. It is similar to the common argument that post-1945, Jews must have many babies to spite Hitler.[5] Textiles were destroyed in the fires of genocide, and so, they must be added back *in*, re-created for the remaining Jews. Gerry was clear, of course, on the fact that these new items could not truly replace those that were lost—so many stitches, from so many murdered hands!—but it was still an additive logic.

When she began creating as a Pomegranate Guild member, Gerry said, "I had visions of very traditional things. Your tallits, your yarmulkes. Ordinary stuff."[6] She went on to describe some innovative ritual culture from Pomegranate Guild members, but these words linger: "ordinary stuff." One important task that faces contemporary Jewish Americans is how to reclaim "ordinary losses" after the Holocaust.[7] Holocaust commemoration in the United States often dwells on that which is large—the scope of the crimes, the numbers murdered, and the *extraordinary* nature of the Third Reich policies and the resulting mass suffering and death for Jews and other minority groups. Obviously, there has already been a great deal of attention to material culture in Holocaust museums. How, though, can we better attune ourselves to that which is *ordinary* and small—not just that which was small in the lives of the Holocaust's victims, but also that which is small and often unnoticed in the lives of those who commemorate them? Sewing, knitting, embroidery ... these are quotidian activities, and yet, through them, Gerry and others like her are performing subtle acts of memorialization in powerful ways. Gerry's story opens up the ways that even when sewing projects are not explicitly Holocaust themed, they may be part of the pervasive presence of Holocaust memorialization in Jewish American life.

In my next two interviews, I spoke with women who were descendants of Holocaust survivors. For them, creating new objects for their families and those around them is a very direct response to this haunting legacy. Bonnie explained her twin inheritance of both Holocaust memory and sewing:

> I'm a first-generation American. My parents are both from Poland. My mother was a Holocaust survivor. My father left Poland before the war started. My mother's parents, sister, and three brothers were all murdered in Auschwitz, and she lived in the shtetl of Sharachev, which is now in Belarus, but was in Poland in the early 1900s, and her mother was a seamstress. In their shtetl there were two thousand people. A thousand were Jews and a thousand non-Jews, and my mother said that her mother sewed for the non-Jews. She would make clothing. My mother, after the war, came to New York, and in her words, she was a finisher by dresses. So, she did the hemming and whatever the finishing was. I don't think that she ever really had all the skills that her mother had, but she did do finishing. She had a sewing machine. I have her sewing machine. She didn't sew a lot, but she did sew, and she always said that I picked up from her mother the genes of creating things.[8]

Family legacies are crucial for Bonnie, who is also dedicated to genealogy and whose output of items is prodigious. During the hours I spent talking with her in her home, I was in awe of not just her talent but the sheer number of quilts, pillows, decorations, bookmarks, and other items she has produced. Later in our interview, when I asked her about the connections between Judaism and her craft practice, Bonnie described a very specific moment when she experienced the connections across different generations while crocheting hundreds of prayer caps for a family *b'nai mitzvah* (coming of age ceremony). She was sitting in a chair in her family room, with memorabilia from family weddings behind her and pictures of her mother's parents in the bookcase beside her:

> I'm sitting, crocheting kippot, and I'm doing them in piles of ten and—I'm going to get a little emotional here. I realized that I was putting them in front of my mother's parents, who perished in the Holocaust, and I began to weep because—it wasn't necessarily spiritual, but it was emotional—and there was such a tie from generation to generation, and I hadn't thought about it before. I'd been sitting there for probably nine months crocheting these kippot and putting them here, and all of a sudden, I looked down, and wow. I mean, here they died because they were Jewish, and their great-great grandchildren are becoming b'nai mitzvah, who are still Jewish. It was emotional but spiritual at the same time—that's what it was.[9]

This anecdote reminds us that religious practice is deeply embodied and that it is situated in powerful spatial contexts. For Bonnie, multiple factors—the disciplined physical activity of crocheting hundreds of kippot, the juxtaposition of her crafting practice with her family mementos—led to an insight about families, generations, and Jewish identity. This is a potent reminder of the importance of paying attention to lived religion. Moments of spiritual affect do not just occur in churches and synagogues, at pilgrimage sites and on holy days. They happen in quiet corners and at unexpected times. Bonnie's anecdote also crystallizes the concept of generative resilience. In this case, the resilience is a sort that spans decades and confronts one of the great tragedies of human history. The astounding nature of Jewish survival and literal generativity through the birth of generations is encapsulated in the creation of these small caps to be worn at a coming-of-age ritual. They are inadvertently placed before an image of the murdered great-great grandparents, like an offering to the ancestors. Provoked by the senses of touch and sight, Bonnie took that moment and focused her awareness on the miraculous nature of her family's continuation after an unspeakable loss.

For Cathy Perlmutter, who is also a descendant of a Holocaust survivor, creating objects is a way of filling in the gaps of what had never been. "My mom was a Holocaust survivor from Poland, so we had no heirlooms, we had nothing," she told me, "I think everyone who's the offspring of a Holocaust survivor has thought about this. A lot. You know, the things that were missing from our family. The things we don't know about their home. Especially because I had a mother who never wanted to talk about it. So, to me it [stitching] means perpetuating the Jewish culture and faith and tradition, and that's an important thing to do."[10]

Cathy expresses a logic similar to Gerry's, but on a more intimate, familial scale. Gerry was thinking abstractly about creating new Judaica on a global stage to make up for the vast stores of material culture lost in the Holocaust. Cathy is also thinking about Jewish continuity writ large, but the move starts from her immediate home, from the objects and heirlooms she did not have growing up.

In my conversations with these three women, I saw how the act of creation was a direct response to destruction and how the looming presence of the Holocaust in either their families or their communities more broadly led them to want to generate new Jewish objects, *any* kinds of Jewish objects, as a kind of repopulation. For Gerry, Bonnie, and Cathy, crafting was an action resonant with absences and presences. It was a way of wrestling with the void, akin to the horror vacui with which this book began. In their logic, it is not enough just to remember the Holocaust in one's head. The best way to combat the sheer inhumanity and incalculable loss of that epoch is to wield new materialities against the violent destruction of past generations—and their objects. The object itself need not be about the Holocaust; *all* Jewish objects, on some level, show resilience and survival after great loss.

## THE GREEN SWEATER

Another category of Holocaust craft artifacts is those that are crafted with the intentional goal of commemorating the Holocaust. I now turn to two such examples. The first of these is connected to one of the central nodes of Holocaust memorialization in North America: the United States Holocaust Memorial Museum, which opened to the public in 1993 and remains one of the most popular tourist destinations in Washington, D.C. In the museum's permanent rotating collection, there is a small green sweater that once belonged to a child named Krystyna Chiger, who now goes by the name Kristine Keren (for clarity, I refer to her by her childhood surname). Her family escaped from Nazi-occupied Poland when she was seven years old. In news interviews and oral histories, Chiger recalls the experience of watching her grandmother knit the sweater before the war: "Wherever I went from place to place, I had one thing I wanted to wear. It was my sweater that my grandmother knitted for me before the war. This is the sweater that I cherished the most.... I saw my grandmother knitting this for me. And when I look at the sweater, I see her face. I almost see her sitting and knitting."[11] In this testimony, seeing the surviving green stitches materially links Chiger to the memory of her grandmother's physical presence, to the repeated ritual of knitting. The sweater is a powerful conduit, a Proustian catalyst of vivid recall.

In 1941, when Chiger was five, her grandmother was transported and killed. In 1943, when the Lvov ghetto was liquidated, Chiger and her parents survived by hiding in the sewers for fourteen months; they eventually escaped from Poland. She became a dentist in Israel and ultimately emigrated to the United States. Through all of this, she kept the sweater with her. Eventually, she donated it to the Holocaust Memorial Museum.[12]

Years later, a Silver Spring anesthesiologist and avid knitter named Lea Stern, who was struck by the sweater when she saw it in an exhibit, found a way to backwards engineer the garment (the curators let her spend some careful hands-on time with the sweater itself, which had returned to storage). Now a pattern for the sweater is available for purchase at the museum's bookshop, as well as on Ravelry, a popular social media and pattern-sharing site for knitters (proceeds benefit the museum).[13] The sweater was featured in news stories in 2015. In one report, museum curator Suzy Snyder said, "We won't always have survivors. The object tells the story where/when they won't be able to."[14] Stern told the reporters, "It represents survival, the will of people to live."[15] One news report also included footage of a meeting between the two women at Chiger's home in New York; Stern has knit many copies of the sweater, and presented one such copy to Chiger herself. "Now I have my sweater back," the older woman said.[16]

This story is evocative on multiple levels. Here, the simulacrum becomes a substitute for the original object, because the object itself—the one touched by the grandmother's hands, fused with her presence—has itself become raised up to the level of historical artifact. The first sweater was given as a gift from grandparent to grandchild; its emotional power stems from the death of the giver and the death-defying struggles of the recipient. What's more, the sweater's memorial power is now destined to outlive its recipient, too. This remnant clothes Chiger in memory, connecting her with her grandmother but also presaging the fact that someday her sweater will be here to tell her story while she will not. Some of the museum's pieces, of course, exist precisely because of the deaths of their owners, rather than because of their survival. Objects from Auschwitz, for example—those objects left behind when their owners went to the gas chambers—have long been a potent site of meaning making in Holocaust commemoration. The green sweater is slightly different because it stands instead as an emblem of survival, a fabric light in the literal darkness of the sewer where Chiger and her family dwelled. We have the sweater because Chiger lived, not because she died. Like the girl in the red dress in *Schindler's List*—the one spot of color in that film, and a particularly haunting aspect of it for many viewers—the girl in the green sweater provides a stark image of color against a tragic past that *did*, of course, happen in color but is so often rendered in sepia tones. Unlike the girl in the red dress, Chiger survives, making this story an outlier and also the kind of narrative that appeals to American audiences.[17]

All heirlooms outlive their givers. This one, though, came from the hands of a grandmother lost to an act of violence that looms large in our collective imagination, giving it an extra layer of pathos and a great sense of loss. I am struck, too, by the existence of the pattern, which seems to exist as an ode to the grandmother's skill while also being an uncanny piece of ephemera. A friend bought me a printed copy of it from the museum gift shop. It is called, simply, "The Green Sweater." Much of it reads like any other knitting pattern. It contains a list of materials, including a suggested yarn; the yarn weight; the needle size (US 1—a 2.25 mm needle, very small); stitch patterns, expressed in the knitter's language of "k1, p5" ("knit one, purl five"); and precise directions. What is different about this knitting pattern is its preface, which begins "Dear Knitters," and then continues with Chiger's story. Stern then writes:

> This small child's sweater represents the resilience of the human spirit. It is something that cannot be destroyed by prejudice and intolerance and it is with these thoughts that I have reconstructed this sweater. It is meant to be as near an exact replica of Krystyna's sweater as possible. I hope I have been as successful in preserving its historical accuracy.... My hope is that in knitting this sweater, Krystyna's story will be told again and again to future generations. In this way, the bravery of Krystyna and her family, as well as the courageous people who helped them will never be forgotten.[18]

Here it is, in perhaps its starkest (and yet also most clichéd) formulation: *resilience*, in this case, a sweater that "represents the resilience of the human spirit." Can a sweater truly encapsulate resilience? My argument throughout this book has been that the *process* of crafting constitutes a form of coping. Here, Stern frames the crafted *object* itself as an ode to overcoming adversity, a symbol of survival. Because of the nature of the interviews I have conducted for this project, in which older women predominated, the sweater makes me think more of the grandmother who knitted it than of the little girl who wore it. The fact that the act of making a replica is so meaningful makes me ponder what is lost, and what is found, when objects are reproduced. It was the materiality of the original sweater, the one her grandmother held and crafted, the one that comforted Chiger in the fetid sewer. This is why giving it to the museum was, ultimately, a difficult decision. When I read her statement about receiving the replica from Stern—"Now I have my sweater back"—I was both moved by the story and personally disquieted by the way it was reported. Perhaps I romanticize the power of the material touch, but to me, though the sweater survives, it has also been lost in its museumification. I cannot, of course, speak for Chiger, but I am personally struck by the fact that she can no longer *touch* the original; the sweater is so fragile that it cannot even be permanently displayed. In that way, of course, the green sweater pattern and the powers of replication do an immense public service: they carry on a story when the only way to preserve an artifact entails limiting access to it. The *practice* of making a replica sweater is done in memory of a grandmother who perished and her granddaughter who survived. Yet the stitches that linked them, though extant, are now in storage. They are returned, uncannily, to the darkness.

I also wonder about those who would be moved to make a replica from this pattern, whether it was purchased on a trip to Washington or downloaded from a website. More than a thousand copies of the pattern have been sold from these two sources. Stern told one reporter, "I've answered hundreds of emails from people all over the world. I've been contacted by children of survivors, people concerned about the rise of hatred and divisions in society, teachers, and others."[19] To make such a sweater— I found several completed ones in users' galleries of finished projects on Ravelry—is to participate in a "fantasy of witnessing" the Holocaust, a simulacrum that commemorates on multiple levels, a phenomenon that is widespread but deeply uncanny and ethically challenging.[20] We cannot typically travel to the sewers of Lvov or hold the actual sweater in our hands, but we can participate actively in Holocaust commemoration by knitting a copy. In a discussion board on Ravelry, one knitter mused that it would be "too painful" to knit.[21] I find that I concur; I own the appropriate weight of green yarn and the right type of needles, but I cannot bring myself to cast it on. I am too haunted by the untouchability of the sweater, the way that the original is no longer an everyday, intimate object. What would I do with a replica? Who would wear it? Could I clothe my own daughter in such a ghostly garment?

## THE ANNE FRANK TZEDAKAH BOX

I encountered a very different Holocaust-themed artifact in my own community through the work of ceramics maker Linda Schwartz. A friend told her she should be making *tzedakah* boxes—simple boxes with a slot, like a bank, that are used to collect money to be donated to charity. Tzeda-kah boxes need not be elaborate—many homes had simple metal *pushkes* (the Yiddish term for such boxes) with little decoration—but fancier ones have become a common item in Judaica shops. They are also a popular craft among the Hebrew school set. Schwartz was doing research on Anne Frank and came across a statement, attributed to Frank: "No one ever became poor by giving." She was inspired to create a tzedakah box in the shape of the Anne Frank house, with the quotation engraved upon it. It is an arresting item. I first saw it in her display at a JCC craft fair. It is also discussed, and pictured, in online interviews with her, and on Etsy, where it is one of her most popular items and is carefully and tastefully described (it does *not* bear the taglines of other items: "makes a wonderful gift for bar/bat mitzvah, wedding").[22] The box does resemble Prinsen-gracht 263, the building in Amsterdam where Frank hid in a secret annex with seven other Jews before being found and deported to various camps, including Bergen-Belsen, where she died. When I noticed the box, I had just visited the Anne Frank House the previous summer, waiting in line for about an hour before walking through the tiny spaces where Frank hid. The exterior of the house on Prinsengracht is dark brick; in contrast, the ceramic house is off-white. The red tile roof that Schwartz designed evokes Amsterdam well. Anne Frank is known for inspiring many things. I had not associated her with charity.

This tzedakah box is just one small example of "the Anne Frank phenomenon," the "vast sprawl" of endeavors dedicated to her memory over the nearly seven decades since her diary's publication.[23] In fact, in the book *Anne Frank Unbound*, one can see that Linda's tzedakah box is not the first to feature Prinsengracht 263. That book's introduction features an "alms box" in porcelain, created for the Jewish Federation of Greater Philadelphia, that more closely resembles the house, though to my gaze it lacks some of the warmth of Schwartz's more abstract creation. To memorialize Frank as a symbol of all Holocaust victims and to hold her up as a beacon for social justice movements is common. There is something deeply haunting, though, about the nature of these material mediations. Just as Anne's first diary (one of multiple physical objects on which the diary we know as a published book was written) is displayed like a holy relic at the Anne Frank House, the house *itself* becomes a symbol that can be replicated and can inspire others to do good deeds. Who can say no to an Anne Frank tzedakah box? The moral imperative to give charity to such a receptacle seems overpowering.

There are hundreds more commemorative Holocaust projects I could have included here—such as the Six Million Stitches Project, an online exhibit of needlework projects originally sparked by Rita Lenkin Hawkins in the late 1990s before her untimely death from cancer.[24] Then there is Trudie Stroebel, a Holocaust survivor whose tapestries became a crucial part of her experience coping with this trauma.[25] Theologian Melissa Raphael turns to sewing as a central pillar for her reparative approach to the ruptures and theodicies of the Shoah's vast inhumanity. She describes women's attempts to knit and sew in the camps, using whatever tattered scraps and bits of fiber they could locate: "Knitting and sewing could be a practical and symbolic means of renewing the connective and protective functions of love and one that bound women to their mothers and grandmothers within a female world now destroyed."[26] Raphael theologizes sewing, arguing, "Sewn and worked cloth is a symbol of the beauty and durability of a covenant of protective love made between persons and between God and persons. . . . Domestic sewing signals a lifelong commitment; a promise to care for the created body."[27] For Raphael, such acts of care are a part of literal, metaphorical, and mystical acts of tikkun (repair) in the face of a regime that quite literally unclothed its victims and exposed them to the world's cold, when it wasn't shooting or gassing them.

Although Raphael's argument rests upon a stereotypically feminized notion of the fiber arts, her vision has great consonance with the language used by many of my informants, who described creation as their response to destruction. As a process, generative resilience rests upon acts of care. Materiality and memory extend this notion by giving repair a temporal dimension. When Linda Schwartz makes an Anne Frank tzedakah box, she is pulling Holocaust memories into the present, the moment of giving, and toward the future of a world she wants to reimagine. When Gerry preserves old textiles and makes new ones, she is crafting a future for her family and community. Both Raphael and the creators portrayed here seem to understand the imperfections of forging ahead after Auschwitz, the impossibility of full redemption. Yet they persevere, creating new objects against this backdrop of destruction.

## MAKING HEIRLOOMS AND STITCHING MEMORIES
For my interviewees who were the descendants of Holocaust survivors, creating the heirlooms their families never had was an important task, one that animated their Jewish crafting. Memory, however, is not just about the Holocaust. The creation of heirlooms and the notion of passing something down to future generations was a thread running through all of my fieldwork conversations and reading. I frequently encountered the refrain that crafters were making, not just *any* objects, but objects that

would be *heirlooms*. Many of my informants reflected on how the future was incorporated into the objects that they made.

An heirloom is a value-added item and repository of memory. The values that are added multiply time and familial connections. The English word "heirloom" signifies an object passed down through a family, literally through the "heir," or financial recipient, of the "loom," which at the time of this term's emergence meant "tool." An adjacent Hebrew term is the phrase *l'dor v'dor*, "from generation to generation," which pops up often in Jewish liturgy and implies a command to pass on one's traditions, especially the teaching of the Torah. This idea of passing Judaism from generation to generation is also, for many of my interviewees, a deeply materialized notion.

Stacey, a Pomegranate Guild member raising teenagers, put it this way: "I also like the generational thing, that you're making things that will be passed down, and that you're creating some family heirlooms that somebody might value someday, even if they don't appreciate them now. Like, I know that bar mitzvah kids don't really appreciate when they get tallis bags, but they will someday. You know, twenty years from now, they will look back and say, 'Oh, somebody made this for me. Isn't that nice?'"[28] For Stacey, a special kind of futurity is built into her projects. The hours of investment into her intricate needlepoint pieces are a way of contributing to communal continuity and future memories, a way of showing care, even as she acknowledges that the average teenager is not a great connoisseur of handmade objects.

Laurel Robinson, the Georgia-based artist and yad maker, told me a funny anecdote from her time working at a Jewish summer camp, where she frequently made small, simple yads for the myriad Torah readings that went on each week at the camp:

> So, another kid that I made one at camp for said to me, "Wow, an heirloom." And I thought well, that's really a weird idea. And it was a young boy, an eighteen-year-old, a twenty-year-old or whatever. And I said, "What do you mean?" And he said, "Well, this will just stay in my family and then I'll give it to my child and ...." It was a kid that was eighteen, and he was thinking that he was having a child. But it hadn't occurred to me that I was making an heirloom.[29]

Robinson's story tilts in the opposite direction from Stacey's. At other times she has labored in great detail over a yad for a specific person or occasion, but in this case, she was quickly making pieces in her spare time as an art counselor, part of her daily routine, handing them out somewhat randomly. She said, "It hadn't occurred to me that I was making an heirloom," whereas most of my other interviewees are quite consciously doing just that. We can also juxtapose her teenage informant with Stacey's perception of the gift recipients she knows. In Stacey's case, she expects teenagers to have an underwhelmed reaction to their gift; the heirloom aspect will come much later. In Robinson's interaction, the teenage boy is the one to quickly ascribe future, potent meaning to the object. This quotation also shows how heirlooms are fashioned by *time* as much as they are by *intent*. The summer camper seemed instinctively to know this. The yad would become an heirloom only once it was passed down.

At their core, heirlooms are about associations with specific people, times, and places that accrue around objects. This is what makes their sentiment "sticky."[30] One particularly adherent and overdetermined example of such sentiment is the creation of memory quilts. Memory quilts are not new, and not uniquely Jewish—we have hundreds of examples of "mourning quilts" created to commemorate either a person or an event throughout American history.[31] I did, however, have the opportunity to speak with Louise Silk, a nationally recognized quilter who specializes in this art. Cathy Perlmutter also makes many such quilts and has shared her thoughts on them.

Silk is the author of *The Quilting Path: A Guide to Spiritual Discovery through Fabric, Thread, and Kabbalah*. In that book, she identifies herself as "a quilting mystic born into a Jewish culture following a Buddhist practice," although in her conversation with me, many years after the book's publication, she used slightly different descriptors, focusing more on Jewishness. In the book, she writes, "My quilting has always been my spiritual practice, but it took me years to comprehend that as my truth."[32] The book includes a series of projects, each of which has prefatory reflective material connected with one *sefirah*, or luminous sphere, of the godhead, as described in classical kabbalah. *The Quilting Path* thus blends the genres of memoir, instruction manual, and inspirational literature. Chapter 8 is called "Fragments of Life: Remembrance Crazy Quilt," and it is dedicated to the sefirah of *netzach*: "dominance, victory, eternity, conquest, the capacity to overcome."[33]

Silk's memory quilts are a major part of both her personal craft practice and her professional quilt business.[34] In her book, Silk describes how she created memory quilts from old clothes after the death of her longtime partner and after her parents' deaths. Both the quilting process and the objects themselves have many functions: "Creating these quilts opens up a space to reflect, recall, weep, lament, sigh, smile, and laugh."[35] Her description of cutting open her father's old clothing is especially poignant: "The strongest memory I have of the actual quilting experience is the first time I cut and ripped off one of the pant legs from my dad's tux. Ripping that leg gave me a powerful direct understanding of his death, the clear reality that I had no choice but to destroy these pants. He had no more use for them. It became my responsibility to let them go and to make them over into something new. I was letting go of Dad and transforming the pants to a different and useful experience."[36]

In Silk's examples, the action of rending clothing, which is a traditional mourning practice in the "Jewish ritual toolbox" is transposed into a slightly different mode.[37] In Jewish tradition, clothing (one's own) is indeed typically rent upon the death of a close family member, but it is not reused (or a symbolic black k'riah ribbon is torn instead). Here, in contrast, the cutting is a part of a process that is not merely destructive but also generative: the clothing of the deceased will be transformed and given new life as part of a new object, providing solace for the mourner through both the meditative activity of sewing and the existence of this tangible link to the past. It is an example of "'piecing' as 'peacing': pieces that make peace between the living and the dead."[38]

In our interview, Silk had more to say about memory quilts. "Everyone's mourning process is different," she told me. In the case of one family, she encountered a woman who was unable to open her husband's closet for two years after his death; now Silk was working on a quilt from his clothes. In contrast, another family brought over huge amounts of clothing right away. "The father died, he had two daughters and four grandchildren, and they made seven quilts for Christmas. He died in November." She discussed more about memory, tactility, and her own experiences with memory objects, and told me about a memory quilt she made for the JCC of Pittsburgh, referring to her craft practices as having a kind of "ritual" to the work. In this case, she said, "I sat in the JCC twice a week, for the month before [an anniversary], and I collected everybody's pictures and memories ... and then I made a quilt for them."[39]

Silk was so enamored of memory quilts that she told me she had actually proposed writing a book about them. The way that she talks about fabric and memory is visceral. "You don't really need very much of something for it to hold memory," she told me.[40] In this formulation, fabric does explicitly *hold* memory; families experience emotion through tactility. Sewers talk about the "memory" of fabric, how its form is affected by *our* form. Thus, "When our parents, our friends, our lovers die, the clothes in their closets still hang there, holding their gestures, both reassuring and terrifying, touching the living with the dead.... When a person is absent or dies, cloth can absorb their actual presence."[41]

Sometimes, the process of making memory quilts for others takes on powerful personal dimensions. On her blog and in our face-to-face conversation, Cathy Perlmutter describe her own memory quilt-making process, which is introspective and ritualized. Like Silk, she acknowledged the emotional pain that accompanies grief, a pain that is especially palpable when a mourner is confronted with materiality. In one blog post, she describes working on a memory quilt for a dear friend who had lost her father, writing of what she observed as "the agony of sorting through his possessions."[42] This particular quilt, made up of the deceased man's shirts, became a window into Perlmutter's typical routine for this type of project. After the clothes have been collected, she writes: "Back in my work room, before I start cutting or arranging, I light a candle, say a prayer, and have a chat with the deceased."[43] The post then moves the reader through the steps of the quilt's creation and, because this was for a friend, included some mentions of how the man's values had been transmitted to his daughter and, in turn, to Perlmutter. In this and several other memorial projects, she conveys how fabric craft is a powerful way to comfort the bereaved, a practice that is a central mitzvah (commandment) in Jewish tradition.

By turning to fabric, rather than writing, as a locus of memory, Silk, Perlmutter, and other quilters like them are reversing a move that historian Constance Classen describes among early modern European Christian women of a certain class. Women like Margaret Cavendish, an English aristocrat, wanted to "spin a garment of memory" in *words*, not silks; these women were criticized for abandoning the activities considered appropriate for their sex and class.[44] This was, of course, a matter of great class privilege at a time when literacy was rare and engaging in handwork was more typically a matter of survival, rather than leisure. Still, here at the turn of the twenty-first century, long after modernity has ushered in a more visual and less tactile culture, memory quilts exemplify what Classen calls "the persistence of touch."[45] When Silk and Perlmutter create memory quilts from the clothing of the deceased, they are forging a new religious sensorium that throws us back to times when touch, not sight, was one of the chief ways people learned. (As Classen documents, in early museums, visitors expected to be able to *touch* objects in order to learn, a practice that fell out of fashion as museum attendance increased among lower classes, as visitors became disciplined into a different way of relating to the displays, and as both the science and politics of preservation changed.)[46]

The power of memory quilts lies in the "animacy" ascribed to the emotions and sensations that they provoke.[47] We can understand our relationship to objects more richly if we consider this concept, which we can use to examine the affective charge surrounding different types of materiality. In linguistics, "animacy is the quality of liveness, sentience, or humanness of a noun or noun phrase that has grammatical, often syntactic, consequences."[48] It is not surprising that, throughout *Painted Pomegranates and Needlepoint Rabbis*, I have frequently slipped into anthropomorphic language when I discuss the objects I have encountered. For the most part, however, I have tried to focus on the actions and words of the humans surrounding the objects. But what if we also take the fields of power exerted by the objects themselves seriously?[49] To encounter this discourse around memory quilts and other items requires us to face the fact that *matter matters*. What is it about *this* T-shirt, *that* pair of dress pants, that so changes the nature of the object created from them?

It is one thing to say, "This is obvious—they belonged to someone beloved by the recipient of the memory quilt." But that fact is not enough to account for Silk's statement about how an item can *hold* memory. I want to take that notion quite seriously, because hers is not the only example in which the specific objects used as raw materials carried a powerful emotional energy. Part of that power comes not just from people but from the thing-ness of the object itself. We can see this process play out closely in another heirloom fabric project.

When I spoke with Bonnie in Southern California, she showed me two family naming pillowcases, circa 2004 and 2009, that she had created for her grandchildren out of family heirloom textiles (Bonnie has three children and, through two of them, five grandchildren). On the back of each pillowcase she affixed a label, which I photographed. It carefully detailed the provenance of each of the earlier pieces she incorporated into this final product. On one pillowcase, there were items that would link the grandchildren to nearly all of their paternal and maternal lines, including a doily made by the first cousin of the infants' "great-great-grandfather [Kopel Kaminsky], who died in the Holocaust." Much of the fabric grafted together to make the pillowcase had once had a different purpose—a tablecloth here, a napkin there, rosettes from another tablecloth affixed as a decoration (fig. 6.1). On the back of the first pillowcase, a white cloth garlanded with intricate brown cross-stitch shows a small stain, a sign of its previous life.

On the front of each pillowcase, Bonnie stitched a formulation that is also common on wimpels (ceremonial swaddling cloths). In Hebrew, she embroidered the words "LeTorah, Ul'Chupah, Ul'ma'asim Tovim" (transliteration hers), which translates to a prayer that these descendants would live a life of "Torah (learning), marriage/companionship (the wedding canopy, or chuppah), and good deeds." After the grandchildren had

FIGURE 6.1. *Bonnie Vorspan, Sela family naming pillowcase, 2004. Photograph by the author.*

been named, she added their names to the pillowcases. "Even with the stains, they're just wonderful," she told me, though at first—like Louise Silk with her father's trousers—she was hesitant to cut into the fabrics.[50] In the end, though, she was delighted with the final product, and she found the entire process meaningful. When I asked her if she had found anything spiritual or religious in her crafting experiences, these were the first examples she turned toward, telling me that working with the "heirloom fabrics" was "spiritual."[51] It was also a practice that was *learned*, that she had seen online done by other crafters; and it is a practice I have seen on the blogs and Facebook groups I follow many times since our conversation.

In this practice of transforming old family fabrics, a special energy is attributed to the materiality of objects. Do all crafters who incorporate old family cloth into their work see it as spiritual or religious? Surely not. In either event, though—and certainly in these examples—a fabric's previous bearer is understood as having altered that fabric through the act of possession, changing its nature. We have porous bodies. We are not neatly sealed off from the world around us through our skin; rather, to use a fabric metaphor, our skin is a loose seam, not a tight one: it is how we link up with the wider material world, just as, at a seam, the grain of one fabric meshes with the next. On a microscopic level, we leave ourselves behind on everything we touch: skin cells, tiny strands of hair, fragrance, bits of food we have eaten, bacteria. The wine stain on Bonnie's family heirloom was just what was visible. What we leave behind when we die is saturated with our material selfhood—hence the pain of poring through such possessions. On a metaphysical level, it is thus not surprising that old fabrics are imagined as holding memory, as carrying on something of the spirit of those we have lost. The "thing-power"—"the curious ability of inanimate things to animate, to act, to produce effects dramatic and subtle"—of the dead's possessions carries great emotional weight.[52] The lost touch of the one who possessed an item is what animates its continuing emotional valence, what makes it hard to give up those objects. How much more emotional value is thus poured into these memorialization objects, through the hours spent stitching?

Holding on to old objects and enshrining them in new ones is a marked contrast to most American consumer trends. As political theorist Jane Bennett writes, "American materialism, which requires buying ever-increasing numbers of products purchased in ever shorter cycles, is anti-materiality. The sheer volume of commodities, and the hyperconsumptive necessity of junking them to make room for new ones, conceals the vitality of matter."[53] When these women rescue old fabrics and retain them in the design of something new, they are taking part in a powerful counterculture, one with roots in *the* counterculture of the 1960s and 1970s and that has even more urgent relevance in the early twenty-first century, here on the cusp of environmental catastrophe.

Craft practices like memory quilts exemplify a formulation of religion as a cultural flow through which humans "intensify joy and confront suffering by drawing on human and suprahuman forces to make homes and cross boundaries."[54] The flows of sentiment around fabric linger somewhere between life and death, between human and suprahuman. In this particular instance, makers confront not just any kind of suffering but mortality. As we will see, age and mortality are key themes for understanding many crafters' dreams for bridging the generations and the fundamental power of crafting itself.

## LINKING THE GENERATIONS IN FABRIC

Throughout my work on *Painted Pomegranates and Needlepoint Rabbis*, many of my informants—almost all of them—spoke about either the ways that they had inherited their craft from previous generations or the skills they hoped to pass on to their offspring. For a large number of these crafters, tracing the connections between multiple generations of stitchers became a way of cementing their identities as creators and a way of linking their family stories with both Jewish tradition and Jewish history. Jews in the nineteenth and early twentieth century were associated with both the reuse of old clothing and the burgeoning garment industry: "For writers, cartoonists, and popular poets, a sack of castoffs and stack of rumpled hats became convenient shorthand for Jews: they were the rag race. Those who created these often-mocking depictions could little anticipate how, in turn, the rag race—the business of buying, selling, stitching, and sewing clothing—would aid the transformation of Jewish life in the United States and England."[55] Today, both these mid-nineteenth-century formations and the industrial age of the sweatshop form a major part of Jewish American popular imaginations, from the papa who owns a rag shop in the classic children's series *All-of-a-Kind Family* to books about sewing in the more recent publications of PJ Library, not to mention memorialization of the Triangle Shirtwaist Factory fire.[56] When my interlocutors tell me about their family histories of craft, they are evoking both the personal and the collective in their musings. They are concerned with the past, grafting themselves into a lineage of crafters that is understood both genetically and historically, and with the future, hoping that their work will be passed down to the next generation.

Danielle, an avid sewer and late Gen Xer living in the Washington, D.C., area, told me, "My maternal grandmother was the one who taught me how to knit, and even though my paternal grandmother, who was the one who sewed, didn't live to see me doing this kind of stuff, that side of the family, every time they see anything that I've made, they always say that I got her, you know like that genetically, that I was gifted with it, so it was feelings she had."[57] Similarly, one of my baby boomer Pennsylvania interviewees introduced her crafting background in this way: "Both sides of my family had artists. My mother's grandfather was a tailor. My mother's mother did crochet and needlepoint and rug hooking. My mom actually had her master's in fine arts." Later in the interview, she said, "I think I got my great-grandfather's genes."[58] I heard many similar stories throughout my research. The history of Jewish participation in the garment trade came up in many brief asides; it lingered as another layer of pride in Jewish stitching. In this way, the late nineteenth- and early twentieth-century Jewish tailor lives on in the memories and self-formation of contemporary crafters.

Elsewhere in Pennsylvania, Laura, a multitalented crafter who knits, weaves, quilts, crochets, paints, and more, told me, "As far back as I can remember, I've had a needle or a piece of cloth in my hand." In her case, she linked her creativity to many sources, including a great-grandmother who was a seamstress: "Her big claim to fame is that she used to work on the czarina's dresses."[59] One of my survey respondents wrote of a paternal grandmother who "was a very talented seamstress; she was the first child in her family to be sent to the United States from Romania during

World War II. Her two brothers perished in the Holocaust. When I sew, I feel like I'm channeling a bit of her ingenuity and creativity."[60] There it is, in its starkest formulation: to survive persecution is to survive, not just in bodies, but also through acts of creative generation.

In the opposite temporal dimension, some of my interviewees told me about the importance of passing on their skills to future generations, especially in their own family. Sandra Lachter, one of the Pomegranate Guild members featured in chapter 4, taught her granddaughter how to sew; one of their special projects was making a new dress for Rosh Hashanah each year.[61] Women with young children wondered when those sons and daughters would be old enough to handle the sharp needles, scissors, rotary cutters, and other tools of this craft in order to learn how to stitch. Sometimes it was the young adult children who were the crafters; when I interviewed one rabbi about her own creative history and the creations in her synagogue, she showed me the elaborate *kittel*, a white robe worn on the High Holy Days, that her daughter, a Fashion Institute of Technology graduate, had made for her, along with the elaborate decorative pieces for the sanctuary that she had designed.[62]

In other cases, an object has been passed down through multiple generations of family users. In a suburb of Washington, D.C., Amanda told me about the fate of one creation from her congregation's active sewing culture:

> We had one gentleman who, he has since passed away, bless his heart, made atarahs [the collars of the prayer shawls] for all of his grandchildren. They were beautiful. Before he died, he needlepointed the front flap for a chuppah, and then I made the chuppah for him. I can't remember the quote that he needlepointed, but it, too, was also stunning. The chuppah is now in Israel. He has about eleven grandchildren, and they will all get married under this chuppah. I believe that three of them have already been married under it, and it will be passed down to the next.[63]

Here, the created item outlives its creator, remaining present for milestone family occasions as new generations carry on. In other homes, I encountered embroidered pillows, like the one Bonnie made, for the baby to lie upon at a b'rit milah (circumcision) or naming ceremony with the names of multiple babies, sometimes spanning more than a decade, stitched upon them; a burgundy velvet chuppah with the names of myriad couples embroidered upon it; and other similar examples.

More often, however, I encountered anxiety about the future of these craft practices, especially among the members of the Pomegranate Guild.

Here, there is membership contraction and concern that the traditions will not be passed on. During my research for this book, four chapters of the guild folded, though new ones, like the Yellow Rose chapter in Texas, have also been founded. In 2019, the biennial celebration that had been planned for that May in Calgary was canceled because of low registration. The Rimon Calgary chapter still held a celebration, attended by many members, but it was not an official biennial.

Arlene, the president of the Philadelphia chapter of the Pomegranate Guild, saw challenges in getting younger Jews invested in craft practices. "What we found over the years is that the next generation is not interested in doing handwork. They want finished and immediate. And as much as we've been trying for several years to get more younger people to come to our meetings, we have not been successful. And we've tried so many things," she said, describing attempts to recruit at local synagogues with young adult families. "But it's like pulling hair, and I don't understand why. Because this is a long tradition that if we don't maintain it, it's going to go away. And people will not learn what's going on. And I guess that's why I feel compelled to do something, to stay in it, and to try to get the next generation to get involved in doing things, but so far we have not been successful in doing that."[64]

During her presidency, Cathy Perlmutter expressed similar concerns. She connected them with today's work culture and a more general decline in American volunteer social groups. "It is very hard, as you know, to find time to sew when you're a young woman with a family and a career!" she told me, gesturing in my direction. "It's virtually impossible. Plus we're in an era, you know, all these ladies tell me that they used to have a Hadassah chapter in their town and it's gone, and they used to have a library guild and they used to have a garden club, and all of it's gone."[65] Still in the workforce, with college-aged children, Perlmutter was one of the younger members of the guild I encountered. "We know that our most natural group to recruit are the newly retired, but it would be great if we could bring in younger women, if we could figure out how to do that," she explained, along similar lines to Arlene.[66] Both Perlmutter and Stacey, a needlepointer who fits squarely into Generation X, thought that a stronger embrace of digital technologies might help the guild to reach new members, who are less likely to affiliate with brick-and-mortar, face-to-face groups and more likely to make connections via social media. (Members of Generation X and millennials are also less likely to join a synagogue, among other metrics.)[67]

Jewish crafting, on the whole, is not going away any time soon. In July 2019, a search for the term "Jewish crafts" on Pinterest yielded 624 "boards" (each board contains between two and hundreds of "pins," links with images) before I gave up and stopped counting the rows of brightly colored links; indeed, this book could go on forever, if I had the opportunity to interview every person on the continent who has made a Jewish craft. Pinterest is, of course, aspirational—most users pin hundreds of projects they will never have the time to actually make. It is also a reflection of a thriving American DIY scene; in 2015 alone, art supplies were a $1.5 billion business.[68] However, there seems to be a gap between the Pomegranate Guild, which is, in its way, a vestige of a postwar era of comparatively higher middle-class incomes and more time for such pursuits among middle- and upper-class Jews, and today's Jewish crafters, who squeeze in whatever bits of creating they can, when they can. The Pomegranate Guild was founded in the 1970s by women who came of age in the postwar period, then thrived during the 1980s, a comparatively booming time in the American economy. It is not the only twentieth-century-founded Jewish institution to be figuring out new strategies in the twenty-first. Though its numbers are smaller, it is not going anywhere; the call for instructors for the 2021 convention just came into my inbox, and the latest *Paper Pomegranate* is filled with images of group meetings and new projects flying off the needles.

As I wrote in this book's introduction, I often found myself in a complicated role as an ethnographer. I, too, have a stake in the preservation of Jewish values and practices. Though this project is an academic one, I am, like many scholars today, someone who studies a community with which they have ties of identity. Practices of Jewish memory and intergenerational transmission fascinated me on a personal level long before studying them became a professional avocation. As a result, though I was always professional in my interviews, my interviewees knew I was Jewish, and the appreciation I expressed for particular objects also came from a sense of sentiment. Needlework is a part of who I am, and I found that the women I spoke with often related to me not just as a scholar but also as a Jew and as a stitcher.

This was something I experienced acutely at the 2017 Pomegranate Guild biennial convention, where I was one of the youngest women present, although one younger Orthodox woman from Texas was probably my junior by at least a decade. In this extraordinarily friendly environment, most of the women were eager to meet new people and to get to know why they were there. I felt deeply cared for and semiadopted by many of the women, with offers to stay with them if I wanted to visit new cities in my research. Even though my stitching skills are fairly rudimentary, I represented a possibility for growth, a youngish (OK, middle-aged)

Jewish woman, raising a Jewish female child, with a direct line to other Jewish women of my generation. At the Pennsylvania knitting group with which I sat in, I was the youngest woman in the group by a significant margin, and though I tried to be relatively quiet in order to avoid interrupting the natural flow of conversation, the women there often asked me about Jewish studies at Lehigh and about my personal and scholarly background. In the transcripts of my formal interviews, I reread numerous moments where interviewees ask me whether I have encountered a particular technique or tried it myself. In my interview with Louise Silk—one of the first I conducted—I found myself explaining my fear of sewing machines, which she encouraged me to get over.

Ethnographers always have layered relationships with the people they write about, and it's very important to remember that we do not all study people who are like us. In this particular study, though, I think that it is crucial to attend to how the nature of Jewish continuity concerns adds a particularly fraught overlay to my positionality. Obviously, I think that the continuation of Jewish craft practices matters: it's what drove me to write this book, into these homes. I often wished that I could help in ways more concrete than as a recorder of stories, finding myself caught up in worry over the Pomegranate Guild's membership numbers and the viability of the entire future of Jewish material culture. Ironically, the time it takes to write a book has truncated my own crafting practice. During fieldwork, I was able to keep it up, in part by necessity, but as I write these words in late 2019, I find I rarely pick up my needles anymore, and some of my projects from the convention remain unfinished—I have been writing instead. Ethnography can provide snapshots of moments in time, perhaps raising up voices that are not always heard or illuminating "micro-practices" that are often missed.[69] But what happens now? Will I have failed my responsibility to the stitchers with whom I spoke, in some way, if I stop stitching—or if I don't pass the capacity to make Jewish objects on to someone younger than me? Does the ethnographer's role extend beyond the page? How can the preservation of *words* matter so much in a book that is predicated on the importance of our sense of *touch*?

These are emotional questions without easy answers. Emotions—*feeling*—brings us to the heart of the matter, to the Judaism of feeling that my interlocutors shared with me and that I have tried to share with you. "Feeling" doesn't just happen in our skin. It is also a synonym for sentiment: "Material culture ... is not principally the expression of ideas or doctrines, but rather the cultural production, circulation, and reception of felt-knowledge."[70] Touching objects *touches us*, sparking emotions.

FIGURE 6.2. *Geraldine Weichman, handprint Passover towel.*
*Photograph by the author.*

When I visited Gerry in Los Angeles, she had a treasure trove of objects carefully laid out on the dining room table. One of these was a hand towel (to be used after ritual handwashing) that she created for Passover in 1981 (fig. 6.2). Within a border of multitoned peach flowers, I saw the outlines of three small hands, embroidered in blue running stitch. Each hand was opened in the priestly blessing, made famous by Leonard Nimoy as a Vulcan greeting on *Star Trek*: the thumb spread apart, the next four fingers split in two. Within each hand was a name: Jeffrey, Jerry, and Joseph. Gerry had traced her grandsons' hands on cardboard, then used those cardboard pieces to lay out her stitch pattern. Beside the towel she had carefully placed a picture of the grandsons—and the original cardboard pattern.

Touch matters. Gerry's matzah cover is a form of felt knowledge on multiple levels. The embodied nature of her grandchildren's hands was sealed onto the linen in a simple yet remarkable transfer process. Standing in her dining room, during the middle days of Passover, thirty-six years later, I could trace those outlines with my own hands; Gerry, now a *great*-grandmother, had linked the generations in fabric. She had combined visuality and tactility in this sentimental artifact. She had, indeed, brought forth countless textiles in these many decades after the Holocaust. I thought about the ritual handwashing that happens during the seder. Gazing again at this picture, a snippet of a Passover song pops into my head. *"Then came the water that quenched the fire,"* a line from a long sequence of objects that each consume or attack one another in the dark, yet raucous tune "Had Gadya" ("An Only Kid"). We cannot always quench the fires of hatred, past or present. Yet, through creation, we can surely try.

# CONCLUSION

. . . . . . . . . . . . . . . . . . . . .

## *The Fabric of Forever*

During an otherwise glorious spring week in Los Angeles, in the middle days of Passover 2017, I was haunted by the ghost of Charlton Heston. Late one night, I flipped the channels on the hotel room television and stumbled onto a screening of *The Ten Commandments* in all its Technicolor glory. It was uncanny, watching Cecil B. De-Mille from a space adjacent to the dream factory itself. Heston, dressed as Moses and overacting, led his people forth from slavery. I had forgotten how much livestock figured in the departure from Egypt scene. *Those sheep would make an awful lot of sweaters*, I mused. And I thought about yarn, and freedom, and the small objects being made daily by Jewish women for their families and friends in this city where big blockbusters are produced for the masses.

Two days later, Charlton Heston—still dressed as Moses—stared up at me from a matzah cover.

I was at Cathy Perlmutter's home, where she showed me a piece she calls *Old Plagues on Them, New Plagues on Us*, which are the phrases she has appliquéd, in gold lamé, across its top and bottom (fig. C.1). The top half of this quilted cover features the familiar Passover plagues enumerated in the book of Exodus: Blood. Frogs. Lice. And so on. The bottom half, however, is overlaid with what Cathy considers to be our modern plagues, as she defined them when she created this object in the spring of 2001. Using pop art and clips from advertisements, she affixed these new horrors to their cloth canvas. "War." "Junk food." "SUVs." "Disney," next to an image of Mickey Mouse. (At this, my own Small World–infused heart quavered. One person's plague is another's delight.) "Laundry." "Tobacco." "Pollution." All of the items evoked powerful affects, channeling the feelings that had been strong ones for Cathy that long-ago spring.

Most strikingly, at the center of these new plagues rests Moses. Not just any version of Moses, of course. This Moses was a reproduced photo from *The Ten Commandments*—the same Moses I had seen on my television screen. In this shot, Moses raises one of the tablets of the law high above his head, about to smash it. On the tablet, Perlmutter affixed the words

FIGURE C.1. *Cathy Perlmutter, Old Plagues on Them, New Plague on Us,* *matzah cover. Photograph by the author.*

of one particular commandment: "Thou shalt not kill." Below the figure's feet, just so we are clear, it says, "Charlton Heston." Across Moses's chest, she stitched a tiny label: "NRA."

And so it came to pass that there, not far from Hollywood, I was holding on to Charlton Heston, matinee idol turned National Rifle Association president, rendered in fabric rather than celluloid. This Moses was not larger than life; he did not speak in the stentorian tones of postwar melodrama. No, this was not the Moses that DeMille wanted us to envision. He was miniaturized and ironed, contained and critiqued in this modern midrash of a quilt. I hadn't asked Perlmutter if she believed in God. What I saw, though, in this piece, was the Jewish notion of "wrestling with God." Jewish art and craft are one site of a practice that, like Perlmutter's plagues, is both old and new: the practice of asking difficult questions about which Jewish stories and ethics matter—and how, and why—in our own time and place. For Perlmutter, that meant naming contemporary American evils in the places that she found them.

*Old Plagues on Them, New Plagues on Us* encapsulates a way of doing Judaism that is vibrant, resilient, and activist. It takes a strong Jewish woman with a large collection of vintage sewing machines to bring Charlton Heston down to size. Telling the story of Passover is an embodied ritual that Jews have pursued, in many ways, for millennia now. Attending a Passover seder remains the most popular ritual among Jews in the United States. It's thus no surprise that in my travels, I found that Passover objects outnumbered all others. Passover is a rite of resilience. The telling of the exodus story in a communal setting is so central to Jewish life that it has endured for centuries. How fitting, then, that creativity is deeply enmeshed with this holiday, not only in quilted matzah covers and ceramic seder plates, but also in so many other ways: homemade *haggadot* (books telling the story), creative table dioramas that resemble the Red Sea, innovative recipes, kids' crafts that might adorn the table.

The story of the exodus—a vital, central narrative that runs through the veins of Jewish self-understanding—is a resilient one. It captivates because it is about survival. Generations endure under harsh conditions, then experience liberation. Further trials await in the desert, but still, they march on, pausing to create beautiful objects along the way—objects that adorn their rituals and sacred objects. At the start of this book, I argued that there is no fixed, singular Jewish identity, and my informants followed this pattern. They all brought different flavors of Jewishness to the table—and like most people who are not in positions of professional Jewish leadership or demography, they were not concerned with precisely defining this category. What *did* link them was their practice of generative resilience through craft. Like Cathy, they were coping with old and new plagues. The Jewish Hearts for Pittsburgh, those small objects from all over the nation that were mighty in number, consoled a grieving city amid the plagues of gun violence and hatred. The green sweater recreation evoked survival in the narrow straits of the ghetto sewers during the Holocaust. The Pomegranate Guild's lively convention was a liberation, a women-led celebration like the timbrels at the shores of the sea. Ketzirah's amulets were a ritual technology of strength in times of trouble. Jewish identity was expressed in many ways among the people in these pages: it could be activism, synagogue ritual, or magic, ethnic, religious, hybrid, or gastronomic. What united all of these iterations of Jewishness was a sense of perseverance.

The crafting of Judaism is a continuous making and unmaking, one that sustains, even when covered in wine stains, from generation to generation. The Passover table also exerts power because it lies at the hinge of the generations. When I set out to write this book, one of my biggest goals was to attend to older Jewish women's voices, the sorts of voices that are often missing from Jewish life. Though I spoke to women of different ages, it is these voices that linger with me most powerfully, and it is with them that we conclude. Barbara Myerhoff's *Number Our Days* remains one of the most significant books to pay close attention to the dimension of age in the field of Jewish studies, and many of her observations remain helpful. She calls the women of the center where she did her fieldwork "bricoleurs," parlaying bits of culture and different activities together, able to devise entire "miniature worlds" in the home.[1] For the women of the Pomegranate Guild, these worlds of creation sometimes became exterior, jutting out into the collective gatherings of their conventions and the occasional public exhibition, but those generative universes retain a strong domestic component. For Myerhoff, the power of such women resides in the everyday: "Because their [the center women's] tasks are particularized, concrete, embedded, and subjective, there is less urgency (not to mention little opportunity) to make them into platforms, public festivals, ideological treatises. They are known as part of living rather than discussions about living, and their very form makes it an inconsistency to formulate them as enduring, collective principles. These understandings are a kind of underground culture, quietly transmitted in situations, no less essential than the starkly evident, grandiose cultural productions we customarily attend."[2] The "underground culture" of crafting, which is both a big business and an intimate production, continues this thread of literal and metaphorical bricolage. When my informants want Jewish stitching to continue, they are saying that these subtle cultures, these hours of careful creation that rarely get the attention of a High Holy Day sermon or a viral op-ed, must endure.

In California, Zelda put it this way, as she summed up what she loves about stitching: "It's very fulfilling. I love it. I feel a connection to the past. I feel that I'm in some way opening a road to the future with it. My children have all these things, they will remember me doing, what I made. And it's a very sacred part of my life, really.... You could see I do a lot of Jewish things. That way, I'm very, very 'orthodox.'"[3] The sacred happens where people say that it happens. Zelda played upon the word "orthodox"—on her own perception of her Jewish observance, which, like the practice of most Jewish Americans, does not adhere to all of the classical elements of Jewish law or include large amounts of public prayer. In a Protestant-dominated culture, belief has become the most important aspect of religion to some Jews, too. Rather than belief *or* formal ritual, she says, what makes her quite playfully orthodox is her devotion to Jewish *objects*, and, most crucially, to objects at the fulcrum of multiple generations. Zelda's objects connect her to the past and to the future, providing a form of Jewish continuity that is sutured to the life of her family and with how she wants to be remembered.

Stitching, like writing and religion, is a place where we encounter mortality. In the *Paper Pomegranate* of September 1981, Faith Feldman Cohen writes, "To many people, men and women—pushing a needle in and yanking it out of some material is just that. *To us*—as needlewomen—it's a stitch taken in the fabric of forever."[4] To stitch is to take part in an act of faith that says not only will you finish the stitching project but, also, that the item may have a life after you are gone. Someone will save it; someone will use it; someone will remember that you made it. Or will they? Our looming worldwide environmental catastrophe makes me think of the thousands of textiles lost in the Holocaust, the ones that Gerry wanted to replace—but on a global scale, a vision of a world without recipients to inherit these heirlooms. It makes me marvel even more deeply at this will to continue creating.

Among the older community members that Barbara Myerhoff met in Venice Beach, "the opposite of honor was not shame but invisibility."[5] This holds true for crafting. It doesn't matter whether the work is a prize winner or someone's kitschy, over-the-top first quilt with uneven seams— the point of these works is that they must be seen, touched, smelled, have wine spilled upon them over dinner. To create is to be remembered. Remembrance is a signpost of resilience. *I was here, animated by a "stitch taken in the fabric of forever," by a hand that survived illness, the death of loved ones, the tumult of life*, the stitches suggest. Crafting makes many Judaisms visible, lifting the quotidian into the realm of something that might not be *eternal*—who can say?—but can extend us beyond the boundaries of our own skin.

# ACKNOWLEDGMENTS

. . . . . . . . . . . . . . . . . . . . . . . . .

This book has been brought to you by the letter "S," for Skinny Pop Popcorn, and by the number 1,180, which is how many miles I ran over the many years it took to write it. Each of these things nourished me and enabled me to reach this day.

More seriously, I owe my largest debt of gratitude to the thirty-three individuals who took the time to speak with me in detailed interviews, the three-hundred-plus people who responded to my 2016 survey, and so many, many more who spoke with me during fieldwork or communicated with me about this topic via email or social media. Without them, *Painted Pomegranates and Needlepoint Rabbis* would not exist. Though only some of their stories are directly referenced here, every point of contact shaped this final work in infinite ways. What you have in your hands is just a small square of an ever expanding, rich tapestry: a universe of crafting. In a book that is in part about the homes we make, I want to pause to acknowledge the homes into which I was warmly welcomed as I wrote it. From homemade madeleines to baked ziti to matzah during Passover, I was always ridiculously well fed. Most important, I was entrusted with a host of stories and images of objects. I do not know if I could ever do justice to them, but I hope that this book, combined with some digital curation and further writing, will bring many of these stitches to light. I have been truly humbled by these interactions.

When I came to Lehigh University in 2015, I could not have imagined what lay in store or just how much my colleagues' support and friendship would mean to me in the coming years. To the best Religion Studies department in the whole wide world—Hartley Lachter, Michael Raposa, Dena Davis, Benjamin Wright, Annabella Pitkin, Khurram Hussain, Robert Rozehnal, Christopher Driscoll, Monica Miller, Lloyd Steffen, Jodi Imler, and the inimitable, one-and-only Marian Gaumer: thank you. You ran with me, you cooked Indian food, you listened, you baked shortbread and bought dumplings, you shared your immense knowledge of whiskey, you read drafts, you watched this whole book progress, and you helped me to survive in more ways than I can detail here. Tara Coyle—*you* are Wonder Woman! The Philip and Muriel Berman Center for Jewish Studies has been my other home since I arrived at Lehigh. I could not be more delighted to be a part of it and to work with my Jewish Studies colleagues there, including Jessica Carr, Hartley Lachter, Nitzan Lebovic, Ben Wright, and Roslyn Weiss. The Center provided critical financial support for this research. I also received a Faculty Research Grant from Lehigh's Office of Research and Graduate Studies. At Lehigh, I owe further thanks to Kate Bullard, Marci Levine, Suzanne Edwards, Danielle Lindemann, Allison Mickel, Julia Maserjian, Allison Kanofsky, Mandy Fraley, Bill Betterman, Holly Zakos, Rob Nichols, Christa Neu, and Lori Friedman.

In my academic fields of Jewish studies and the study of religion in the Americas, I am lucky to know a host of amazing people who have helped to shape this work through conversations, immensely thoughtful readings of drafts, and digital cheerleading. To Laura Levitt: you are an amazing mentor in every sense of the word and a model of engaged scholarship who truly brings so many fields together and binds all of us up in the warmth of cashmere. I owe particular thanks to Rachel Gross, Cara Rock-Singer, Mira Sucharov, Shira Kohn, and Jessica Cooperman, who all provided feedback at crucial points in the process. This book was also shaped by conversations and correspondence, sometimes brief, sometimes lengthy, with Amy Milligan, Andrea Lieber, Chava Weissler, Anthony Petro, Samira Mehta, Ayala Fader, Lea Taragin Zeller, Vanessa Ochs, Alan Berger, Sofia Vinsce, Miri Freud-Kandel, Adam Ferziger, Naomi Seidman, Rudolf Klein, Rose Stair, Sara Hirschhorn, Rachel Gordan, Benji Rolsky, Brett Krutzsch, Courtney Bender, Ken Koltun-Fromm, Mary-Jane Rubenstein, Jennifer Caplan, Angela Tarango, Rachel McBride Lindsey, Amy DeRogatis, Isaac Weiner, Rachel Kranson, Gila Silverman, and Maria Damon. Portions of *Painted Pomegranates and Needlepoint Rabbis* benefited from presentations at the American Academy of Religion, the Association for Jewish Studies, the American Jewish Historical Society Biennial Scholars' Conference, the Oxford Summer Institute on Modern and Contemporary Judaism, the University of Kentucky, and Congregation B'rith Shalom in Bethlehem, Pennsylvania.

I am immensely grateful that *Painted Pomegranates and Needlepoint Rabbis* found a home at UNC Press. Elaine Maisner, thank you for your keen editorial insight and faith in this project from its beginning. Many thanks also to Catherine Hodorowicz and Andrew Winters. The truly constructive comments from the anonymous readers for the press were invaluable and strengthened the final book immensely.

Social media gets a bad rap sometimes, but it makes the writing process much less lonely. Some of the colleagues who read drafts are friends I first met on the Internet. I can't name everyone, but to all of the friends who have cheered on my #craftingdrafting posts on Facebook and Instagram: thank you for keeping me going.

While writing *Painted Pomegranates and Needlepoint Rabbis*, I faced a serious health crisis that imperiled this project, and much more. In that context, I need to thank many people near and far who got me and my family to this season (some names will repeat here): Rosemary Corbett, Erika Dyson, Tamar Ron Marvin, Jill Ratzan, Rabbi Rebecca Einstein Schorr, Suzanne Edwards, Jessica Schocker Zolotsky, Rabbi Moshe Re'em and Adina Re'em, Dustin and Lorena Nash, Audrey Ettinger and Michael Finley, Alicia Zahn, Shari Spark, Kathy

Zimmerman, Brian and Emily Ford, Danielle and Joshua Kroo, Alyssa Pure, Jessica and Nick Volchko, Amy Golding, Hartley Lachter and Jessica Cooperman, Cara Rock-Singer, Laura Levitt, Andrea and Zach Goldsmith, Annabella Pitkin, Khurram and Meegan Hussain, Daniela Viale and Daniel Leisawitz, Cheri Silverstein and Yariv Fadlon, Judy Lasker, Marian Gaumer, Dena Davis, Caryn Lederer, Kerri Berney, Adam Greenwald, Pamela Garretson, Amy Johansson, Keith and Diana Goldberg, Anna Margulis Bradley, Dr. Tyler Gifford, Dr. Garrett Nash, Dr. Iris H. Wei, Dr. Andrea Cercek, Natasha Pinheiro, and Joe Bacani: Thank you. There are not enough words to convey my emotions or to name all of the ways you each made this book a reality.

Finally, to my immediate family: I wouldn't be able to write without all of you. Thank you to my mother-in-law extraordinaire, Rosalie Sacks Levine, for all of her care, support, and wisdom over the years. As I've said to you many times, I'm lucky to have been born in 1978, because it means I got to marry the son of a Barnard-educated feminist, which makes all the difference in the world in more ways than one. I am also so lucky to have married into your amazing extended family, who are too numerous to thank here, but I hope they know how much I love all of them. Thank you for always being there for all of us. To my parents, Miriam and Ray Eichler: thank you for imbuing me with a love of Judaism, objects, and books. When it comes to this particular book, thank you especially for sharing your family stories and objects with me, and for all of the driving (especially in traffic!), babysitting, and emotional support these past few years have entailed. Mom, thank you for showing me what it means to make things with your hands, and that it matters. Dad, thank you for your abundant curiosity and for all of the music. I listened to a lot of it while I wrote. To Maccabee and Thalia: As Ben Folds sings, "I am the luckiest." Thank you both for understanding that all of the travel and late nights at my office are part of who I am. Thalia: you are the smartest, most beautiful, sportiest, kindest human being I know, and you always have wise advice—especially about calming down and seeing the good in the world. Maccabee: You have kept me steady for over two decades now, and I can't imagine finally closing my computer and coming home to a better partner. To infinity ... and beyond ...

# NOTES

· · · · · · · · · · ·

### PROLOGUE

1. Bennett, *Vibrant Matter*.

2. Classen, *Book of Touch*, 2.

3. Schaeffer, *Religious Affects*; Kosofsky-Sedgwick, *Touching Feeling*; Corrigan, *Feeling Religion*.

4. Levitt, *Jews and Feminism*; Joselit and Braunstein, *Getting Comfortable in New York*.

5. Hirsch, *Family Frames*, 22.

6. Although sales may of course end before this book is published, I found several versions of this rabbi for sale on eBay and Etsy in July 2019; I procured screen shots of these sales and include links in the bibliography. These three, all from canvases identical to the one my grandmother used, ranged in price from $36 to $295: "Framed Needlepoint Art Wall Hanging Jewish Rabbi Holding a Torah Scroll Judaism"; "Vintage Framed Judaica Rabbi Needlepoint Artwork"; "Vintage Needlepoint Framed Art Rabbi with Torah Judaica Artwork Wall Decor 14" × 11"."

7. Rockland, *Work of Our Hands*, 7. Tupa wrote this book under the name Mae Shafter Rockland.

8. One square was made by a much younger male cousin who later went to art school. Thanks, Miki Flores-Amper!

9. Murphy, *Zen and the Art of Knitting*; Silk, *Quilting Path*; Skolnik and MacDaniels, *Knitting Way*; Manning, *Compassionate Knitting*.

### INTRODUCTION

1. Piercy, *Art of Blessing the Day*, 3.

2. I take the idea of the "horizon" from the work of queer theorist José Esteban Muñoz. Muñoz, *Cruising Utopia*.

3. Kaplan, *Judaism as a Civilization*.

4. Cohen, *Beginnings of Jewishness*; Satlow, *Creating Judaism*. On the Protestant influence on United States culture, including that which we think of as secular, see Fessenden, *Culture and Redemption*.

5. Jewish material culture obviously extends well beyond the boundaries of North America. For a study of embroidery groups in Israel, see Salamon, *Israel in the Making*.

6. Tolkien, *Return of the King*, loc. 4055.

7. Weisenfeld, *New World A-Coming*.

8. McDannell, *Material Christianities*; Plate, *Key Terms in Material Religion*; Plate, *History of Religion in Five-and-a-Half Objects*; Morgan, *Embodied Eye*; Meyer, "Mediation and Immediacy." The journal *Material Religions* is another notable site for this burgeoning subfield.

9. Cohen, *Beginnings of Jewishness*.

10. Baker, *Jew*, 3.

11. Imhoff, *Masculinity and the Making of American Judaism*; Kelman, "Jewish Identity Ain't What It Used to Be."

12. Stavrakopolou and Barton, *Religious Diversity in Ancient Israel and Judah*. Although I had first read about the existence of nineteenth-century Jewish catechisms, including one by Isaac Leeser, a long time ago, I have learned so much more about them from important work-in-progress by Professor Laura Yares of Michigan State University.

13. Schultz, *Tri-Faith America*; Moore, *G.I. Jews*; Batnitzky, *How Judaism Became a Religion*; Cooperman, *Making Judaism Safe for America*. Cooperman carefully traces the roots of this phenomenon back into the earlier part of the twentieth century. Much of my thinking on this subject has been influenced by conference presentations by Professor Rachel Gordan, whose work on this topic is forthcoming. As Lila Corwin Berman has demonstrated, in the nineteenth century, Jewish leaders still frequently described the specialness of Jewish "blood," which they saw as a positive thing. Berman, *Speaking of Jews*.

14. Jacobson, *Roots Too*; Gilman, *Multiculturalism and the Jews*.

15. Smith, "Religion, Religions, Religious."

16. My approach to religion has been deeply influenced by scholars who follow in the spirit of sociologist Émile Durkheim's work. Though Durkheim's text is dated and includes many problematic components (such as its reliance on the notion of "the primitive"), his basic argument—that religion arises from community and that it is, in fact, the very nature of the social world, the community itself, that humans venerate (in other words, the social *is* the divinity)—remains a powerful intervention. Durkheim, *Elementary Forms of Religious Life*. On the "church of baseball," see Chidester, "Church of Baseball."

17. Lofton, *Consuming Religion*, 13.

18. Taves, *Religious Experience Reconsidered*, 16. Taves writes, "Building on Durkheim, I distinguish between things that people view as special or that they set apart, on the one hand, and the systems of belief and practices that some people associate with some special things, on the other. The former involves a simple ascription (of specialness) and the latter a composite ascription (of efficacy to practices associated with special things) characteristic of what we think of as *religions* or *spiritualities*" (17).

19. Furthermore, how we conceptualize "the secular" is deeply influenced by Protestant Christianity, especially in the United States. Fessenden, *Culture and Redemption*.

20. Ammerman, *Everyday Religion*. Although I focus on people and their objects, these flows also apply to nature (including animals and other organisms and nonbuilt objects).

21. "Religious Landscape Survey." The "religious nones" became a particularly notable category of study following the Pew Forum's major 2014 study, which found that 22.8 percent of all Americans identified as "religious nones," which include atheists, agnostics, and "nothing in particular." Scholars have shown great interest in this category of Americans while also nuancing our understanding of American religious life through qualitative work. There are many problems with describing these Americans as religious "nones," because even a cursory glance at the Pew data shows that a high percentage of "nones" engage in practices we would call religious, such as praying, suggesting that their problem is with institutional forms of religion and being pinned down to labels—not with all forms of religion and spirituality per se. For further work nuancing the notion of the "nones" (who also have increased in the General Social Survey), see Lim, Putnam, and MacGregor, "Secular and Liminal."

22. Too often, scholars in the subfield of American religions fail to consider where Jews fit in their theories and conversations, and similarly, scholars of American Jewish life do not always sufficiently consider the broader context of American religions in their work, though this is changing.

23. Rabin, *Jews on the Frontier*; Mehta, *Beyond Chrismukkah*.

24. Here I am especially influenced by Courtney Bender's work on "kitchen talk," the fluid, informal way that ideas about religion and ethnicity emerge while speakers are engaged in other tasks. Bender, *Heaven's Kitchen*.

25. Myerhoff, *Number Our Days*, 14.

26. Prell, "Barbara Myerhoff."

27. Brown, *Mama Lola*.

28. I had hoped to include many more important examples of Jewish craft and art in this book but found that I was already deluged with material. I hope to study these in future projects but note a few here for interested readers. Two are based in San Francisco: the Jewish Studio Project, led by Rabbi Adina Allen, and Atiq, founded by Adina Polen. The other is an international project, based in Canada, called Torah Stitch by Stitch, in which stitchers from all over the world cross-stitched Torah verses, which were then put together in an exhibition (the goal is eventually to stitch the entire Torah). The websites for all three of these examples are in the bibliography.

29. Magid, *American Post-Judaism*, 57–59.

30. Kelman et al., *Counting Inconsistencies*, 2.

31. Janet Walton, quoted in DeBoar, *Visual Arts in the Worshipping Church*, 181. Gadamer, *Relevance of the Beautiful*, 34–35.

32. Langlands, *Cræft*, 20.

33. *Merriam-Webster's Collegiate Dictionary*, 11th ed., s.v. "art," n., 4a.

34. Schachter, *Image, Action, and Idea in Contemporary Jewish Art*, 10–16.

35. Jefferson, "Beyond Cultural Labeling."

36. Brennan, *Transmission of Affect*.

37. A debate on this issue between Miriam Peskowitz and Carol Christ played out in the journal *Feminist Studies in Religion* and is reproduced in Castelli, *Women, Gender, Religion*, 29–48.

38. Fader and Gottlieb, "Occupy Judaism."

39. Stolow, "Introduction," 3.

40. Kaell, "Of Gifts and Grandchildren."

41. Cataneo, "Grabbing Back the Pussy."

CHAPTER 1

1. Heather Arak-Kanofsky interview.

2. Heather Arak-Kanofsky interview.

3. Kulick and Meneley, *Fat*.

4. Fletcher and Sarkar, "Psychological Resilience."

5. On race, spirituality, and resilience in African American communities, see Johnson, *Race, Religion, and Resilience in the Neoliberal Age*.

6. Tweed, *Crossing and Dwelling*, 54; Orsi, *Heaven and Earth*, 2.

7. Butler, *Gender Trouble*; Stryker and Whittle, *Transgender Studies Reader*, 12–15; McNabb, *Nonbinary Gender Identities*.

8. Levitt, "Intimate Engagements."

9. Castelli, *Women, Gender, Religion*, 29–48.

10. Unless otherwise noted, all biblical quotations are from the New Revised Standard Version of the Hebrew Bible.

11. Because it features a baby in its mother's womb, this verse is also frequently used by antiabortion activists. Runions, "Political Theologies of the Surveiled Womb?"

12. Eilberg-Schwartz, *God's Phallus*; Wolfson, "Crossing Gender Boundaries in Kabbalistic Ritual and Myth." Feminist anthropologist Carol Delaney criticizes the emphasis on masculine control of generativity and the ways that it results in male control over the fate of offspring. Delaney, *Abraham on Trial*.

13. Trishagumuri, "Willendorf Venus, 11 cm."

14. Plaskow, *Coming of Lilith*.

15. Prell, *Women Remaking American Judaism*, 1–26; Plaskow, *Standing Again at Sinai*; Adler, *Engendering Judaism*; Hyman, "Jewish Feminism Faces the American Women's Movement."

16. Butler, *Gender Trouble*; Sedgwick, *Epistemology of the Closet*; Jacobs, Thomas, and Lang, *Two-Spirit People*.

17. Fausto-Sterling, "Five Sexes, Revisited."

18. "Crafting Judaism Survey."

19. "Crafting Judaism Survey."

20. What contemporary Americans think of as a traditional mother is itself a fiction built out of post–World War II middle-class ideals that have rarely existed for the majority of Americans. Coontz, *Way We Never Were*.

21. Mishnah Shabbat 7:2.

22. Schachter, *Image, Action, and Idea in Contemporary Jewish Art*, 43.

23. Levitt, *American Jewish Loss after the Holocaust*; Khan, *Reproducing Jews*.

24. Aber, *Art of Judaic Needlework*, 2, emphasis added.

25. Heinz, *Adapting to Abundance*. It is also important to note that "Israelites" are not technically "Jews"; the institutions that become part of "normative Judaism" don't begin to develop until the Babylonian exile, at the very earliest. Some scholars would not use the term "Judaism" until the Second Temple period, or later. Cohen, *Beginnings of Jewishness*.

26. Laurel Robinson interview.

27. Antler, *You Never Call! You Never Write!*; Prell, *Fighting to Become Americans*, 21–50.

28. Gilman, *Jew's Body*.

29. Gay, *Hunger*, loc. 1313, Kindle.

30. Miller, *Comfort of Things*.

31. Louise Silk interview.

32. Jarema, "Marie Kondo Books Debate"; Land, "Class Politics of Decluttering"; Thomas, "Domesticity and Spirituality."

33. Lofton, *Consuming Religion*; Moreton, *To Serve God and Walmart*.

34. Heather Arak-Kanofsky interview.

35. Rebhum, *Jews and the American Religious Landscape*, 25–50.

36. "Art of Infertility."

37. Friedman, "When You're Facing Infertility."

38. Heather Stoltz interview.

39. Heather Stoltz interview.

40. Stoltz, "Torn (Artist vs. Mother)."

41. Stoltz, "Hanging by a Thread."

42. Stoltz, "Being Jewish Kind of Sucks Now That I'm a Mom."

43. Benjamin, *Obligated Self*, locs. 687, 500.

44. Stoltz, "Being Jewish Kind of Sucks Now That I'm a Mom."

45. This phenomenon has also uncannily overlapped with charges of sexual harassment against many of the men who produced these studies. Rosenblatt, Berman, and Stahl, "How Jewish Academia Created a #MeToo Disaster."

46. Kirshenblatt-Gimblett, "Cut That Binds."

47. Baumgarten, *Mothers and Children*, 102, 117–18.

48. Geizhals, "Rise of the Wimpel."

49. Robin Kessler Einstein interview.

50. Robin Kessler Einstein interview.

51. Wertz and Wertz, *Lying-In*.

52. Zelda interview.

53. Klassen, *Blessed Events*.

54. Cohen, *Why Aren't Jewish Women Circumcised?*; Labovitz, "Do I Have Something Yet?" Circumcision is a practice some Jews criticize for various reasons. For many Jewish feminists, the focus on the male body as the one that is essential for marking the covenant with God is yet another example of how Jewish men are privileged as the main subject of Jewish laws and personhood. More recently, some Jews have criticized circumcision for the same reason that some non-Jewish feminists criticize the procedure: because it alters a baby's body, removing sensitive flesh, without the child's consent to have his body modified. Some Jews (numbers are not available, but likely a minority) have developed new ceremonies such as a *b'rit shalom* (covenant of peace) as an alternative to circumcision. Ingall, "To Cut or Not to Cut."

55. Delaney, *Abraham on Trial*; Zierler, "In Search of a Feminist Reading of the Akedah."

56. Robin Kessler Einstein interview.

57. Barthes, *Camera Lucida*, 26.

58. Peachy Levy interview.

59. Cvetkovitch, *Depression*, locs. 2437, 2411.

60. Schaefer, *Religious Affects*; Corrigan, *Feeling Religion*.

61. Schaeffer, *Evolution of Affect Theory*, 3.

62. Thompson, *Jewish on Their Own Terms*, 1–20; Rosenblatt, Berman, and Stahl, "How Jewish Academia Created a #MeToo Disaster." For an earlier iteration of a continuity crisis, see Sanua, *Let Us Prove Strong*, 100–134.

63. "Crafting Judaism Survey."

64. Flora Rosefsky interview.

65. Zelda interview.

66. Weissler, "Art *Is* Spirituality."

67. Schaefer, "Beautiful Facts," 69.

68. Imhoff, *Masculinity and American Judaism*, 158.

69. For an important history of the progress of gender studies in American religion, see Petro, "Race, Gender, Sexuality, and Religion in North America."

70. Griffith, *Born Again Bodies*; Strings, *Fearing the Black Body*.

71. McDannell, *Material Christianity*, 272.

72. Kirshenblatt-Gimblett, "The Cut That Binds."

73. Roof, *Spiritual Marketplace*.

CHAPTER 2

1. Mishnah Pirkei Avot 5:22; Amanda interview.

2. Milgram, *Handmade Midrash*.

3. Stolow, "Introduction," 14–16.

4. Smith, *Body of the Artisan*, 6.

5. Stolow, "Introduction," 3.

6. Stolow, "Introduction," 5.

7. Barber, *Women's Work*, 42–70.

8. Peskowitz, *Spinning Fantasies*, 13.

9. Mendelsohn, *Rag Race*; Barber, *Women's Work*.

10. Perlmutter, *Gefiltequilt*; Jacobs, *Sarah in NYC*.

11. Jacobs, *Sarah in NYC*.

12. Jacobs, "Black and White Fire."

13. Jacobs, "Black and White Fire."

14. Jacobs, "Black and White Fire."

15. Jacobs, "Black and White Fire."

16. Rashi on Song of Songs 5:16 and Devarim (Deuteronomy) 33:2. For examples from kabbalah, see Idel, *Absorbing Perfections*, 47.

17. Walton, "Lilith's Daughters, Miriam's Chorus."

18. At least, that is Jonathan Rosen's argument in *The Talmud and the Internet*, a book that is elegant and yet already dated—it was published in the year 2000, an aeon in Internet age. The comparison may not *entirely* hold up, but it is an interesting one with which to think.

19. Wagner, *Godwired*, 16.

20. I do not want to essentialize women's experiences: they vary widely. There is no stable category of women's experiences, although many of my informants would argue the opposite.

21. Drucker, *White Fire*, xii.

22. Jacobs, "Domestic Science."

23. Jacobs, "Some Additional Thoughts about Our Mother's Linens."

24. "Kohenet Hebrew Priestess Institute." The institute trains cohorts of women—inclusive of trans and genderqueer individuals who want to take part—to officiate rituals, provide guidance, become Jewish educators, pursue activism, and take part in a variety of other fields.

25. Lesser, *devotaj*.

26. Lesser, "Custom Healing Bundle Amulet."

27. Lesser, "Evil Eye Amulet."

28. Ketzirah Lesser interview.

29. Ketzirah Lesser interview.

30. Ketzirah, "Looks So Cool."

31. Ochs, *Inventing Jewish Ritual*, 5–7.

32. Ketzirah Lesser interview.

33. On transmitting the divine, see Bender, *New Metaphysicals*, 93–94.

34. Sarah Jacobs interview. On the history of spiritual transmission as it intertwines with electricity in American history, see Stolow, "Spiritual Nervous System," 85.

35. McCluskey, "This Man Who Knits Sweaters to Match Landmarks."

36. Holson, "It's Sweater Weather Forever."

37. Holson, "It's Sweater Weather Forever."

38. O'Molloy, "The Man Who Turns Scenery into Sweaters."

39. Benjamin, *Illuminations*, 221–23.

40. Shimoni, "The Baltimore Knitter Who Unraveled the Internet."

41. Zax, "Man Who Made Those Viral Sweaters"; Hafford, "Your New Hero Knits Sweaters of Places."

42. Quoted and reproduced in Hafford, "Your New Hero Knits Sweaters of Places."

43. Kelner, *Tours that Bind*.

44. Stoil, "The Baltimore Knitter Who Unraveled the Internet."

45. Macdonald, *No Idle Hands*; Franger, "Survival-Empowerment-Courage."

46. Cataneo, "Grabbing Back the Pussy."

47. Fader and Gottlieb, "Occupy Judaism."

48. Cataneo, "Grabbing Back the Pussy."

49. Cataneo, "Grabbing Back the Pussy."

50. Jayna Zweiman, foreword to Mandell, *Crafting Dissent*, xiv.

51. "Jennifer" interview.

52. Cataneo, "Grabbing Back the Pussy."

53. Bender, "Studying Up."

54. Key—but by no means exhaustive—examples of the "lived religions" approach include Orsi, *Maddona of 115th St.*; Bender, *Heaven's Kitchen*; and Hall, *Lived Religion in America*.

55. Oringel, "Secret Jewish History of the Pussyhat."

56. Jacobs, Twitter thread.

57. Peskowitz, *Spinning Fantasies*, 49–76.

58. In the academic world, one of the more famous such debates took place between Miriam Peskowitz and Carol Christ, both formidable scholars who had a spirited back and forth about women and work by hand, in the *Journal of Feminist Studies in Religion*. The debate was reproduced fully in Castelli, *Women, Gender, Religion*.

59. Kimmelman and Leavitt, "American Women Crafting Cloth," 55.

60. "Quiltropolis."

61. Kezirah Lesser interview.

62. "Danielle" interview.

63. Cathy Perlmutter interview. On messianic Jews, see Kaell and Imhoff, "Lineage Matters."

64. I have been given permission to cite the *Paper Pomegranate* in my research; it is an astounding archive.

65. Kimmelman and Leavitt, "American Women Crafting Cloth," 56.

66. Minahan and Cox, "Stitch 'n Bitch," 11, 18.

67. Three of the most prominent scholars in this field are Heidi Campbell, Stewart Hoover, and Nabil Echchaibi. See especially Campbell, "Understanding the Relationship between Religion Online and Offline"; Campbell, *Digital Religion*; Echchaibi and Hoover, "Media Theory"; and Hoover, *Media and Religious Authority*.

68. Kimmelman and Leavitt, "American Women Crafting Cloth," do not do this, but some of the sources they cite do.

69. Modern, "eBay and the Historical Imagination."

70. Sometimes, I annotate in red using an Apple Pencil on my iPad—a simulation worthy of its own examination.

CHAPTER 3

1. Josephson, "Empowered World," 117. Josephson argues that in premodern Japan, "empowered prayer was an important therapeutic technology" (118).

2. Laurel Robinson interview, May 20, 2017.

3. Laurel Robinson interview.

4. Laurel Robinson interview.

5. Douglas, foreword to Marcel Mauss, x.

6. "Purim: The Rowdiest Day of the Year."

7. Laurel Robinson interview.

8. Paine, *Religious Objects in Museums*, 113.

9. Gross, *Beyond the Synagogue*.

10. Berlin, "Book of Esther and Ancient Storytelling"; Beal, *Book of Hiding*.

11. Laurel Robinson interview.

12. Ulrich, *Age of Homespun*, 29.

13. Kranson, *Ambivalent Embrace*, 15.

14. Joselit, *Wonders of America*, 102.

15. Kranson, *Ambivalent Embrace*, 138.

16. Kranson, *Ambivalent Embrace*, 156–57.

17. Strassfeld and Strassfeld, *Second Jewish Catalog*, 322.

18. Chidester, *Authentic Fakes*, 5.

19. Chidester, *Authentic Fakes*, 48.

20. Shuman, "Ritual Exchange and Excess Meaning," 504.

21. Ulrich, *Age of Homespun*.

22. "Dana" interview.

23. Amanda interview.

24. Laura interview.

25. Bartra, *Crafting Gender*, 162.

26. Lindsey, *Communion of Shadows*, 64–112.

27. Rockland, *Work of Our Hands*, 7.

28. Bergson, *Matter and Memory*, 24.

29. Zelda interview.

30. Kaell, "Of Gifts and Grandchildren," 134.

31. "Crafting Judaism Survey."

32. "Crafting Judaism Survey."

33. "Crafting Judaism Survey."

34. Gross, "People of the Picture Book"; Kornfeld, "Revaluing Story Time."

35. Kelner, *Tours That Bind*.

36. Chidester, *Authentic Fakes*, vii.

37. Bataille, *Visions of Excess*, 118.

38. "Crafting Judaism Survey."

39. "Crafting Judaism Survey."

40. "Crafting Judaism Survey."

41. "Crafting Judaism Survey."

42. *Oxford English Dictionary*, s.v. "precious."

43. Geraldine Weichman interview.

44. "Gertrude" interview.

45. Bonnie Vorspan interview.

46. "Maya" interview.

47. "Maya" interview.

48. "Maya" interview.

49. Sandra Lachter interview.

50. Heather Stoltz interview.

51. Stoltz, "Flinging Prayer."

52. Maurette, *Forgotten Sense*, 5.

53. Kaell, "Of Gifts and Grandchildren," 133.

CHAPTER 4

1. Oldenburg, *Great Good Place*; Oldenburg, *Celebrating the Third Place*; Tweed, *Crossing and Dwelling*, 57.

2. *Paper Pomegranate* 1, no. 1:1. This microhistory of the Pomegranate Guild is drawn from a combination of sources, including the entire forty-plus year archive of the group's newsletters, the group's website, and interviews with members.

3. *Paper Pomegranate* 1, no. 2.

4. *Paper Pomegranate* 1, no. 1:3.

5. *Paper Pomegranate* 1, no. 2:1–2.

6. *Paper Pomegranate* 1, no. 2:6.

7. *Paper Pomegranate* 4, no. 3:2.

8. Geraldine Weichman interview, April 16, 2017.

9. "About the Guild."

10. "About the Guild."

11. "About the Guild."

12. Bonnie Vorspan interview.

13. Sandra Lachter interview.

14. Sandra Lachter interview.

15. Geraldine Weichman interview.

16. Magid, *American Post-Judaism*, 59.

17. On denominations, see Diner, *New Promised Land*, 97–102; and Sarna, *American Judaism*, 282–93. Denominations also developed in nineteenth-century Germany and are present in many countries, but they became particularly pronounced in the United States due to the influence of Christianity's vibrant denominational growth in a nation with no state church.

18. Wertheimer, *New American Judaism*, 10. To demonstrate their fluidity and variance, Wertheimer includes the examples of Reform Jews reinserting prostration into worship during the Great Aleinu prayer and Conservative Jews doing mindfulness.

19. Weissler, *Making Judaism Meaningful*.

20. Hazon, "Hazon." Other examples of such organizations include Jewish Farm School and Urban Adamah. Sack-Pikus, "Outsider Looks at the Jewish Genealogy Phenomenon." On the Jewish food movement and some approaches to remaking agriculture, see Krone, "Shmita Manifesto."

21. Goldstein, *Price of Whiteness*; Brodkin, *How Jews Became White Folks*; Kaye/Kantrowitz, *Colors of Jews*.

22. Kelman et al., *Counting Inconsistencies*.

23. Parfitt, *Jews of Africa*.

24. Rock-Singer, "Chicken Soup."

25. Bonnie Vorspan interview.

26. Bonnie Vorspan interview.

27. Cathy Perlmutter interview.

28. "Stacey" interview.

29. Lindi interview.

30. Arlene Diane Spector interview.

31. Mehta, *Beyond Chrismukkah*, 83, 123, 136–60; Krutzsch, "Editor's Letter."

32. Plaut, *Kosher Christmas*, 3–4.

33. "Stacey" interview.

34. Peachy Levy interview.

35. Levy, *Threads of Judaism*; "Torah Mantle"; *Peachy Levy: Threads of Judaism*.

36. Antler, *Jewish Radical Feminism*; Diner, Kohn, and Kranson, *Jewish Feminine Mystique*.

37. Kelman, "Reading a Book Like an Object," loc. 2826.

38. Bonnie Vorspan interview.

39. Ammerman, *Everyday Religion*.

40. Oldenberg, *Great Good Place*.

41. On the history of women's advancement in various movements, see Prell, *Women Remaking American Judaism*, 109–230.

42. Bender, *Heaven's Kitchen*, 90–116.

43. "Jan" interview, October 17, 2018.

44. Berman, "Jewish History beyond the Jewish People," 274.

45. Parker, *Subversive Stitch*, 15.

46. "Prayer Shawl Ministry Home Page."

47. Bowman, *Prayer Shawl Ministries*, xxxii.

48. Bowman, *Prayer Shawl Ministries*, 85.

49. Bowman, *Prayer Shawl Ministries*, 43.

50. Jorgenson and Izard, *Knitting into the Mystery*, 51.

51. Bowman, *Prayer Shawl Ministries*, 66–74.

52. Bowman, *Prayer Shawl Ministries*, 27.

53. Bowman, *Prayer Shawl Ministries*, 79.

54. Boyarin, *Unheroic Conduct*.

55. Flora Rosefsky interview, May 22, 2017.

56. "Prayer Shawl Ministry Home Page."

57. On ancient examples, see Peskowitz, *Spinning Fantasies*. On medieval and early modern examples, see Parker, *Subversive Stitch*.

58. Quoted in Parker, *Subversive Stitch*, xix.

59. Masuzawa, *In Search of Dreamtime*.

60. Pike, *New Age and Neopagan Religions in America*.

61. Wilcox, *Queer Nuns*; Bender, *New Metaphysicals*; Cooperman, *Fighting to Make Judaism Safe for America*; Krutzsch, *Dying to Be Normal*; Mehta, *Beyond Chrismukkah*.

62. Brennan, *Transmission of Affect*.

63. Translations here are from the Jewish Publication Society, rather than the NRSV.

CHAPTER 5

1. Macdonald, *No Idle Hands*, 33.

2. Macdonald, *No Idle Hands*, 35.

3. Sturken, *Tangled Memories*, 185–86.

4. Kimmelman and Leavitt, "American Women Crafting Cloth," 59.

5. Greer, "Craftivism."

6. Greer, "A Look at the Social Justice Sewing Academy!"

7. Fisk, "To Make, and Make Again," 172.

8. Draguca, "Interview with Jayna Zweiman."

9. Devine, "Honoring International Women's Day."

10. Imhoff, "Why Disability Studies Needs to Take Religion Seriously."

11. Cataneo, "Grabbing Back the Pussy."

12. Oringel, "Secret Jewish History of the Pussyhat."

13. Bowman, "Love Trumps Hate," 118.

14. "Lily," email communication with author, May 15, 2019.

15. Maryann, email communication with author, May 15, 2019.

16. Markus, "Craftivism from Philomena to the Pussyhat," 24.

17. "Dana" interview.

18. Anonymous interview, May 9, 2017.

19. Markus, "Craftivism from Philomena to the Pussyhat," 22.

20. Lang, "Women's March in Year 3"; North, "Women's March Changed the American Left"; Vesoulis, "Women First Marched to Challenge Trump"; Ziri, "To March or Not to March?"

21. Antler, *Jewish Radical Feminism*, 349.

22. Quoted in Kaplan, *Abraham Joshua Heschel*, 225.

23. Bernstein, "Pussy Hats Galore."

24. Cvetkovitch, *Depression*, loc. 2033.

25. Cvetkovitch, *Depression*, loc. 2203.

26. Markus, "Through the Eye of a Needle."

27. Cvetkovitch, *Depression*, loc. 2118.

28. Roberston, Mele, and Tavernise, "11 Killed in Synagogue Shooting."

29. Bondarenko, "Jews Chant 'We've Seen This Before'"; Wofford, "In a Time of Trump"; "We've Seen This Before."

30. Hinda Mandell interview.

31. Hinda Mandell interview.

32. Facebook group, "Jewish Hearts for Pittsburgh."

33. Hinda Mandell interview.

34. Hinda Mandell interview.

35. Ellen Dominus Broude interview.

36. Ellen Dominus Broude interview.

37. Facebook communication from member of Jewish Hearts for Pittsburgh group, May 2019.

38. Ellen Dominus Broude interview.

39. "Linda," email communication with author, May 15, 2019.

40. Ellen Dominus Broude interview; Pitz, "Crafters Create Jewish Hearts for Pittsburgh."

41. Jewish Hearts for Pittsburgh.

42. Bender, *New Metaphysicals*, 1–5, 36.

43. Pitz, "Crafters Create Jewish Hearts for Pittsburgh."

44. Jewish Hearts for Pittsburgh.

45. Hinda Mandell interview.

46. Ellen Dominus Broude interview.

47. Hinda Mandell interview.

48. "Anti-Semitic Incidents Remained at Near-Historic Levels in 2018."

49. Email communication with author, May 14, 2019.

50. Rachel Kranson, email communication with author, December 6, 2018.

51. Tabachnik, "'Jewish Hearts' Spread Message of Love throughout City."

52. "Global Outpouring Fuels 'Jewish Hearts for Pittsburgh' Program."

53. Ellen Dominus Broude interview.

54. Facebook communication, "Elizabeth," May 15, 2019.

55. Stoltz, "Dark Days."

56. Heather Stoltz interview.

57. Stoltz, "Shattered Childhood."

58. Heather Stoltz interview.

59. Heather Stoltz interview.

60. Heather Stoltz interview.

61. Linda Schwartz interview.

62. Schwartz's political vantage point has a context; she fits within decades of twentieth-century Jewish American liberalism. See, for example, Dollinger, *Quest for Inclusion*.

63. Peachy Levy interview.

64. Petro, "Ray Navarro's Jesus Camp," 923.

65. Literat and Balsamo, "Stitching the Future of the AIDS Quilt," 139.

66. Krutzsch, *Dying to Be Normal*, 25–28; Literat and Balsamo, "Stitching the Future of the AIDS Quilt," 139–40.

67. Wilcox, *Queer Nuns*, 138.

68. Wilcox, *Queer Nuns*, 86.

69. Bryan-Wilson, *Fray*, 272.

CHAPTER 6

1. Geraldine Weichman interview.

2. Diner, *We Remember with Reverence and Love.* Diner's landmark study brought to light how discourse around the destruction of European Jewry had in fact been important to American Jews soon after World War II, whereas previous historiography had placed its importance later, in the 1960s and 1970s.

3. Linenthal, *Preserving Memory*; Weissman, *Fantasies of Witnessing*; Flanzbaum, *Americanization of the Holocaust*.

4. Geraldine Weichman interview.

5. For a criticism of this trope, see Levitt, *American Jewish Loss after the Holocaust*, 177. I have criticized this biologically driven, teleological argument elsewhere, asking that we consider other ways of conceiving of futures. Eichler-Levine, *Suffer the Little Children*, 3.

6. Geraldine Weichman interview, April 16, 2017.

7. Levitt, *American Jewish Loss after the Holocaust*.

8. Bonnie Vorspan interview.

9. Bonnie Vorspan interview.

10. Cathy Perlmutter interview.

11. Conneen, "Silver Spring Woman Inspired."

12. "Cherished Object"; "Handknit Sweater Worn by a Young Girl"; Blakemore, "Hand Knit Sweater."

13. Stern, "Green Sweater."

14. Conneen, "Silver Spring Woman Inspired."

15. Conneen, "Silver Spring Woman Inspired."

16. Conneen, "Silver Spring Woman Inspired."

17. Krystyna Chiger wrote a memoir by this title: *The Girl in the Green Sweater: A Life in Holocaust's Shadow.*

18. Stern, "Green Sweater."

19. Ghert-Zand, "Knitters Worldwide Recreate Sweater."

20. Weissman, *Fantasies of Witnessing.*

21. "Green Sweater Survived the Holocaust."

22. Art of Life Clay.

23. Kirshenblatt-Gimblett and Shandler, *Anne Frank Unbound*, 7.

24. Six Million Stitches Project.

25. Eckerling, "Embroidering the Past." Exhibitions of Stroebel's work are opening as this book goes to press, and a book on her work is slated to appear shortly before this one.

26. Raphael, *Female Face of God at Auschwitz*, 140.

27. Raphael, *Female Face of God at Auschwitz*, 141.

28. "Stacey" interview. "Tallis" is the Yiddish/Ashkenazi pronunciation of the Hebrew word *tallit*. The use of an ending "t" reflects a speaker whose pronunciation was more influenced by modern Israeli Hebrew. Some Jews toggle back and forth between pronunciations.

29. Laurel Robinson interview.

30. Ahmed, *Cultural Politics of Emotion*, 84.

31. Kiracofe, Johnson, and Huff, *American Quilt*, 170.

32. Silk, *Quilting Path*, ix.

33. Silk, *Quilting Path*, 129.

34. Silk, "Memory Quilts."

35. Silk, *Quilting Path*, 131.

36. Silk, *Quilting Path*, 132.

37. Ochs, *Inventing Jewish Ritual*, 5.

38. Stallybrass, "Worn Worlds," 36. Stallybrass draws this wordplay from the work of Elaine Hedges.

39. Louise Silk interview.

40. Louise Silk interview.

41. Stallybrass, "Worn Worlds," 28, 30.

42. Perlmutter, "Memorial Quilt from Tee Shirts."

43. Perlmutter, "Memorial Quilt from Tee Shirts."

44. Quoted in Classen, *Deepest Sense*, 83.

45. Classen, *Deepest Sense*, 138.

46. Classen, "Touch in the Museum," 275–86.

47. Chen, *Animacies*, 1–12.

48. Chen, *Animacies*, 24.

49. Bennett, *Vibrant Matter*. Bennett, in turn, is drawing upon work by philosopher Bruno Latour.

50. Bonnie Vorspan interview.

51. Bonnie Vorspan interview.

52. Bennett, *Vibrant Matter*, 6.

53. Bennett, *Vibrant Matter*, 4.

54. Tweed, *Crossing and Dwelling*, 54.

55. Mendelsohn, *Rag Race*, 8.

56. Taylor, *All-of-a-Kind Family*; Marshall, *Grandma Rose's Magic*; Edwards, *Hat for Mrs. Goldman*; Haddox, *Uprising*; "Remember the Triangle Fire Coalition."

57. "Danielle" interview.

58. Anonymous interview.

59. Laura interview.

60. "Crafting Judaism Survey."

61. Sandra Lachter interview.

62. Rabbi Melody Davis interview.

63. Amanda interview.

64. Arlene Spector interview.

65. Cathy Perlmutter interview.

66. Cathy Perlmutter interview.

67. Roughly 31 percent of American Jews report belonging to a synagogue; among Jews age 18–49, the number is 27 percent. Pew Research Center Survey of U.S. Jews, 60.

68. Zumbach, "Growing Arts and Crafts Market"; Dobush, "Crafter's Paradise."

69. Perez, *Religion in the Kitchen*.

70. Morgan, *Embodied Eye*, 147.

CONCLUSION

1. Myerhoff, *Number Our Days*, 263.

2. Myerhoff, *Number Our Days*, 267–68.

3. Zelda interview, April 18, 2017.

4. Cohen in *Paper Pomegranate* 5, no. 2:10–11.

5. Myerhoff, *Number Our Days*, 144.

# BIBLIOGRAPHY

. . . . . . . . . . . . . . . . . . . .

PRIMARY SOURCES

*Interviews*

Amanda, May 8, 2017, Silver Spring, Md.

Anonymous, May 9, 2017

Heather Arak-Kanofsky, October 5, 2016, Pen Argyl, Pa.

Ellen Dominus Broude, December 11, 2018, telephone

"Dana," May 8, 2017, Washington, D.C.

"Danielle," May 9, 2017, Arlington, Va.

Rabbi Melody Davis, May 3, 2017, Easton, Pa.

Robin Kessler Einstein, April 17, 2017, Orange County, Calif.

"Gertrude," April 17, 2017, Los Angeles

Sarah Jacobs, May 5, 2017, New York

"Jan," October 17, 2018, Nazareth, Pa.

"Jennifer," March 20, 2017, Allentown, Pa.

Sandra Lachter, August 9, 2017, Allentown, Pa.

Laura, January 26, 2018, Pen Argyl, Pa.

Ketzirah Lesser, May 9, 2017, Washington, D.C.

Peachy Levy, April 16, 2017, Los Angeles

Lindi, May 21, 2017, Atlanta, Ga.

Hinda Mandell, January 3, 2019, telephone

"Maya," May 17, 2016, Kutztown, Pa.

Cathy Perlmutter, April 17, 2017, Pasadena, Calif.

Laurel Robinson, May 20, 2017, Macon, Ga.

Flora Rosefsky, May 22, 2017, Atlanta

Linda Schwartz, February 22, 2017, Easton, Pa.

Louise Silk, February 23, 2017, Center Valley, Pa.

Arlene Diane Spector, February 23, 2018, Philadelphia

"Stacey," May 22, 2017, Atlanta

Heather Stoltz, January 17, 2018, New York

Bonnie Vorspan, April 18, 2017, San Fernando Valley, Calif.

Geraldine Weichman, April 16, 2017, Los Angeles

Zelda, April 18, 2017, Los Angeles


*Survey Data*

"Crafting Judaism Survey." Although I closed this survey in late 2016, the
questions can be found on the original Google Forms site I used at the link

below. I used this survey as a way of gathering initial data on what kinds of Jewish creative ventures were out there (early on, I considered including areas like music and dance, then quickly realized that would not be feasible). When I began this project, my goal was to study anyone who identified on the gender spectrum somewhere approaching "woman." Thus, I included survey boxes for genderqueer and other nonbinary identities but did not solicit men, though a few responded anyway; ultimately, as I moved through my research, I decided it was also important to consider a few men in this project, though it remained primarily about individuals who identify as women. The survey was a first foray into seeing what big themes were out there—and if there were a lot of people doing creative ventures. It also allowed me to see which forms of creativity were most popular; I eventually narrowed this study to the fiber arts and a few other tactile forms of creativity, such as ceramics. https://docs.google .com/forms/d/1tvH_aDtj4NJJRROZIbj8Pb1C8nV7MWJfjYTCjXJ-jTQ.

*Other Primary Sources*

Aber, Ita. *The Art of Judaic Needlework: Traditional and Contemporary Designs*. New York: Charles Scribner's Sons, 1979.

"About the Guild." Pomegranate Guild of Judaic Needlework. https://www .pomegranateguild.org/about.html.

"Anti-Semitic Incidents Remained at Near-Historic Levels in 2018; Assaults against Jews More Than Doubled." *ADL*, April 30, 2019. https://www .adl.org/news/press-releases/anti-semitic-incidents-remained-at-near -historic-levels-in-2018-assaults.

The ART of Infertility. http://www.artofinfertility.org/#!/info/artwork/untitled.

Art of Life Clay. https://www.etsy.com/shop/LindaSchwartzCeramic.

Atiq Jewish Maker Institute. https://www.atiqmakers.org.

Bernstein, Nat. "Pussy Hats Galore." *Jewcy*, January 31, 2017. http://jewcy.com /jewish-social-justice/pussy-hats-galore.

Blakemore, Erin. "The Hand Knit Sweater That Helped a Little Girl Survive the Holocaust." *History Stories*, July 31, 2018. https://www.history.com /news/sweater-holocaust-girl-survivor.

Bondarenko, Veronika. "Jews Chant 'We've Seen This Before' as Protest Campaign against Donald Trump Kicks Off." *Forward*, June 22, 2016. https://forward.com/news/breaking-news/343179/jews-chant-weve-seen -t-in-trump-tower-demonstration-as-bend-the-arc-kicks-o.

Braun, Rachel. *Embroidery and Sacred Text: New Designs in Judaic Needlework*. Pennsauken, NJ: BookBaby, 2016.

Cataneo, Emily. "Grabbing Back the Pussy: An Interview with Jayna Zweiman on the Pussy Hat Movement." *Jewish Women, Amplified* (blog), March 14, 2017. https://jwa.org/blog/grabbing-back-pussy-architects-of-pussy-hat -movement-speaks-out.

"A Cherished Object: Kristine Keren's Green Sweater." *Curators Corner* (blog), United States Holocaust Memorial Museum. https://www.ushmm.org /collections/the-museums-collections/curators-corner/a-cherished-object -kristine-kerens-green-sweater.

Chiger, Krystyna, with Daniel Reiser. *The Girl in the Green Sweater: A Life in Holocaust's Shadow*. New York: St. Martin's, 2012.

Conneen, Mike. "Silver Spring Woman Inspired by Holocaust Survivor's Knitted Sweater." *WJLA*, May 27, 2015. https://wjla.com/news/local /silver-spring-woman-inspired-by-holocaust-survivor-s-knitted-sweater -114307.

Devine, Anna. "Honoring International Women's Day: Q&A with Pussyhat Project Co-Founder Jayna Zweiman." *Harvard University Graduate School of Design* (blog), March 8, 2017. https://www.gsd.harvard.edu/2017/03 /pussyhat-project-interview.

Dobush, Grace. "Crafter's Paradise." *Quartz*, April 4, 2017. https://qz.com /928235/the-business-of-creativity-is-worth-44-billion.

Draguca, Brianna. "An Interview with Jayna Zweiman, Founder of the Pussyhat Project Inspired by the Women's March." *Teen Vogue*, January 21, 2017. https://www.teenvogue.com/story/pussyhat-project-womens-march -jayna-zweiman-interview.

Edwards, Michelle. *A Hat for Mrs. Goldman*. Illustrated by G. Brian Kas. New York: Schwarz and Wade, 2016.

"Framed Needlepoint Art Wall Hanging Jewish Rabbi Holding a Torah Scroll Judaism." Item for sale on eBay, accessed July 29, 2019. https://www.ebay .com (no longer available).

Friedman, Ruth Balinsky. "When You're Facing Infertility, a Synagogue Can Be the Most Painful Place to Go; Let's Change That." *Washington Post*, March 30, 2016.

Geizhals, Rachel. "The Rise of the Wimpel." *Forward*, June 2, 2010. https:// forward.com/articles/128478/the-rise-of-the-wimpel.

Ghert-Zand, Renee. "Knitters Worldwide Recreate Sweater Worn by Girl Who Survived Holocaust in Sewer." *Times of Israel*, October 22, 2019. https:// www.timesofisrael.com/knitters-worldwide-recreate-sweater-worn-by -girl-who-survived-holocaust-in-sewer.

"Global Outpouring Fuels 'Jewish Hearts for Pittsburgh' Program." *WPXI*, accessed May 20, 2019. https://www.wpxi.com (video no longer available).

"The Green Sweater Survived the Holocaust." *Ravelry* discussion board, accessed July 27, 2019. https://www.ravelry.com/discuss/jewish-fiberaholics /3239734.

Greer, Betsy. "Craftivism: Definition." *Craftivism* (blog), http://craftivism.com /definition.

———. "A Look at the Social Justice Sewing Academy!" *Craftivism* (blog),

June 10, 2017. http://craftivism.com/blog/look-social-justice-sewing
-academy.

Haddox, Margaret Peterson. *Uprising*. New York: Simon and Schuster, 2011.

Hafford. "Your New Hero Knits Sweaters of Places and Then Goes to Those
Places." *Refinery 29*, January 8, 2017. https://www.refinery29.com/en
-us/2017/01/135270/guy-knits-sweaters-places-photos-visit.

"Handknit Sweater Worn by a Young Girl while Hiding in the Lvov Sewers."
United States Holocaust Memorial Museum. https://collections.ushmm
.org/search/catalog/irn515606.

"Hazon." Hazon. https://hazon.org.

Holson, Laura M. "It's Sweater Weather Forever." *New York Times*, April 3,
2018.

The Jewish Studio Project. https://www.jewishstudioproject.org.

Jacobs, Jill. Twitter thread, June 26, 2019. https://twitter.com/rabbijilljacobs
/status/1144029098924109825.

Jacobs, Sarah. "Black and White Fire." *Sarah in NYC* (blog), March 14, 2017.
https://sewnewyork.blogspot.com/2017/03/yesterday-my-case-of-yucks
-had.html.

———. "Domestic Science." *Sarah in NYC* (blog), April 26, 2017. http://
sewnewyork.blogspot.com/2017/04/domestic-science.html.

———. *Sarah in NYC* (blog). http://sewnewyork.blogspot.com.

———. "Some Additional Thoughts about Our Mother's Linens." *Sarah in
NYC* (blog), April 9, 2017. http://sewnewyork.blogspot.com/2017/04/some
-additional-thoughts-about-our.html.

Jarema, Kerri. "The Marie Kondo Books Debate Has Classist Racist
Undertones That Can't Be Ignored." *Bustle*, January 15, 2019. https://
www.bustle.com/p/the-marie-kondo-books-debate-has-classist-racist
-undertones-that-cant-be-ignored-15796044.

Jewish Hearts for Pittsburgh. Facebook group. https://www.facebook.com
/groups/1152904931542954.

Jorgenson, Susan S., and Susan S. Izard. *Knitting into the Mystery: A Guide to
the Shawl-Knitting Ministry*. Harrisburg, Pa.: Morehouse, 2003.

Kohenet Hebrew Priestess Institute. http://www.kohenet.com.

Land, Stephanie. "The Class Politics of Decluttering." *New York Times*, July 18,
2016.

Lang, Marisa J. "The Women's March in Year 3." *Washington Post*, January 18,
2019.

Lesser, Ketzirah. "Custom Healing Bundle Amulet." Item for sale at *devotaj* on
Etsy, accessed May 28, 2017. https://www.etsy.com (no longer available).

———. *devotaj* (blog). http://devotaj.tumblr.com.

———. "Evil Eye Amulet." Item for sale at *devotaj* on Etsy, accessed May 28,
2017. https://www.etsy.com (no longer available).

———. "Looks So Cool . . . ." https://www.instagram.com/p/BUcVQt3AerS.

Manning, Tara Jon. *Compassionate Knitting: Inviting Contemplative Practice to the Craft*. Boston: Tuttle Books, 2004.

Marshall, Linda Elovitz. *Grandma Rose's Magic*. Minneapolis, Minn.: Kar-Ben, 2014.

McCluskey, Megan. "This Man Who Knits Sweaters to Match Landmarks Is the Hero the Internet Needed." *Time*, April 4, 2018.

Milgram, Jo. *Handmade Midrash: Workshop in Visual Theology*. Philadelphia: Jewish Publication Society, 1992.

Murphy, Benadette. *Zen and the Art of Knitting: Exploring the Links between Knitting, Spirituality, and Creativity*. Avon, Mass.: Adams Media, 2002.

North, Anna. "The Women's March Changed the American Left." *Vox*, December 21, 2018. https://www.vox.com/identities/2018/12/21/18145176 /feminism-womens-march-2018-2019-farrakhan-intersectionality.

O'Molloy, Colm. "The Man Who Turns Scenery into Sweaters." *BBC*, February 13, 2017. https://www.bbc.com/news/av/world-us-canada-38960970/the -man-who-turns-scenery-into-sweaters.

Oringel, Amy. "The Secret Jewish History of the Pussyhat." *Forward*, March 7, 2017. http://forward.com/culture/365099/the-secret-jewish-history-of -the-pussyhat.

*Paper Pomegranate* 1, no. 1 (June 1977); 1, no. 2 (September 1977); 4, no. 3 (December 1980); 5, no. 2 (September 1981).

*Peachy Levy: Threads of Judaism*. Foreword by Rabbi David Ellenson, essays by Rabbi Norman J. Cohen and Laura Kruger. Exh. cat. New York: Hebrew Union College, Jewish Institute of Religion, 2007. http://huc.edu/research /museums/huc-jir-museum-new-york/exhibition-archive/peachy-levy -threads-judaism.

Perlmutter, Cathy. *GefilteQuilt* (blog). http://gefiltequilt.blogspot.com.

———. "Memorial Quilt from Tee Shirts, Button Down Shirts, and a Bedsheet (or Two)." *Gefiltequilt* (blog), May 7, 2017. https://gefiltequilt.blogspot.com /2017/05/memorial-quilt-from-tee-shirts-button.html.

Piercy, Marge. *The Art of Blessing the Day: Poems with a Jewish Theme*. New York: Alfred A. Knopf, 2007.

Pitz, Marylynne. "Crafters Create Jewish Hearts for Pittsburgh and More Than 40 Volunteers Hang Them in City." *Pittsburgh Post-Gazette*, November 17, 2018.

"Prayer Shawl Ministry Home Page." The Prayer Shawl Ministry. https://www .shawlministry.com.

"Purim: The Rowdiest Day of the Year." *Jewish Museum* (blog), February 16, 2017. https://stories.thejewishmuseum.org/purim-the-rowdiest-day-of -the-year-1807d56b1ab7.

Quiltropolis. http://www.quiltropolis.net/default.htm.

Remember the Triangle Fire Coalition. http://rememberthetrianglefire.org.

Robertson, Campbell, Christopher Mele, and Sabrina Tavernise. "11 Killed in Synagogue Massacre." *New York Times*, October 27, 2018.

Rockland, Mae Shafter. *The Work of Our Hands: Jewish Needlecraft for Today.* New York: Schocken Books, 1973.

Sack-Pikus, Sallyann Amdur. "An Outsider Looks at the Jewish Genealogy Phenomenon." *Avotaynu: The International Review of Jewish Genealogy* 3 (Fall 2014): 3–5.

Silk, Louise. "Memory Quilts." http://www.silkquilt.com/memoryquilts.

———. *The Quilting Path: A Guide to Spiritual Discovery through Fabric, Thread, and Kabbalah.* Woodstock, Vt.: Skylight Paths, 2006.

Six Million Stitches Project. https://sites.google.com/site/sixmillion stitchesproject/home.

Skolnik, Linda, and Janice MacDaniels. *The Knitting Way: A Guide to Spiritual Self-Discovery.* Woodstock, Vt.: Skylight Paths, 2005.

Stern, Lea. "The Green Sweater." Pattern for sale at the United States Holocaust Memorial Museum, Washington, D.C.

———. "The Green Sweater." Pattern for sale on *Ravelry.* https://www.ravelry .com/patterns/library/the-green-sweater.

Stoil, Rebecca Shimoni. "The Baltimore Knitter Who Unraveled the Internet." *Times of Israel.* January 11, 2017.

Stoltz, Heather. "Being Jewish Kind of Sucks Now That I'm a Mom." *Kveller*, April 16, 2018. https://www.kveller.com/being-jewish-feels-like-a-burden -now-that-im-a-mom.

———. "Dark Days: Where Does It End?" *Sewing Stories: Fiber Art That Tells a Story.* https://sewingstories.com/portfolio-item/dark-days-where-does -it-end.

———. "Flinging Prayer." *Sewing Stories: Fiber Art That Tells a Story.* https:// sewingstories.com/portfolio-item/flinging-prayer.

———. "Hanging by a Thread." *Sewing Stories: Fiber Art That Tells a Story.* http://sewingstories.com/portfolio-item/hangingbyathread.

———. "Shattered Childhood." *Sewing Stories: Fiber Art That Tells a Story.* https://sewingstories.com/portfolio-item/shattered-childhood.

———. "Torn (Artist vs. Mother)." *Sewing Stories: Fiber Art That Tells a Story.* https://sewingstories.com/2017/02/16/torn-artist-vs-mother.

Strassfeld, Sharon, and Michael Strassfeld, eds. *The Second Jewish Catalog.* Philadelphia: Jewish Publication Society, 1976.

Tabachnik, Toby. "'Jewish Hearts' Spread Message of Love throughout City." *Pittsburgh Jewish Chronicle*, November 29, 2018. https://jewishchronicle .timesofisrael.com/jewish-hearts-spread-message-of-love-throughout -city/.

Taylor, Sydney. *All-of-a-Kind Family.* New York: Dell Yearling, 1981.

Tolkien, J. R. R. *The Return of the King*. New York: Houghton Mifflin Reissue, 2012. Kindle.

"Torah Mantle." Skirball Cultural Center, Los Angeles. https://www.skirball .org/media/image/1291.

Torah Stitch by Stitch: An International Project. https://torahstitchbystitch.org.

"The Willendorf Venus (11 cm)." *Trishagumuri* (blog), August 20, 2017. https://trishagurumi.com/the-willendorf-venus.

Vesoulis, Abby. "Women First Marched to Challenge Trump: Now They Are Challenging Each Other." *Time*, January 19, 2019. https://time.com /5505787/womens-march-washington-controversy.

"Vintage Framed Judaica Rabbi Needlepoint Artwork." Item for sale by BirchardHayes on Etsy. https://www.etsy.com/listing/666652123/vintage -framed-judaica-rabbi-needlepoint. .

"Vintage Needlepoint Framed Art Rabbi with Torah Judaica Artwork Wall Decor 14" × 11"." Item for sale by LiliasAntiques on Etsy. https://www.etsy .com/listing/724169575/vintage-needlepoint-framed-art-rabbi.

"We've Seen This Before: A Campaign of Bend the Arc Jewish Action." Bend the Arc. https://www.weveseenthisbefore.org.

Wofford, Ben. "In a Time of Trump, Millennial Jews Awaken to Anti-Semitism." *Politico*, October 2, 2016. https://www.politico.com/magazine /story/2016/10/donald-trump-anti-semitism-young-jews-214314.

Zax, Talya. "The Man Who Made Those Viral Sweaters Has One for Every Jewish Holiday." *Forward*, January 10, 2017. https://forward.com/culture /359546/the-man-behind-those-viral-homemade-sweaters-has-made-one -for-every-jewish/.

Ziri, Danielle. "To March or Not to March? Women's March Divides Progressive Jewish Women in the United States." *Haaretz*, January 14, 2019.

Zumbach, Lauren. "Growing Arts and Crafts Market Isn't Just for Kids." *Chicago Tribune*, April 29, 2016.

SECONDARY SOURCES

Adler, Rachel. *Engendering Judaism: An Inclusive Theology and Ethics*. Boston: Beacon, 1999.

Ahmed, Sara. *The Cultural Politics of Emotion*. 2nd ed. New York: Routledge, 2014.

Ammerman, Nancy, ed. *Everyday Religion: Observing Modern Religious Lives*. New York: Oxford University Press, 2007.

Antler, Joyce. *Jewish Radical Feminism: Voices from the Women's Liberation Movement*. New York: New York University Press, 2018.

———. *You Never Call! You Never Write! A History of the Jewish Mother*. New York: Oxford University Press, 2007.

Baker, Cynthia. *Jew*. New Brunswick, N.J.: Rutgers University Press, 2017.

Barber, Elizabeth Wayland. *Women's Work, the First 20,000 Years: Women, Cloth, and Society in Early Times*. New York: W. W. Norton, 1994.

Barthes, Roland. *Camera Lucida: Reflections on Photography*. Translated by Richard Howard. New York: Hill and Wang, 1981.

Bartra, Eli, ed. *Crafting Gender: Women and Folk Art in Latin America and the Caribbean*. Durham, N.C.: Duke University Press, 2003.

Bataille, George. *Visions of Excess: Selected Writings, 1927–1939*. Edited by Allan Stoekl. Translated by Allan Stoekl, with Carl R. Lovitt and Donald M. Leslie Jr. Minneapolis: University of Minnesota Press, 1985.

Batnitzky, Leora. *How Judaism Became a Religion: An Introduction to Modern Jewish Thought*. Princeton, N.J.: Princeton University Press, 2011.

Baumgarten, Elisheva. *Mothers and Children: Jewish Family Life in Medieval Europe*. Princeton, N.J.: Princeton University Press, 2013.

Beal, Timothy K. *The Book of Hiding: Gender, Ethnicity, Annihilation, and Esther*. New York: Routledge, 1997.

Bender, Courtney. *Heaven's Kitchen: Living Religion at God's Love We Deliver*. Chicago: University of Chicago Press, 2003.

———. *The New Metaphysicals: Spirituality and the American Religious Imagination*. Chicago: University of Chicago Press, 2010.

———. "Studying Up: The Skyscraper View and Modern Perspectives on American Religion." The Alice Eckhardt Lecture, Lehigh University, October 28, 2015.

Benjamin, Mara H. *The Obligated Self: Maternal Subjectivity and Jewish Thought*. Bloomington: Indiana University Press, 2018. Kindle.

Benjamin, Walter. *Illuminations: Essays and Reflections*. Edited and with an introduction by Hannah Arendt. Translated by Harry Zohn. New York: Schocken Books, 1968.

Bennett, Jane. *Vibrant Matter: A Political Ecology of Things*. Durham, N.C.: Duke University Press, 2010.

Bergson, Henri. *Matter and Memory*. Translated by N. M. Paul and W. S. Palmer. New York: Zone Books, 1991.

Berlin, Adele. "The Book of Esther and Ancient Storytelling." *Journal of Biblical Literature* 120, no. 1 (2001): 3–14.

Berman, Lila Corwin. "Jewish History beyond the Jewish People." *AJS Review* 42, no. 2 (2018): 269–92.

———. *Speaking of Jews: Rabbis, Intellectuals, and the Creation of an American Public Identity*. Berkeley: University of California Press, 2009.

Bowman, Donna. "Love Trumps Hate: Images of Political Love from Pussyhat Makers." In *Taking It to the Streets: Public Theologies of Activism and Resistance*, edited by Jennifer Baldwin, 115–28. New York: Lexington Books, 2019.

————. *Prayer Shawl Ministries and Women's Theological Imagination*. New York: Lexington Books, 2016.

Boyarin, Daniel. *Unheroic Conduct: The Rise of Heterosexuality and the Invention of the Jewish Man*. Berkeley: University of California Press, 1997.

Brennan, Teresa. *The Transmission of Affect*. Ithaca, N.Y.: Cornell University Press, 2004.

Brown, Karen McCarthy. *Mama Lola: A Vodou Priestess in Brooklyn*. Berkeley: University of California Press, 2001.

Bryan-Wilson, Julia. *Fray: Art+Textile Politics*. Chicago: University of Chicago Press, 2017.

Butler, Judith. *Gender Trouble: Feminism and the Subversion of Identity*. New York: Routledge, 1991.

Campbell, Heidi A. "Understanding the Relationship between Religion Online and Offline in a Networked Society." *Journal of the American Academy of Religion* 80, no. 1 (2012): 64–93.

————, ed. *Digital Religion: Understanding Religious Practice in New Media Worlds*. New York: Routledge: 2013.

Castelli, Elizabeth, with Rosamond C. Rodman, ed. *Women, Gender, Religion: A Reader*. New York: Palgrave Macmillan, 2001.

Chen, Mel Y. *Animacies: Biopolitics, Racial Mattering, and Queer Affect*. Durham, N.C.: Duke University Press, 2012.

Chidester, David. *Authentic Fakes: Religion and American Popular Culture*. Berkeley: University of California Press, 2005.

————. "The Church of Baseball, the Fetish of Coca-Cola, and the Potlach of Rock 'n' Roll: Theoretical Models for the Study of Religion in American Popular Culture." *Journal of the American Academy of Religion* 64, no. 4 (1996): 743–65.

Classen, Constance. *The Deepest Sense: A Cultural History of Touch*. Urbana: University of Illinois Press, 2012.

————. "Touch in the Museum." In *The Book of Touch*, edited by Constance Classen, 275–86. New York: Berg, 2005.

Cohen, Shaye J. D. *The Beginnings of Jewishness: Boundaries, Varieties, Uncertainties*. Berkeley: University of California Press, 2005.

————. *Why Aren't Jewish Women Circumcised? Gender and Covenant in Judaism*. Berkeley: University of California Press, 2005.

Coontz, Stephanie. *The Way We Never Were: American Families and the Nostalgia Trap*. New York: Basic Books, 1992.

Cooperman, Jessica. *Fighting to Make Judaism Safe for America: World War I and the Origins of Religious Pluralism*. New York: New York University Press, 2018.

Corrigan, John, ed. *Feeling Religion*. Durham, N.C.: Duke University Press, 2017.

Cvetkovitch, Ann. *Depression: A Public Feeling*. Durham, N.C.: Duke University Press, 2011. Kindle.

DeBoar, Lisa. *Visual Arts in the Worshipping Church*. Grand Rapids, Mich.: Eerdmans, 2016.

Delaney, Carol. *Abraham on Trial*. Princeton, N.J.: Princeton University Press, 1998.

Diner, Hasia. *We Remember with Reverence and Love: American Jews and the Myth of Silence after the Holocaust, 1945–1962*. New York: New York University Press, 2009.

Diner, Hasia, Shira Kohn, and Rachel Kranson, eds. *A Jewish Feminine Mystique? Jewish Women in Postwar America*. New Brunswick, N.J.: Rutgers University Press, 2010.

Dollinger, Marc. *Quest for Inclusion: Jews and Liberalism in Modern America*. Princeton, N.J.: Princeton University Press, 2000.

Douglas, Mary. Foreword to Marcel Mauss, *The Gift: The Form and Reason for Exchange in Archaic Societies*. New York: Routledge, 1990.

Drucker, Malka. *White Fire: A Portrait of Women Spiritual Leaders in America*. Woodstock, Vt.: Skylight Paths, 2003.

Durkheim, Émile. *The Elementary Forms of the Religious Life*. Translated by Karen E. Fields. New York: Free Press, 1995.

Echbaibi, Nabil, and Stewart Hoover. "Media Theory and the 'Third Spaces of Digital Religion,'" accessed February 26, 2020. https://thirdspacesblog.files.wordpress.com/2014/05/third-spaces-and-media-theory-essay-2-0.pdf.

Eichler-Levine, Jodi. *Suffer the Little Children: Uses of the Past in Jewish and African American Children's Literature*. New York: New York University Press, 2013.

Eilberg-Schwartz, Howard. *God's Phallus: And Other Problems for Men and Monotheism*. Boston: Beacon, 1995.

Fader, Ayala, and Owen Gottlieb. "Occupy Judaism: Religion, Digital Media, and the Public Sphere." *Anthropological Quarterly* 88, no. 3 (2015): 759–93.

Fausto-Sterling, Anne. "The Five Sexes, Revisited." *Sciences*, July 2000, 19–23.

Fessenden, Tracy. *Culture and Redemption: Religion, the Secular, and American Literature*. Princeton, N.J.: Princeton University Press, 2006.

Fisk, Anna. "'To Make, and Make Again': Feminism, Craft, and Spirituality." *Feminist Theology* 20, no. 2 (2012): 160–74.

Flanzbaum, Helene, ed. *The Americanization of the Holocaust*. Baltimore: Johns Hopkins University Press, 1999.

Fletcher, David, and Mustafa Sarkar. "Psychological Resilience: A Review and Critique of Definitions, Concepts, and Theory." *European Psychologist* 18, no. 1 (2013): 12–23.

Franger, Gaby. "Survival-Empowerment-Courage: Insights into the History and Developments of Peruvian *Arpilleras.*" In *Stitching Resistance: Women, Creativity, and Fiber Arts*, edited by Marjorie Agosin, 101–20. Kent, U.K.: Solis, 2014.

Gadamer, Hans-Georg. *The Relevance of the Beautiful and Other Essays.* Edited by Robert A. Berasconi. Cambridge: Cambridge University Press, 1987.

Gay, Roxanne. *Hunger: A Memoir of (My) Body.* New York: Harper Perennial, 2017. Kindle.

Gilman, Sander. *The Jew's Body.* New York: Routledge, 1997.

———. *Multiculturalism and the Jews.* New York: Routledge, 2006.

Goldstein, Eric L. *The Price of Whiteness: Jews, Race, and American Identity.* Princeton, N.J.: Princeton University Press, 2006.

Griffith, R. Marie. *Born Again Bodies: Flesh and Spirit in American Christianity.* Berkeley: University of California Press, 2004.

Gross, Rachel. *Beyond the Synagogue: Jewish Nostalgia as Religious Practice.* New York: NYU Press, 2021.

———. "People of the Picture Book." In *Religion and Popular Culture in America.* 3rd ed., edited by Bruce David Forbes and Jeffrey H. Mahan, 177–93. Berkeley: University of California Press, 2017.

Hall, David D., ed. *Lived Religion in America: Toward a History of Practice.* Princeton, N.J.: Princeton University Press, 1997.

Heinz, Andrew. *Adapting to Abundance.* New York: Columbia University Press, 1992.

Hirsch, Marianne. *Family Frames: Photography, Narrative, and Postmemory.* Cambridge, Mass.: Harvard University Press, 1997.

Hoover, Stewart M., ed. *The Media and Religious Authority.* University Park: Pennsylvania State University Press, 2016.

Hyman, Paula. "Jewish Feminism Faces the American Women's Movement: Convergence and Divergence." In *American Jewish Women's History: A Reader*, edited by Pamela S. Nadell, 297–312. New York: New York University Press, 2003.

Idel, Moshe. *Absorbing Perfections: Kabbalah and Interpretation.* New Haven, Conn.: Yale University Press, 2002.

Imhoff, Sarah. *Masculinity and the Making of American Judaism.* Bloomington: Indiana University Press, 2017.

———. "Why Disability Studies Needs to Take Religion Seriously." *Religions* 8, no. 9 (2017): 186.

Jacobs, Sue-Ellen, Wesley Thomas, and Sabine Lang, eds. *Two-Spirit People: Native American Gender Identity, Sexuality, and Spirituality.* Urbana: University of Illinois Press, 1997.

Jacobson, Matthew Frye. *Roots Too: White Ethnic Revival in Post–Civil Rights America.* Cambridge, Mass.: Harvard University Press, 2008.

Jefferson, Margo. "Beyond Cultural Labeling, beyond Art versus Craft." *New York Times*, March 22, 2005.

Johnson, Cedric C. *Race, Religion, and Resilience in the Neoliberal Age*. New York: Palgrave Macmillan, 2016.

Joselit, Jenna Weissman. *The Wonders of America: Reinventing Jewish Culture, 1880–1950*. New York: Henry Holt, 1994.

Joselit, Jenna Weissman, and Susan Braunstein, eds. *Getting Comfortable in New York: The American Jewish Home, 1880–1950*. New York: Jewish Museum, 1990.

Josephson, Jason Ananda. "An Empowered World: Buddhist Medicine and the Potency of Prayer in Japan." In *Deus in Machina: Religion, Technology, and the Things in Between*, edited by Jeremy Stolow, 117–42. New York: Fordham University Press, 2012.

Kaell, Hillary. "Of Gifts and Grandchildren: American Holy Land Souvenirs." *Journal of Material Culture* 17, no. 2 (2012): 133–51.

Kaell, Hillary, and Sarah Imhoff. "Lineage Matters: DNA, Race, and Gene Talk in Judaism and Messianic Judaism." *Religion and American Culture* 27, no. 1 (2017): 95–127.

Kaplan, Edward. *Abraham Joshua Heschel: Prophetic Witness*. New Haven, Conn.: Yale University Press, 2007.

Kaplan, Mordecai. *Judaism as a Civilization: Toward a Reconstruction of American-Jewish Life*. Philadelphia: Jewish Publication Society, 2010.

Kaye/Kantrowitz, Melanie. *The Colors of Jews: Racial Politics and Radical Diasporism*. Bloomington: Indiana University Press, 2007.

Kelman, Ari. "Reading a Book Like an Object: The Case of the Jewish Catalog." In *Thinking Jewish Culture in America*, edited by Ken Koltun-Fromm, 109–30. Lexington, Ky.: Lexington Books, 2013. Kindle.

———. "Jewish Identity Ain't What It Used to Be." *Learning about Learning* (blog), May 17, 2014. http://blogs.brandeis.edu/mandeljewished/?p=1735.

Kelman, Ari, Aaron Hahn Tapper, Isabel Fonseca, and Aliya Saperstein. *Counting Inconsistencies: An Analysis of American Jewish Population Studies, with a Focus on Jews of Color*. https://jewsofcolorfieldbuilding.org/wp-content/uploads/2019/05/Counting-Inconsistencies-052119.pdf.

Kelner, Shaul. *Tours That Bind: Diaspora, Pilgrimage, and Israeli Birthright Tourism*. New York: New York University Press, 2010.

Khan, Susan. *Reproducing Jews: A Cultural Account of Assisted Reproduction in Israel*. Durham, N.C.: Duke University Press, 2000.

Kimmelman, Marilyn, and Rebecca Leavitt. "American Women Crafting Cloth: From Bees to Blogs." In *Stitching Resistance: Women, Creativity, and Fiber Arts*, edited by Marjorie Agosin, 55–64. Kent, U.K.: Solis, 2014.

Kiracoff, Roderick, and Mary Elizabeth Johnson. *The American Quilt: A History of Cloth and Comfort, 1750–1950*. New York: Crown, 2004.

Kirshenblatt-Gimblett, Barbara. "The Cut That Binds: The Western Ashkenazic Torah Binder as Nexus between Circumcision and Torah." In *Celebration: Studies in Festivity and Ritual*, edited by Vincent Turner, 136–46. Washington, D.C.: Smithsonian Institution Press, 1984.

———. *Fabric of Jewish Life: Textiles from the Jewish Museum Collection.* New York: Jewish Museum, 1977.

Kirshenblatt-Gimblett, Barbara, and Jeffrey Shandler, eds. *Anne Frank Unbound: Media, Imagination, History.* Bloomington: Indiana University Press, 2012.

Klassen, Pamela. *Blessed Events: Religion and Homebirth in America.* Princeton, N.J.: Princeton University Press, 2001.

Kornfeld, Moshe. "Revaluing Story Time." Presentation, Association for Jewish Studies Annual Meeting, December 19, 2016, San Diego, Calif.

Kranson, Rachel. *Ambivalent Embrace: Jewish Upward Mobility in Postwar America.* Chapel Hill: University of North Carolina Press, 2017.

Krone, Adrienne. "'A Shmita Manifesto': A Radical Sabbatical Approach to Jewish Food Reform in the United States." *Scripta Instituti Donneriani Aboensis* 26 (2015): 303–25.

Krutzsch, Brett. *Dying to Be Normal: Gay Martyrs and the Transformation of American Sexual Politics.* New York: Oxford University Press, 2019.

Kulick, Don, and Anne Meneley. *Fat: The Anthropology of an Obsession.* New York: Tarcher, 2005.

Labovitz, Gail. "Do I Have Something Yet? And If So, What?" *Our Torah*, December 30, 2016. https://www.aju.edu/ziegler-school-rabbinic-studies /our-torah/back-issues/do-i-have-something-yet-and-if-so-what.

Langlands, Alexander. *Cræft: An Inquiry into the Origins and True Meaning of Traditional Crafts.* New York: W. W. Norton, 2018.

Levitt, Laura. *American Jewish Loss after the Holocaust.* New York: New York University Press, 2007.

———. "Intimate Engagements: A Holocaust Lesson." *Nashim* 7 (2004): 190–205.

———. *Jews and Feminism: The Ambivalent Search for Home.* New York: Routledge, 1997.

Lim, Chaeyoon, Robert D. Putnam, and Carol Ann MacGregor. "Secular and Liminal: Discovering Heterogeneity among Religious Nones." *Journal for the Scientific Study of Religion* 49, no. 4 (2010): 596–618.

Lindsey, Rachel McBride. *A Communion of Shadows: Religion and Photography in Nineteenth-Century America.* Chapel Hill: University of North Carolina Press, 2017.

Linenthal, Edward. *Preserving Memory: The Struggle to Create America's Holocaust Museum.* New York: Columbia University Press, 2001.

Literat, Ioana, and Anne Balsamo. "Stitching the Future of the AIDS

Quilt: The Cultural Work of Digital Memorials." *Visual Communication Quarterly* 21, no. 3 (2014): 138–49.

Lofton, Kathryn. *Consuming Religion*. Chicago: University of Chicago Press, 2017.

Macdonald, Anne L. *No Idle Hands: A Social History of American Knitting*. New York: Ballantine Books, 1988.

Magid, Shaul. *American Post-Judaism: Identity and Renewal in a Postethnic Society*. Bloomington: Indiana University Press, 2013.

Mandell, Hinda, ed. *Crafting Dissent: Handicraft as Protest from the American Revolution to the Pussyhats*. New York: Rowman and Littlefield, 2019.

Markus, Sandra. "Craftivism from Philomena to the Pussyhat." In *Crafting Dissent: Handicraft as Protest from the American Revolution to the Pussyhats*, edited by Hinda Mandell, 15–32. New York: Rowman and Littlefield, 2019.

———. "Through the Eye of a Needle: Craftivism as an Emerging Mode of Civic Engagement and Cultural Participation." Ph.D. diss., Teacher's College, Columbia University, May 2019.

Maurette, Pablo. *The Forgotten Sense: Meditations on Touch*. Chicago: University of Chicago Press, 2018.

Mazusawa, Tomoko. *In Search of Dreamtime: The Quest for the Origin of Religion*. Chicago: University of Chicago Press, 1993.

McDannell, Colleen. *Material Christianity: Religion and Popular Culture in America*. New Haven, Conn.: Yale University Press, 1995.

McNabb, Charlie. *Nonbinary Gender Identities: History, Culture, Resources*. New York: Rowman and Littlefield, 2018.

Mehta, Samira K. *Beyond Chrismukkah: The Jewish-Christian Interfaith Family in the United States*. Chapel Hill: University of North Carolina Press, 2018.

Mendelsohn, Adam D. *The Rag Race: How Jews Sewed Their Way to Success in America and the British Empire*. New York: New York University Press, 2014.

Miller, Daniel. *The Comfort of Things*. Cambridge: Polity, 2008.

Minahan, Stella, and Julie Wolfrrame Cox. "Stitch 'n Bitch: Cyberfeminism, a Third Place and the New Materiality." *Journal of Material Culture* 12, no. 1 (2007): 5–21.

Modern, John Lardas. "eBay and the Historical Imagination." *Immanent Frame* (blog), April 9, 2015. http://blogs.ssrc.org/tif/2015/04/09/ebay-and-the-historical-imagination.

Moore, Deborah Dash. *GI Jews: How World War II Changed a Generation*. Cambridge, Mass.: Belknap Press of Harvard University Press, 2006.

Moreton, Bethany. *To Serve God and Walmart: The Making of Christian Free Enterprise*. Cambridge, Mass.: Harvard University Press, 2010.

Morgan, David. *The Embodied Eye: Religious Visual Culture and the Social Life of Feeling*. Berkeley: University of California Press, 2012.

Muñoz, José Esteban. *Cruising Utopia: The Then and There of Queer Futurity*. New York: NYU Press, 2009.

Myerhoff, Barbara. *Number Our Days: A Triumph of Continuity and Culture among Jewish Old People in an Urban Ghetto*. New York: Touchstone, 1980.

Ochs, Vanessa. *Inventing Jewish Ritual*. Philadelphia: Jewish Publication Society, 2007.

Orsi, Robert. *Between Heaven and Earth: The Religious Worlds People Make and the Scholars Who Study Them*. Princeton, N.J.: Princeton University Press, 2004.

———. *The Madonna of 115th St.: Faith and Community in Italian Harlem*. 2nd ed. New Haven, Conn.: Yale University Press, 2002.

Paine, Crispin. *Religious Objects in Museums: Private Lives and Public Duties*. New York: Bloomsbury, 2013.

Parfitt, Tudor. *Black Jews in Africa and the Americas*. Cambridge, Mass.: Harvard University Press, 2013.

Parker, Rozsika. *The Subversive Stitch: Embroidery and the Making of the Feminine*. New York: Bloomsbury, 2019.

Perez, Elizabeth. *Religion in the Kitchen: Cooking, Talking, and the Making of Black Atlantic Traditions*. New York: New York University Press, 2016.

Peskowitz, Miriam. *Spinning Fantasies: Rabbis, Gender, and History*. Berkeley: University of California Press, 1997.

Petro, Anthony. "Ray Navarro's Jesus Camp, AIDS Activist Video, and 'The New American Catholicism.'" *Journal of the American Academy of Religion* 85, no. 4 (2017): 920–56.

———. "Race, Gender, Sexuality, and Religion in North America." In *Oxford Research Encyclopedia of Religion*, February 2017. https://doi.org/10.1093/acrefore/9780199340378.013.488.

Pike, Sarah. *New Age and Neopagan Religions in America*. New York: Columbia University Press, 2004.

Plaskow, Judith. *The Coming of Lilith: Essays on Feminism, Judaism, and Sexual Ethics, 1972–2003*. Boston: Beacon, 2005.

———. *Standing Again at Sinai: Judaism from a Feminist Perspective*. New York: Harper One, 1991.

Plate, S. Brent. *A History of Religion in Five-and-a-Half Objects*. Boston: Beacon, 2014.

———, ed. *Key Terms in Material Religion*. London: Bloomsbury, 2015.

Plaut, Joshua Eli. *A Kosher Christmas: 'Tis the Season to Be Jewish*. New Brunswick, N.J.: Rutgers University Press, 2012.

"A Portrait of Jewish Americans: Findings from a Pew Research Center Survey of U.S. Jews." Pew Research Center, 2013.

Prell, Riv-Ellen. "Barbara Myerhoff." *Jewish Women: A Comprehensive Historical Encyclopedia.* March 20, 2009. Jewish Women's Archive. https://jwa.org/encyclopedia/article/myerhoff-barbara.

———. *Fighting to Become Americans: Jews, Gender, and the Anxiety of Assimilation.* Boston: Beacon, 1999.

———, ed. *Women Remaking American Judaism.* Detroit, Mich.: Wayne State University Press, 2007.

Rabin, Shari. *Jews on the Frontier: Religion and Mobility in Nineteenth-Century America.* New York: NYU Press, 2017.

Raphael, Melissa. *The Female Face of God in Auschwitz: A Jewish Feminist Theology of the Holocaust.* New York: Routledge, 2003.

Rebhum, Uzi. *Jews and the American Religious Landscape.* New York: Columbia University Press, 2016.

"Religious Landscape Survey." Pew Research Center, Religion and Public Life. http://www.pewforum.org/religious-landscape-study.

Rock-Singer, Cara. "Chicken Soup: Women and the Making of the Modern Jewish Home and Nation." In *Beyond Chicken Soup: Jews and Medicine in America,* 52–70. Exh. cat. Baltimore: Jewish Museum of Maryland, 2015.

Roof, Wade Clark. *Spiritual Marketplace: Baby Boomers and the Remaking of American Religion.* Princeton, N.J.: Princeton University Press, 1999.

Rosen, Jonathan. *The Talmud and the Internet: A Journey between Worlds.* New York: Picador, 2001.

Rosenblatt, Katie, Lila Corwin Berman, and Ronit Stahl. "How Jewish Academia Created a #MeToo Disaster." *Forward,* July 19, 2018. https://forward.com/opinion/406240/how-jewish-academia-created-a-metoo-disaster.

Runions, Erin. "Political Theologies of the Surveiled Womb?" *Political Theology* 16, no. 4 (2015): 301–4.

Salamon, Hagar. *Israel in the Making: Stickers, Stitches, and Other Critical Practices.* Bloomington: Indiana University Press, 2017.

Sanua, Marianne Rachel. *Let Us Prove Strong: The American Jewish Committee, 1945–2006.* Waltham, Mass.: Brandeis University Press, 2007.

Satlow, Michael. *Creating Judaism: History, Tradition, Practice.* New York: Columbia University Press, 2006.

Schachter, Ben. *Image, Action, and Idea in Contemporary Jewish Art.* University Park: Pennsylvania State University Press, 2017.

Schaefer, Donovan O. "Beautiful Facts: Science, Secularism, and Affect." In *Feeling Religion,* edited by John Corrigan, 69–92. Durham, N.C.: Duke University Press, 2017.

———. *The Evolution of Affect Theory: The Humanities, the Sciences, and the Study of Power.* Cambridge: Cambridge University Press, 2019.

———. *Religious Affects: Animality, Evolution, and Power.* Durham, N.C.: Duke University Press, 2015.

Schultz, Kevin. *Tri-Faith America: How Catholics and Jews Held Postwar America to Its Protestant Promise.* New York: Oxford University Press, 2011.

Sedgwick, Eve Kosofsky. *Epistemology of the Closet.* Berkeley: University of California Press, 2008.

Shuman, Amy. "Food Gifts: Ritual Exchange and the Production of Excess Meaning." *Journal of American Folklore* 113, no. 450 (2000): 495–508.

Smith, Jonathan Z. "Religion, Religions, Religious." In *Critical Terms in Religious Studies,* edited by Marc C. Taylor, 269–84. Chicago: University of Chicago Press, 1998.

Smith, Pamela H. *The Body of the Artisan: Art and Experience in the Scientific Revolution.* Chicago: University of Chicago Press, 2006.

Stallybrass, Peter. "Worn Worlds: Clothes, Mourning, and the Life of Things." In *Cultural Memory and the Construction of Identity,* edited by Dan Ben-Amos and Liliane Weissberg, 27–44. Detroit, Mich.: Wayne State University Press, 1999.

Stavrakopolou, Francesca, and John Barton, eds. *Religious Diversity in Ancient Israel and Judah.* London: T&T Clark, 2010.

Stolow, Jeremy. "Introduction: Religion, Technology, and the Things in Between." In *Deus in Machina: Religion, Technology, and the Things in Between,* edited by Jeremy Stolow, 1–24. New York: Fordham University Press, 2013.

———. "Spiritual Nervous System: Reflections on a Magnetic Cord Designed for Spirit Communication." In *Deus in Machina: Religion, Technology, and the Things in Between,* 83–116. New York: Fordham University Press, 2013.

Strings, Sabrina. *Fearing the Black Body: The Racial Origins of Fat Phobia.* New York: New York University Press, 2019.

Stryker, Susan, and Stephen Whittle, eds. *The Transgender Studies Reader.* New York: Routledge, 2006.

Sturken, Marita. *Tangled Memories: The Vietnam War, the AIDS Epidemic, and the Politics of Remembering.* Berkeley: University of California Press, 1997.

Taves, Ann. *Religious Experience Reconsidered: A Building Block Approach to the Study of Religion and Other Special Things.* Princeton, N.J.: Princeton University Press, 2009.

Thomas, Jolyon Baraka. "Domesticity and Spirituality: Kondo Is Not an Animist." *Marginalia* (blog), *Los Angeles Review of Books,* February 8, 2019. https://marginalia.lareviewofbooks.org/domesticity-spirituality-kondo-not-animist.

Thompson, Jennifer. *Jewish on Their Own Terms: How Intermarried*

*Couples Are Changing American Judaism*. New Brunswick, N.J.: Rutgers University Press, 2013.

Tweed, Thomas. *Crossing and Dwelling: A Theory of Religion*. Cambridge, Mass.: Harvard University Press, 2006.

Ulrich, Laurel Thatcher. *The Age of Homespun: Objects and Stories in the Creation of an American Myth*. New York: Vintage, 2002.

Wagner, Rachel. *Godwired: Religion, Ritual, and Virtual Reality*. New York: Routledge, 2011.

Walton, Rivkah M. "Lilith's Daughters, Miriam's Chorus: Two Decades of Feminist Midrash." *Religion and Literature* 43, no. 2 (2011): 115–27.

Weiner, Isaac. *Religion Out Loud: Religious Sound, Public Space, and American Pluralism*. New York: New York University Press, 2013.

Weiner, Isaac, and Amy DeRogatis. The American Religious Sounds Project. https://religioussounds.osu.edu.

Weisenfeld, Judith. *New World A-Coming: Black Religion and Racial Identity during the Great Migration*. New York: New York University Press, 2017.

Weissler, Chava. "Art *Is* Spirituality! Practice, Play, and Experiential Learning in the Jewish Renewal Movement." *Material Religion* 3, no. 3 (2007): 354–79.

———. *Making Judaism Meaningful: Ambivalence and Tradition in a Havurah Community*. New York: AMS Press, 1989.

Weissman, Gary. *Fantasies of Witnessing: Postwar Efforts to Experience the Holocaust*. Ithaca, N.Y.: Cornell University Press, 2004.

Wertheimer, Jack. *The New American Judaism: How Jews Practice Their Religion Today*. Princeton, N.J.: Princeton University Press, 2018.

Wertz, Richard W., and Dorothy C. Wertz. *Lying-In: A History of Childbirth in America*. New Haven, Conn.: Yale University Press, 1989.

Wilcox, Melissa M. *Queer Nuns: Religion, Activism, and Serious Parody*. New York: NYU Press, 2018.

Wolfson, Elliot. "Crossing Gender Boundaries in Kabbalistic Ritual and Myth." In *Ultimate Intimacy: The Psychodynamics of Jewish Mysticism*, edited by Mortimer Ostow, 255–352. London: Karnac Books, 1995.

Zierler, Wendy. "In Search of a Feminist Reading of the Akedah." *Nashim* 9 (June 2005): 10–26.

Zeller, Benjamin, Nora Rubel, Marie W. Dallam, and Reid Nelson, eds. *Religion, Food, and Eating in North America*. New York: Columbia University Press, 2014.

Zollman, Joellyn Wallen. "The Gifts of the Jews: Ideology and Material Culture in the Synagogue Gift Shop." *American Jewish Archives Journal* 58, nos. 1–2 (2006): 51–77.

# INDEX

· · · · · · · · · ·

*Page numbers in italics refer to illustrations.*

Holocaust, 30; survivors of, 19, 154, 155, 156, 162

Holocaust Memorial Museum (Washington, D.C.), 154, 157–58

*horror vacui* (fear of a vacuum), 31–32, 34, 38, 44, 157

Industrial Revolution, 52

infertility, 22, 30, 33; among Jewish women, 34

Instagram, 57, 61, 62, 63, 65

Isaac (biblical), 44; *akedah* (binding of Isaac), 44, 45

Israel, 171

Israelites, 30–31, 34, 106, 124, 127, 191n25

Izard, Susan, 121

Jacobs, Sarah, *60*

JCC (Jewish Community Center), 109, 123, 132, 143, 148, 161, 165

Jerusalem temple, 12

Jesus, 90, 111

Jewish Art Salon, 147

*Jewish Catalog* (Siegel, Strassfeld, and Strassfeld, 1973), 82, 114

Jewish Farm School, 108, 197n20

Jewish Federation of Greater Philadelphia, 161

Jewish Gen, 108

Jewish Hearts for Pittsburgh, 17, 22–23, 136–38, *137*, 141–46, *144*, 149–50, *151*, 179; and contributing geographical regions, 138

Jewish Museum (New York City), 78

Jewish Orthodox Feminist Alliance, 97

Jewish Star. *See* Star of David

The Jewish Studio Project, 189n28

Jones, Cleve, 129, 149

Jorgenson, Susan, 121

*JudaiQuilt* (website), 70

Judaism: etymological origins of, 14

—defined as: culture, 19; ethnic category, 14, 15; everyday practice, 26, 119; process, 12, 14, 15; racial category, 14, 15; religious category, 14–15

—denominations and practices: Ashkenazi, 15, 41, 49, 52, 81, 109, 154; Ashkenazi men, 12, 63; Ashkenazi women, 18–19, 20, 48, 108, 116; Chabad, 145; Conservative, 19, 107, 115, 197n18; importance of, 197n17; kabbalah, 164; Kohen (priestly class), 62, 105; "Litvish," 53; Orthodox, 19, 107, 180; postdenominational Judaism, 19, 107–8; Reconstructionist, 19, 107, 115; Reform, 19, 107, 115, 116, 197n18; Sephardic, 76, 108

—history of: American Jewish communities, 16, 20, 170, 178; Jews and garment trade, 169–70; Jews and American religious history, 48

—Jewish perspectives on: conversion, 14; Holocaust, 154–57; masculinity, 123; pronatalism, 30, 38, 46, 49; racial heterogeneity, 133. *See also* material culture

Kaddish (Jewish memorial prayer), 140

*ketubah* (Jewish marriage contract), 91

kiddush (lunchtime Sabbath meal), 79

King, Martin Luther, Jr., 148

*kippah. See* prayer cap

*kittel* (robe worn on High Holy Days), 171

knitting, 5, 48, 61–64, 87, 94–96, 97, 157, 162, 170; amateur, 66; biblical references to, 27, 52; as embodied action, 46; and gender, 18, 28–29, 150; hand-knits, 8, 120; historical origins of, 69; and intention, 92; knitting circle, 16, 17; knitting needles, 33, 64, 66, 118, 133, 159; knitting patterns, 65; Pennsylvania knitting circle, 22, 116–20, 126, 174. *See also* Prayer Shawl Ministry; pussyhats; sweaters

*kohenet* (Hebrew priestess), 56, 58, 60

Kohenet Hebrew Princess Institute, 56, 193n24

*k'riah* ribbon (torn ritual mourning ribbon), 146–47, 165

Kristallnacht, 147

Kuperberg, Adrienne, 101

Lachter, Sandra, *86, 88*, 106, 171

Latin (language), 52

Latinx bodies, 49

Lefkowitz, Muriel Kamins, *25*

Lesser, Ketzirah, 56–60, *59*, 70, 73, 179

Levy, Peachy, 45, 113–14, 149, 154

Lilith (biblical), 28

The Little Knittery, 67

Los Angeles, 42, 45, 63, 64, 153, 154, 175, 177; East Los Angeles, 67; Hollywood, 178. *See also* Pomegranate Guild of Judaic Needlework—regional chapters

Lovelace, Ada, 74

*lulav. See* Sukkot

Lurianic legend, 152

Lvov (Poland), 158, 160

Maccabee, Judah, 2

magic, 101, 103, 117, 123–24, 126, 179; as ritual technology, 124

Mandell, Hinda, 136–38, 141–42, 145

Maryland, 16, 50, 61, 83

Maryland Sheep and Wool Festival, 51

material culture, 13, 21, 36, 47, 49, 80, 107, 174; American, 169; and "animacy," 166–69; and Holocaust, 155–57; and memory, 153; and religious texts, 73; and travel, 64; women's presence in, 45

matzah, 32, 57; afikomen, 7, 57; *shu-mura matzah* (handmade matzah), 63. *See also* covers: matzah; embroidery: matzah covers

*megillah. See* Purim

*melakhot* (work forbidden on the Sabbath), 30, 68–69

memes, viral, 61, 63, 65

memory, 26

*menorah. See* Hannukah

midrash (Jewish interpretive tradition), 26, 50, 54–55, 178

mikvah (ritual bath), 58

Milk, Harvey, 129

Milwaukee, 131

*minhag* (tradition), 40, 52, 140

*minyan* (quorum), 10

Miriam (biblical), 98, 99

*mitzvah* (commandment, good deed), 120, 122, 166; *hiddur mitzvah* (beautification of a commandment), 6, 32, 106

Moscone, George, 129

Moses (biblical), 98, 127, 177–78

mourning, 38

Muslim, 139, 145

Myerhoff, Barbara, 18–19

NAMES Project Foundation, 129

Naomi (biblical), 111

*Naomi and Ruth*, 111, *112. See also* Spector, Arlene Diane

needles, 123–24, 170, 171, 180

needlepoint, 17, 35, 74, 115, 138, 163, 170–72; canvas, 73; chuppah, 171; pillows, 32; rabbis, 1–9, *3*, 12, 21, 187n6; wimpel, 40

Netflix, 33

New Age movement, 49, 126, 141

New York, 16, 35, 96, 104, 138, 146, 147, 155, 158; Long Island, 4, 6, 103, 124; New York City, 53, 78, 103, 104, 132, 142; Rochester, 137; Upstate, 123

Nimoy, Leonard, 175

Noah (biblical), 43

WHERE RELIGION LIVES

Jodi Eichler-Levine, *Painted Pomegranates and Needlepoint Rabbis: How Jews Craft Resilience and Create Community* (2020).

Tony Tian-Ren Lin, *Prosperity Gospel Latinos and Their American Dream* (2020).

Lauren R. Kerby, *Saving History: How White Evangelicals Tour the Nation's Capital and Redeem a Christian America* (2020).